The University of New Mexico
At Gallup

Zollinger Library

Bridging the
Achievement Gap

Bridging the Achievement Gap

John E. Chubb
Tom Loveless
Editors

BROOKINGS INSTITUTION PRESS
Washington, D.C.

Library of Congress Cataloging-in-Publication data

Bridging the achievement gap / John Chubb and Tom Loveless, editors.
    p.   cm.
Includes bibliographical references and index.
   ISBN 0-8157-1400-9 (cloth : alk. paper)—
   ISBN 0-8157-1401-7 (pbk. : alk. paper)
   1. Educational equalization—United States. 2. Academic achievement—
United States. I. Chubb, John E. II. Loveless, Tom, 1954–
   LC213.2 .B74   2002
   379.2'0973—dc21   2002012471

9 8 7 6 5 4 3 2 1

The paper used in this publication meets minimum requirements of the
American National Standard for Information Sciences—Permanence of Paper
for Printed Library Materials: ANSI Z39.48-1992.

Typeset in Adobe Garamond

Composition by
Betsy Kulamer
Washington, D.C.

Printed by
R. R. Donnelley and Sons
Harrisonburg, Virginia

ℬ THE BROOKINGS INSTITUTION

The Brookings Institution is an independent organization devoted to nonpartisan research, education, and publication in economics, governance, foreign policy, and the social sciences generally. Its principal purposes are to aid in the development of sound public policies and to promote public understanding of issues of national importance. The Institution was founded on December 8, 1927, to merge the activities of the Institute for Government Research, founded in 1916, the Institute of Economics, founded in 1922, and the Robert Brookings Graduate School of Economics and Government, founded in 1924. The Institution maintains a position of neutrality on issues of public policy. Interpretations or conclusions in Brookings publications should be understood to be solely those of the authors.

Foreword

All of us here at Brookings attach special importance to education. Educating ourselves is what we do in our capacity as individual scholars; educating the public is a major part of our mission as an institution. We're the only Washington-based think tank that identifies itself on the web as ".edu" rather than ".org." In the wide range of public policy issues on which we focus our energies, none is more important than the state of education in America. It is against that backdrop that we're proud to be the home of the Brown Center on Education, which is currently flourishing under the directorship of Tom Loveless.

The pages that follow represent the latest example of the crucial work that Tom and his colleagues are doing to identify the problems besetting American education and to propose solutions. One of the most important and vexing of those problems is the disparity in academic performance between white students, on the one hand, and African American and Hispanic students, on the other. The so-called achievement gap is one of the most stubborn and pernicious manifestations of racial inequality in our country. It is part of the reason that this legacy of the past persists from one generation to the next. Because white students achieve at levels significantly higher than others, they graduate from high school and college at much higher rates, earn significantly higher incomes, and suffer far fewer of the social ills associated with low levels of education. These differences magnify the divisions and tensions that have long plagued relationships between the races in this country. For at least half a century, since the Supreme Court declared in its landmark 1954 ruling on *Brown* v. *Board of Education* that separate but equal education is unconstitutional, the nation has worked to give children of all backgrounds equal access to better quality education. The country has in fact made enormous progress in eliminating racial segregation among schools, increasing and equalizing spending on schools, and toughening academic standards for schools. But students have not made commensurate strides. After some encouraging movement during the 1970s and 1980s, the achievement gap increased in the 1990s and remains frustratingly wide today.

Progress may not, however, be quite as elusive as the national trends suggest. A number of small-scale initiatives spanning the educational and political spectrum—from class-size reduction to phonics-based reading programs to vouchers for private schools—are beginning to show very promising signs of raising the achievement of black and Hispanic students at rates that equal or sometimes exceed those for white students. The growing evidence of the effectiveness of these reforms taken together suggests that policymakers could help schools bridge the achievement gap, raising the achievement of students from all backgrounds to acceptable levels. That exciting promise is the subject of this volume, which provides the first comprehensive look at the most encouraging of such initiatives nationwide.

In the spring of 2000, John Chubb, chief education officer for Edison Schools and a former senior fellow at Brookings, approached Tom Loveless with the idea for this volume. Edison Schools is a private management company that provides a comprehensive reform model to public schools in over twenty states nationwide, most often schools that are low achieving and attended primarily by African American and Hispanic students. The Brookings Press had in 1998 published the definitive study of the nature of the achievement gap, *The Black-White Test Score Gap*, edited by Christopher Jencks and Meredith Phillips, so it was natural for us to take the first thorough look at any progress toward reducing that gap. John and Tom proceeded to assemble the strongest group of scholars analyzing various approaches to the achievement gap, and papers were presented publicly at a Brookings forum in February 2001. The papers that make up this volume have benefited from commentary provided at the forum and developments since. The result is a tough-minded but generally encouraging view of potential responses to this vital national challenge.

Brookings would like to thank the organizations that provided financial support for this project: Edison Schools, Inc., for supporting the conference and the Spencer Foundation for supporting publication of the book. The authors thank the panelists at the forum who provided diverse and valuable perspective on the papers—practical, theoretical, and methodological: Jens Ludwig, Tom Toch, Julia Lara, Dominic Brewer, Dan Goldhaber, Ronald Ferguson, David Levin, Vonnelle Middleton, John Pannell, and Pamela Massey.

STROBE TALBOTT
President, Brookings Institution

October 2002
Washington, D.C.

Contents

Bridging the
Achievement Gap

1

Bridging the Achievement Gap

JOHN E. CHUBB AND TOM LOVELESS

Overstating the importance of the achievement gap is not easy. The difference in educational achievement between white students, on the one hand, and African American and Hispanic students, on the other, is large and persistent. In the last decade it has gotten worse. The average black or Hispanic student, in elementary, middle, or high school, currently achieves at about the same level as the average white student in the lowest quartile of white achievement. These differences have dire consequences once students leave school. Blacks and Hispanics are much less likely than whites to graduate from high school, acquire a college or advanced degree, or earn a living that places them in the middle class. Blacks and Hispanics are much more likely than whites to suffer the social problems that often accompany low income. If the achievement gap could be reduced, the fortunes of blacks and Hispanics would not only be raised, but the social and economic differences that intensify the country's racial tensions would also be ameliorated.

The achievement gap has been extensively documented. In 1966, in the first truly comprehensive examination of student achievement in the United States, a team of federally sponsored researchers, led by the eminent sociologist James Coleman, found a large black-white achievement gap—which it attributed primarily to family backgrounds, of the students themselves and of their classmates. In 1970 the federal government launched the National Assessment of Educational Progress (NAEP), a random testing of American students every two to four years and a means, for the first time, to track student achievement nationwide. These tests showed black and Hispanic students to be roughly four years behind white students on average by age seventeen. In addition, the 1970s saw large numbers of blacks and Hispanics seeking college admission and scoring approximately a standard deviation behind whites on the SAT.

Over the ensuing years, data from the NAEP, the SAT, and increasingly common state and district testing programs continued to show a racial gap in achievement. Scholars debated its causes—family, peer groups, culture, discrimination, heredity, and schooling. Policymakers lamented its intractability. Gains made by blacks and Hispanics from the late 1970s to the late 1980s on national measures eroded in the 1990s. And these declines occurred during perhaps the most aggressive era of school reform in the nation's history. A fair conclusion, as the definitive volume on the subject (*The Black-White Test Score Gap,* edited by Christopher Jencks and Meredith Phillips) reached in 1998, is that far more is known about the nature of the achievement gap—its causes and its consequences—than about how to fix it.

The situation, however, may finally be changing. Achievement trends, discouraging as they may be, do not give a complete picture of developments in student achievement. Around the country a number of specific efforts are showing that the achievement gap can be bridged. Schools and school reforms are boosting the achievement of Hispanic and, especially, African American students to levels nearing those of whites. Disparate in approach and involving relatively few students, these efforts are nonetheless important. They are potentially replicable. They offer lessons that might be learned and applied widely. They offer hope that the achievement gap might one day, soon, be reduced meaningfully. This book provides, for the first time in one place, the evidence of these efforts—evidence that when taken together is remarkably encouraging.

Over a decade ago, the state of Tennessee launched one of the most important experiments in education reform to investigate the effects of class size on student achievement. Project STAR was designed as a large-scale experiment with random assignment of students to treatment and control groups; that is, to classes of regular or small size or regular size with a teacher's aide. It represented the most powerful of research designs and a rarity in public policy—everyone eligible for a new policy benefit (in this case, a smaller class) wants or expects to receive it. Class-size reduction also happens to be one of the more popular, albeit expensive, reforms being implemented in school systems throughout America today.

In their chapter, "Would Smaller Classes Help Close the Black-White Achievement Gap?" Alan B. Krueger and Diane M. Whitmore put the data from Project STAR to what might be considered the ultimate test. The students in the project, who were in grades K–3 when they experienced different sized classes, have now either finished high school or dropped out. Krueger and Whitmore explore the long-term effects of smaller classes on student achievement. They found that, while all types of students enrolled in smaller classes achieved at higher levels than students enrolled in regular classes (with or without aides) during the years they were in grades K–3, the achievement advantage of smaller classes largely disappeared for white students once they returned to regular-size classes in fourth grade. For black students, however, the achievement advantage diminished in grade four but then stabilized at about 5 national percentiles over the long haul, reducing the black-white achievement gap for those students by 15 percent. What is more, the advantages of smaller classes showed up in participation rates of taking the SAT and the American College Test (ACT). Black students enrolled in smaller classes in their primary years took college entrance exams, years later, at an 8 percent higher rate than black students in regular classes. This amounts to more than a 50 percent reduction in the black-white gap in college entrance exam participation—and a potentially significant reduction in differences in college attendance rates for blacks and whites.

These differences are to be taken seriously because they are enduring products of well-designed experimental interventions. But class size is not the only reform for which experimental evidence is becoming available. School vouchers, a reform of arguably the greatest potential significance, have been implemented through randomized field trials in multiple settings over the last five years. Vouchers, which entitle students to attend any public or private school willing to accept the voucher for all or part of the cost of attendance, could stimulate dramatic change in America's schools. Poorly performing schools could easily lose all of their students and revenue as students choose to use their vouchers to go elsewhere. Schools offering quality education, whether public or private, existing or entirely new, would flourish. Vouchers could bring about change not only in the practices of schools, as they seek to maintain or build enrollment, but also in the mix of schools in existence.

The effects of vouchers are hardly a simple matter to predict. Families could make poor choices. Poor families and poorly educated families, including the families of many black and Hispanic youngsters, could make the worst choices. Schools could cater to families without improving education.

The marketplace might provide better schooling for some but worse schooling for others, and, as a result, the rich could get richer and the poor could get poorer. These issues have been the most vigorously debated in education reform—in part, because they deal with the fundamental organizing principles of public education, but in part because so little direct evidence exists to resolve them.

Paul E. Peterson and William G. Howell, in "Voucher Programs and the Effect of Ethnicity on Test Scores," review the most direct evidence of how vouchers might work. Three state governments—Florida, Ohio, and Wisconsin—and private philanthropists in several major cities currently provide vouchers for students from low-income families. In several of these programs, students are awarded vouchers through a lottery, creating the opportunity to study the effects of the voucher experimentally. Students using vouchers can be compared with students who sought but failed to win vouchers. Peterson and Howell carry out these comparisons over two years in Dayton, Ohio, New York City, and Washington, D.C., where the vouchers are provided by philanthropy. Their key finding is that black students show a clear benefit from attending private school as compared with black students attending public school. The same is not true for white or Hispanic students. Their achievement is no higher in private school than in public. While the effect is not identical for blacks across all cities, it averages 6.3 percentiles, a full third of the black-white test score gap in these data and a clear sign that underachievement by blacks may have much to do with the schools black students attend.

Whether a school is public or private, understanding what schools precisely do to benefit students is important. Over the last decade, reformers have attempted to specify more thoroughly the elements of effective schooling, and they have produced in the process a number of comprehensive reform models. Among these are the Modern Red School House, Direct Instruction, America's Choice, Edison Schools, and, the most widely adopted, Success for All. These models go well beyond changing curriculum or instruction, the traditional domains of school reform. They attempt to change school practice from how they organize to how they teach to how they work with families to, in some cases, everything schools do. All of these models share one other thing in common: they have been adopted primarily by schools serving economically disadvantaged students and students of color.

Robert E. Slavin and Nancy A. Madden are the architects of Success for All, which was created in 1987 and is used today by nearly one million students in forty-eight states and eighteen hundred schools, virtually all with high levels of poverty. In "'Success for All' and African American and Latino Student Achievement," Slavin and Madden review the effects of Success for All on reading achievement in several different settings. First, they consider thirty-five schools, including some six thousand students, where matched control schools could provide reliable measures of program effects. In these thirty-five schools, which are majority African American or Hispanic, Success for All schools achieved about 0.5 standard deviations higher at each elementary grade level than control schools and were one full grade level ahead of the controls by fifth grade. Second, Slavin and Madden review an independent study of Success for All and other reform programs in Memphis, Tennessee, where students are nearly all African American. (The independent study was conducted by famed school accountability expert and scholar William Sanders.) The students in Success for All made the top gains in the city. Third, a study of every school in the state of Texas using Success for All showed black students exceeding the statewide improvement rate on the Texas Assessment of Academic Skills (TAAS), the state's accountability test, by 50 percent. Hispanic gains were better, too, but by lesser amounts.

If Success for All is showing in large numbers how the achievement of traditionally low-achieving groups can be moved forward, other programs are showing in small numbers but just as dramatically what a difference excellent schooling can make. Alex Molnar and a team of researchers from the University of Wisconsin–Milwaukee investigate Wisconsin's Student Achievement Guarantee in Education (SAGE) program. Beginning in 1995, Wisconsin offered schools serving large numbers of poor children an extra $2,000 for each low-income student. The money was to be spent on four reforms: (1) reducing pupil-teacher ratios in kindergarten through third grade, (2) keeping campuses open from early morning to late evening, (3) implementing a rigorous curriculum, and (4) providing professional development activities to instructional staff. Soon after the program began, class-size reduction became the focal point of SAGE in most of the participating schools, and the program expanded from 30 schools the first year to 566 schools in 2001.

The researchers, in "Wisconsin's SAGE Program and Achievement through Small Classes," analyze the test scores of SAGE students as they moved from first through third grades, comparing their achievement with non-SAGE students at similar schools. The findings are positive for SAGE. In reading, math, and language arts, SAGE students gained more than the comparison group in first and third grades—and registered approximately equal gains in second grade. Moreover, after three years in the programs, even though significant gains were evidenced by all racial groups, African American students gained more than whites. The black-white gap narrowed by about a third without white students losing ground. In the non-SAGE comparison schools, the achievement gap slightly expanded. In terms of finding politically feasible solutions to bridging the achievement gap, this is an important development. Policies that are perceived to close gaps at the expense of majority students—busing in the 1970s may be the clearest example—are destined to draw strong political opposition. Thus, Wisconsin may have developed a program that is both educationally sound and politically attractive.

Texas is another state that has targeted the achievement gap. Laurence A. Toenjes and a team of researchers from the University of Houston analyze the impact of the Texas testing and accountability system, in "High-Stakes Testing, Accountability, and Student Achievement in Texas and Houston." In the mid-1980s, Texas was a pioneer in designing a high-stakes accountability system. Several incentives were introduced, from students being required to pass tests before they could graduate from high school or participate in team sports to individual schools being rewarded or sanctioned based on students' test scores. The Texas Assessment of Academic Skills is a battery of criterion-referenced tests serving as the linchpin of the system. To promote equity, Texas was one of the first states to require that schools annually report disaggregated TAAS scores, allowing for the monitoring of progress by each major ethnic and racial group. That requirement was incorporated into the Leave No Child Behind Act, the federal education legislation signed by President George W. Bush in 2002.

The Houston researchers document how all three of Texas's major ethnic groups have registered solid academic gains on the TAAS. For the state as a whole, 55.6 percent of students passed the tests in 1994. In 1999 the passing rate had grown to 78.3 percent. The improvement was most pronounced for Hispanics and African Americans. The Hispanic passing rate jumped from 41.1 percent to 70.1 percent. The passing rate of African Americans nearly doubled, from 33.3 percent to 64.0 percent. The passing rate for whites improved from 69.4 percent to 87.9 percent. In recent years, critics have questioned whether the TAAS gains are real. The researchers address these concerns by analyzing TAAS data from several different angles—using mean scores instead of passing rates, comparing cohorts, and focusing only on Houston. They also evaluate enrollment data to determine whether an increase in student dropout rates may have inflated the TAAS scores. They conclude that the gains are real and that the achievement gap has narrowed substantially in Texas.

In their chapter, "Schools That Work," Abigail Thernstrom and Stephan Thernstrom offer a detailed look into three schools, one in Los Angeles, one in Houston, and one in New York City's borough of the Bronx, that are driving student achievement to eye-popping gains. The three schools are the progenitor (Los Angeles) and first working models of the Knowledge Is Power Program, or KIPP. These schools have taken students from black, Hispanic, and highly disadvantaged backgrounds and raised them from the lowest quartile of the national achievement distribution to the top quartile. These schools have made attendance at competitive universities a reality for students who would normally not attend college at all.

The Thernstroms argue that despite the bleak history of the achievement gap, which they review in detail, there is reason for optimism. No evidence exists that past school reform has attempted to create schools with the vision, determination, and fundamentally sound practice found at KIPP. Yet, if schools could put into place what the founders of KIPP first experienced with a special teacher in Los Angeles and then established in public schools in Houston and the Bronx in the mid-1990s, then clearly, as the tired conviction of educators goes, "all children can learn." The challenge is taking the successes that can be so great in a few schools and carrying them over to many schools.

David Klein, in "High Achievement in Mathematics: Lessons from Three Los Angeles Elementary Schools," identifies a weak curriculum as a major source of inequality in achievement and a strong curriculum as a means of closing gaps. Klein describes three elementary schools in the Los Angeles area: Bennett-Kew, William H. Kelso, and Robert Hill Lane. The schools serve predominantly disadvantaged students. At Bennett-Kew, for example, 77 percent of students qualify for free or reduced-price lunch, 51 percent are African American, 48 percent are Latino, and 29 percent are limited in English proficiency. This demographic profile is, regrettably, one that many people automatically associate with low test scores. Yet on California's annual academic assessments, the three schools consistently score at levels typical of schools in the state's most privileged neighborhoods.

The three elementary schools mainly resist faddish, cutting-edge approaches to teaching and relentlessly focus on teaching the core skills of reading and mathematics. Teachers instruct students on this knowledge and test regularly to make certain that pupils have learned it. In other words, the teachers in these schools teach students solid content. They do not facilitate, guide, or explore. Whole language is out; phonics is in. Calculators and National Council of Teachers of Mathematics math reform are out; arithmetic is in. Process approaches to writing are out; grammar, spelling, and punctuation are in. Bilingual education is out; English immersion and class assistants who help students develop facility with the English language are in.

The schools' principals—Nancy Ichinaga, Marjorie Thompson, and Sue Wong—fought hard to establish and maintain an academic focus at their schools and, by cultivating close ties with parents, have built an ethos of achievement from the classroom to the home. Klein concludes that clear, high-quality standards, textbooks and learning materials that convey high expectations to students, and teachers with sufficient content knowledge to make students reach beyond what they currently know are the key ingredients to school success—and to boosting the achievement of poor and minority students.

Samuel R. Lucas and Adam Gamoran examine the controversial practice of tracking in high school, in "Tracking and the Achievement Gap." They compare data on high school sophomores from two national surveys—High School and Beyond, conducted in 1980, and the National Education Longitudinal Study, conducted in 1990. Critics of tracking have long charged that the practice treats minority students unfairly, channeling them into low-track classes in which very little learning takes place. Lucas and Gamoran are interested in how changes in students' course taking in the 1980s affected achievement gaps and in assessing whether different track indicators—the manner in which a student's track location is reported—alter the measurement and interpretation of tracking's effects.

Did changes in tracking in the 1980s affect achievement gaps? The benefit of taking college-track courses grew during the decade. With all racial groups enrolling in more rigorous, college prep courses in 1990—African Americans, in particular—the black-white gap was cut in half. In 1980 Hispanic students were at a disadvantage in enrolling in college prep classes. However, by 1990 this disadvantage had evaporated, and the chances of blacks, whites, and Hispanics enrolling in the college track were about equal. These findings held true regardless of whether track membership was based on student self-reports or information gleaned from school transcripts. Asian students held an advantage in college-track placement in 1990. Lucas and Gamoran's research is a reminder that achievement gaps other than black-white and Hispanic-white deserve closer attention. Because of Asian students' advantage in gaining access to high-track courses, and the achievement benefit offered there, Lucas and Gamoran conclude that race continued to be a determinant of track location in 1990 and that track location continued to maintain or exacerbate race-linked differences in achievement.

What about Washington, D.C.? Ann Flanagan and David Grissmer argue that the federal government has an important role to play in closing the achievement gap. They document that the most glaring inequalities in financial resources are between, not within, states and argue that interstate disparities necessitate a more vigorous federal effort in equalizing resources. In 1995–96, for example, after adjusting for cost-of-living differences, Mississippi spent $4,900 per pupil while New Jersey spent $9,090. Current federal outlays are not large enough to narrow the gap appreciably. In 1996 Mississippi received $590 per pupil from Washington, while New Jersey received $340 per pupil. Flanagan and Grissmer firmly believe that increased spending can make a difference in narrowing achievement differences, especially when focused on low-achieving students.

Flanagan and Grissmer, in "The Role of Federal Resources in Closing the Achievement Gap," disaggregate NAEP scores by race, region, and locality to illustrate how achievement gaps vary geographically. The widest gaps are in the Midwest and Northeast. Students living in rural and suburban areas of the Midwest and Northeast—almost 30 percent of students nationally— score at levels rivaling the highest achieving students in the world. But students in the central cities of these regions, most of whom are impoverished and black, have some of the lowest test scores in the country. The gap is huge. In the rural South, students score lower than in other regions of the country, but the gap between white and black students is at its narrowest. Flanagan and Grissmer acknowledge that expanding the federal role in education may not always be justified. But, they argue, a larger federal role is warranted in attacking problems that transcend state boundaries. To have the greatest impact on the achievement gap, Flanagan and Grissmer recommend that federal efforts should target minimizing interstate resource differences, supporting sound educational research, and improving teacher quality.

This book is cause for encouragement. In it, some of education's most renowned scholars present a wealth of evidence that education's achievement gap can be bridged. They document how states, districts, and schools are making significant strides in boosting the performance of poor and minority students. Among the most promising strategies are curricula focused on reading and other core academic skills, smaller classes, getting students to take tougher courses, annual testing and reporting of disaggregated achievement data, creating schools with a culture of achievement, and vouchers offered to parents in big-city school districts. These solutions span the ideological spectrum. Both liberals and conservatives can be counted as their advocates.

Any optimism should be tempered, however, by recognizing that many obstacles remain and much work is yet to be done. The book's success stories primarily feature programs at the elementary school level. Success stories about middle and high school levels are more rare. Sound educational programs are notoriously difficult to replicate, often breaking down and losing their effectiveness when tried under different conditions and with new students and new teachers. Implementation problems or unintended effects may arise. The California class reduction program is a prime example, as a sudden shortage of teachers and classroom space placed school systems, especially urban systems, under great strain. Having a good idea is not enough. More experiments are needed to pinpoint the conditions under which even the most promising solutions will work optimally. Independent evaluations of costs and benefits are also needed so that public dollars go into programs getting the most bang for the buck.

Bridging the achievement gap is a national imperative. It can be done. The following pages provide a blueprint for moving beyond mere measurement of the problem and finally finding effective solutions.

2

Would Smaller Classes Help Close the Black-White Achievement Gap?

ALAN B. KRUEGER AND DIANE M. WHITMORE

A distressingly large gap is evident in academic achievement between white and black students.[1] On the 1999 National Assessment of Educational Progress (NAEP) exam, for example, the average seventeen-year-old black student scored at the 13th percentile of the distribution of white students on the math exam and at the 22nd percentile on the reading exam. Although part of this test score gap may result from racial biases in features of achievement tests, part of it reflects real differences in skills.[2] Moreover, the black-white gap in academic achievement appears to be an important contributing factor to the black-white gap in income, health, crime, and other outcomes.[3] W. E. B. Dubois correctly predicted that the problem of the twentieth century would be the color line. The problem of the twenty-first century might be the color line in academic achievement.

While the sources of the black-white achievement score gap are not well understood, identifying strategies to help reduce the gap clearly should be a priority for researchers and public policymakers alike. This paper considers the effect of reducing class size on student achievement. Contrary to the Coleman report and the summaries of the literature by Eric A. Hanushek, a consensus is emerging that students' standardized achievement scores do increase as a result of attending smaller classes.[4] Resources matter. Nonetheless, lowering class size is one of the more costly educational interventions commonly contemplated. Our 2001 cost-benefit analysis suggests that,

Figure 2-1. *Trends in Average Reading and Math Scores by Race, Seventeen-Year-Olds*

Standard deviation

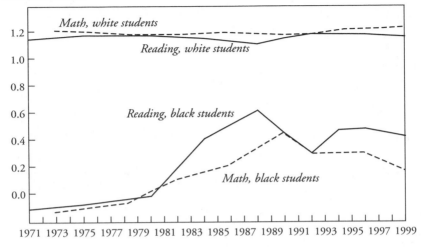

Source: Data are from U.S. Department of Education, National Center for Education Statistics.
Note: Scores are expressed as the raw score less the 1996 subject-specific mean raw score for all seventeen-year-olds, the difference is divided by the 1996 cross-sectional standard deviation for all seventeen-year-olds, and 1.0 is added to the resulting normalized score.

when all students are considered, the benefits of smaller classes in terms of the monetary value of achievement gains are about equal to the additional costs, assuming an initial class-size level of twenty-three students and a discount rate of 5.5 percent.[5] A finding of a normal rate of return from reducing class size should not be a surprise or a disappointment because it suggests that local schools are maximizing their allocation of resources. Moreover, reducing class size could still be a particularly desirable policy goal if disadvantaged groups benefit comparatively more from attending smaller classes.

Trends in the Black-White Achievement Gap

To illustrate the dimensions of the achievement gap, Figure 2-1 displays black and white seventeen-year-old students' average scores on the NAEP math and reading exam, normalized so the nationwide score and standard deviation in 1996 both equal one.[6] Figure 2-2 displays the corresponding results for nine-year-olds. Despite a small dip in the late 1980s, on this scale (which is admittedly wide) white students' achievement scores have been

Figure 2-2. *Trends in Average Reading and Math Scores by Race, Nine-Year-Olds*

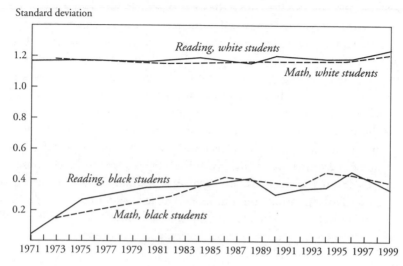

Standard deviation

Source: Data are from U.S. Department of Education, National Center for Education Statistics.
Note: Scores are expressed as the raw score less the 1996 subject-specific mean raw score for all nine-year-olds, the difference is divided by the 1996 cross-sectional standard deviation for all nine-year-olds, and 1.0 is added to the resulting normalized scores.

stagnant since the early 1970s. In the early 1970s, black students in both age groups scored about 1.2 standard deviations less on both the math and reading test than white students did.

The NAEP data indicate that the black-white reading gap among seventeen-year-olds has declined by almost half and the math gap declined by almost a third.[7] Nevertheless, a sizable gap remains. In 1999 black students scored 0.7 standard deviation lower on reading and 1.0 standard deviation lower on math. Also worrisome, the progress in narrowing the racial achievement gap appears to have stalled out since the late 1980s, and the gap has widened somewhat between 1994 and 1999.

Similar to the data from the NAEP exam, data from the SAT exam show a narrowing of the black-white score gap since the 1970s, although the closing continued into the 1980s and the gap did not start to expand until the mid-1990s.[8] In 1976, for example, white students scored 1.16 standard deviations higher on the math portion and 1.08 standard deviations higher on the verbal portion. By 1991 the gap narrowed to 0.85 and 0.81 standard deviation, respectively. In 2000, using the re-centered exam, the gaps were slightly higher at 0.85 and 0.92 standard deviation, respectively. The SAT exam is not designed to be representative of the population and is affected by changes in the composition of test takers, so the results are difficult to interpret. This problem aside, the SAT exam indicates that black students have made progress, although an enormous achievement score gap remains.

To gain some perspective on what it means for the distribution of black students' scores to be centered 0.9 standard deviation below that of other students, suppose that a highly selective college accepts only students who score in the top 5 percent of the distribution and that scores are normally distributed. Then black students would have to score 2.55 standard deviations above the mean of their distribution to be admitted—a hurdle cleared by only 0.5 percent of students. At an even more selective college, one that has a top 1 percent admissions cutoff, say, only 0.06 percent of black students would be admitted. If the mean test performance of black students increased by 0.2 standard deviation, the number of black students who clear this admissions hurdle would double. Raising the distribution of black students' test scores would greatly increase racial diversity at elite colleges.

Previous Literature

A common reaction to work on class size is: "Why bother to look at class-size effects? Hasn't Eric Hanushek definitively shown that hundreds of studies find no systematic relationship between class size and student achievement? Resources just don't matter." Alan B. Krueger argues that this skepticism is unsupported by the research literature.[9] First, Hanushek's latest tabulation of the literature is based on fifty-nine articles on class size and forty-one on expenditures per student, twenty-two of which were included in both; there are not hundreds of studies. Second, the literature seems larger than it is because Hanushek often extracts multiple estimates from the same paper and then treats all estimates as separate, independent studies. Hanushek, for example, extracted 277 estimates of the effect of class size from fifty-nine studies.[10] The number of estimates taken from each study varies widely. As many as twenty-four estimates were extracted from each of two papers (which used the same data set) and only one estimate was extracted from seventeen studies apiece. Third, and most important, the number of estimates Hanushek extracted from a study is systematically related to the study's findings, with fewer estimates taken from studies that tend to find positive effects of smaller classes or greater expenditures per student.

Each estimate that Hanushek extracted was coded as positive, negative, or unknown sign and as either statistically significant or insignificant. The estimates were then tabulated (see column 1 of table 2-1). A consideration of the

Table 2-1. *Reanalysis of Studies of Class Size and Expenditures per Pupil*

Result	Class size			Expenditures per student		
	Weighted by number of estimates extracted (1)	Equally weighted studies (2)	Studies weighted by journal impact factor (3)	Weighted by number of estimates extracted (4)	Equally weighted studies (5)	Studies weighted by journal impact factor (6)
Positive and statistically significant	14.8%	25.5%	34.5%	27.0%	38.0%	28.0%
Positive and statistically insignificant	26.7%	27.1%	21.2%	34.3%	32.2%	30.0%
Negative and statistically significant	13.4%	10.3%	6.9%	6.7%	6.4%	10.0%
Negative and statistically insignificant	25.3%	23.1%	25.4%	19.0%	12.7%	10.0%
Unknown sign and statistically insignificant	19.9%	14.0%	12.0%	12.9%	10.7%	21.0%
Ratio positive to negative	1.07	1.57	1.72	2.39	3.68	2.90
p value	0.500	0.059	0.034	0.0138	0.0002	0.0010

Note: Columns 1 and 4 are from Eric A. Hanushek, "Assessing the Effects of School Resources on Student Performance: An Update," *Educational Evaluation and Policy Analysis*, vol. 19, no. 2 (1997), pp. 141–64, table 3, and they implicitly weight studies by the number of estimates that were taken from each study. Columns 2, 3, 5, and 6 are from Alan B. Krueger, "Economic Considerations and Class Size," Working Paper 447 (Princeton University, Industrial Relations Section, September 2000). Columns 2 and 5 assign each study the fraction of estimates corresponding to the result based on Hanushek's coding, and calculate the arithmetic average. Columns 3 and 6 calculate a weighted average of the data in column 2, using the journal impact factors as weights. A positive result means that a small class size or greater expenditures are associated with improved student performance. Columns 1–3 are based on fifty-nine studies, and columns 4–6 are based on forty-one studies. p value corresponds to the proportion of times the observed ratio, or a higher ratio, of positive to negative results would be obtained in fifty-nine or forty-one independent Bernoulli trials in which positive and negative results were equally likely.

way a few of the studies were treated illustrates some of the problems with this approach.

Two studies by Charles R. Link and James G. Mulligan each contributed twenty-four estimates, or 17 percent of all estimated class-size effects.[11] Both papers estimated separate models for math and reading scores by grade level (third, fourth, fifth, or sixth) and by race (black, white, or Hispanic), yielding $2 \times 4 \times 3 = 24$ estimates apiece. The earlier paper (1986) addressed the merits of a longer school day using an 8 percent subsample of the data set from the later paper (1991). Class size was only included in the regression specifications reported in the earlier paper as an interaction term with classmate ability levels, which generally pointed to a beneficial effect of attending a small class. Nevertheless, Hanushek coded twenty-four estimates as statistically insignificant and unknown sign.

E. Cohn and S. D. Millman estimated a series of education production functions using a sample size of fifty-three secondary schools in Pennsylvania.[12] Hanushek selected eleven ordinary least squares (OLS) estimates, ten of which were negative, but he excluded the authors' preferred two-stage least squares (2SLS) estimates, which corrected for simultaneity bias and were consistently more positive. In addition, the OLS estimates controlled for both the average class size in a high school and the pupil-teacher ratio, making the class-size variable difficult to interpret.

Only one estimate was extracted from a study by Anita Summers and Barbara Wolfe, who analyzed data for 627 sixth-grade students in 103 elementary schools.[13] They mentioned that data were also analyzed for 533 eighth-grade students and 716 twelfth-grade students, with similar class-size results, but these results were not included in Hanushek's tabulation. Summers and Wolfe provided two sets of regression estimates: one with pupil-specific school inputs and another with school averages of school inputs.[14] They also provided pupil-level estimates of class-size effects for subsamples of low-, middle-, and high-achieving students, based on students' initial test scores.[15] Yet Hanushek selected only one estimate from this paper—the main effect from the student-level regression. Why the estimates reported for the various subsamples were excluded is unclear.

Any reasonable standard would not place eleven times more weight on Cohn and Millman's study than on Summers and Wolfe's. By using estimates as the unit of observation, Hanushek implicitly weights studies by the number of estimates he extracted from them. There is no reason that study quality should be related to the number of estimates extracted. Some of the studies from which Hanushek extracted multiple results have estimated problematic specifications. For example, a dozen studies simultaneously controlled for expenditures per student and students per teacher. In such a specification, School A can have a smaller class than School B only by paying its teachers less or crimping on other resources, which is not the policy experiment most people have in mind when they think about reducing class size.[16]

Table 2-1 summarizes Krueger's reanalysis of Hanushek's literature review. Column 1 treats all estimates that Hanushek extracted equally. These results led Hanushek to conclude, "There is no strong or consistent relationship between school inputs and student performance."

When all studies are given equal weight, however, the literature does exhibit systematic evidence of a relationship between school inputs and student achievement. To weight the studies equally, each study is assigned the proportion of estimates that are positive and significant, negative and significant, and so on, according to Hanushek's coding, and then the arithmetic average is taken over all studies (see column 2 of table 2-1). The number of studies that find positive effects of expenditures per student outnumbers those that find negative effects by almost 4:1. The number of studies that find a positive effect of smaller classes exceeds the number that find a negative effect by 57 percent. Differences of these magnitudes are unlikely to have occurred by chance.

We would argue that studies form a more natural unit of observation for this type of literature summary than estimates because studies are accepted for publication, not individual estimates. A weak paper can perhaps overcome the skepticism of a referee by including more estimates. In addition, most of the multiple estimates were either drawn from papers that used the same sample of students to examine different outcomes (math tests, reading tests, composite tests, and so on), so the estimates within a paper are not independent, or drawn from papers that carved up one sample into ever smaller subsamples, so the results were statistically imprecise. Finally, and probably most important, weighting all studies equally reduces the impact of researcher discretion in choosing which estimates to select.

To crudely (but objectively) assign more weight to higher quality studies, the studies are assigned a weight equal to the 1998 impact factor of the journal that published the article, using data from the Institute for Scientific Information. The impact factors are based on the average number of citations to articles published in the journals in 1998. Impact factors are available for forty-four of the fifty-nine class-size studies in the sample; the other fifteen studies were published in books, conference volumes, or unpublished monographs. Studies not published in journals were assigned the impact factor of

18 ALAN B. KRUEGER AND DIANE M. WHITMORE

the lowest ranked journal. The weighted mean of the percentages is presented in column 3 of table 2-1. Although obvious problems arise with using journal impact factors as an index of study quality (for example, norms and professional practices influence the number of citations), citation counts are a widely used indicator of quality, and the impact factor should be a more reliable measure of study quality than the number of estimates Hanushek extracted.[17] The results are similar when either the arithmetic mean or journal-impact-weighted mean is used.

Columns 4, 5, and 6 of table 2-1 repeat this same exercise using Hanushek's tabulated results for expenditures per student. Studies that find a positive effect of school spending outnumber those that find a negative effect by nearly 4:1. As a whole, we believe that when fairly summarized the literature does suggest that school resources matter—or at least it suggests that one should be less confident in the view that they do not matter.

Of particular interest is how class size affects achievement for black students. Table 2-2 summarizes the methods and findings of studies that provide separate estimates by race. The first five studies in table 2-2 were included in Hanushek's survey. We expanded the list by including some studies published after Hanushek's survey was written. We include a 2000 study edited by B. M. Stecher and G. W. Bohrnstedt, which evaluates the class-size reduction initiative in California; early work on the Project STAR class-size reduction experiment by Jeremy D. Finn and Charles M. Achilles; Alex Molnar and others' study of Wisconsin's Student Achievement Guarantee in Education (SAGE) program; and papers by Marie T. Mora and Michael Boozer and Cecilia Rouse, who use the National Education Longitudinal Study (NELS) data.[18] One limitation of some of these studies for our purposes is that class size was often included as one variable in a kitchen-sink model because the authors did not intend for their estimated class-size effect to receive attention. For example, Charles R. Link and James G. Mulligan controlled for both class size and hours of subject-specific instruction.[19] If teachers in smaller classes can spend less class time on discipline and administration, they likely spend more time instructing students on math and reading. Holding instruction time constant but varying class size confounds the estimated effect of smaller classes.

To facilitate comparison, we scaled the coefficients to reflect the impact of a seven-student decrease in class size, which is the average class-size reduction in Project STAR. Where possible, we standardized the results to report test score effects in terms of standard deviations and reported standard errors. In some cases, however, the studies provided insufficient information to perform these calculations.

Table 2-2. *Summary of Class-Size Studies That Provide Separate Estimates by Race*

Study	Description	Findings for a seven-student reduction in class size
Ehrenberg and Brewer (1994)	Uses High School and Beyond individual-level data to look at effects of teachers and school resources on gain in test scores and on dropout behavior. Both equations include pupil-teacher ratio, expenditure per student, base-year test score, student gender, family income and size, parents' education level, a dummy variable indicating whether the school is in an urban setting, the percentage of students in the school that are black, the percentage that are Hispanic, the percentage that are low-income, the difference between the percentage of black (Hispanic) faculty and black (Hispanic) students, and teachers' experience, education level, and quality of their undergraduate institution. The dropout equation is estimated by a probit model, and the gain model is estimated by ordinary least squares (OLS) using a Heckman correction for dropouts. Median sample size is 1,003.	Change in test score gain (standard errors) Blacks: 0.140 (0.108) Whites: 0.038 (0.029) Change in dropout rate (standard errors) Blacks: −0.322 (0.358) Whites: −0.007 (0.023)
Link and Mulligan (1991)	Estimates separate OLS regression models for individual-level Comprehensive Test of Basic Skills (CTBS) math and reading scores for third, fourth, fifth, and sixth grade using the sustaining effects data set. Explanatory variables include pre-test score, class size, gender, hours of instruction, a dummy variable indicating whether the teacher recommends compensatory education, same race percentage of classmates, racial busing percentage, and the mean and standard deviation of classmates' pre-test scores. Median sample size is 6,023.	Average change in test score, scaled by standard deviation (standard errors) Blacks: −0.001 (0.014) Whites: −0.004 (0.007)
Winkler (1975)	Examines the effect of the racial composition of a school on eighth grade Stanford reading scores using student data from a large urban California school district in 1964–65. The model also includes aggregate pupil/teacher ratio in grades one through eight, student intelligence quotient (IQ) measured in first grade, number of siblings, number of cultural items in home, parents' homeownership status, teacher salary, total administrative spending, share of peers with low socioeconomic status (SES), the change in share between elementary and middle school, the share of black students and the change in share between elementary and middle school, and share of teachers from prestigious colleges. Median sample size is 387.	Change in test score for eight years of class-size reduction, scaled by standard deviation (standard errors) Blacks: 0.117 (0.156) Whites: 0.166 (0.170)

continued on next page

Table 2-2. Summary of Class-Size Studies That Provide Separate Estimates by Race (continued)

Study	Description	Findings for a seven-student reduction in class size
Card and Krueger (1992)	Estimates the effect of pupil-teacher ratio on returns to education. Uses census data on wages in 1960, 1970, and 1980 for Southern-born men aggregated to state-by-cohort cells, linked to school characteristics in segregated states from 1915 to 1966. Uses weighted least squares to estimate by race the effect on return to education of pupil-teacher ratio, and state, year, and cohort dummy variables. Sample size is 180.	Change in payoff to one year of education (standard errors) Blacks: 0.410 (0.347) Whites: 0.219 (0.389)
Sengupta and Sfeir (1986)	Sample contains fifty school-level observations on sixth graders in California. Dependent variables are math, reading, writing, and spelling test scores. Explanatory variables are average teacher salary, average class size, percent minority, and interaction between percent minority and class size. Half of the eight models also control for nonteaching expenditures per pupil. Estimates translog production functions by least absolute deviation (LAD).	Change in average test score, scaled by standard deviation Blacks: 0.711 Whites: –0.411
Stecher and Bohrnstedt (2000)	Evaluates the statewide class-size reduction in California enacted in 1996–97, which aimed to reduce the average class size in grades K–3 from twenty-eight to no more than twenty. Uses third grade Stanford achievement test data for reading, math, language, and spelling. Presents differences between third grade scores in schools with and without class-size reduction, after controlling for underlying differences in schools' (untreated) fifth grade scores.	Overall effect size is 0.073 standard deviation. Math and language tests have somewhat larger effect sizes in schools with high percentages of minority, low-income, and English-learner students.
Mora (1997)	Uses individual-level National Education Longitudinal Study (NELS) data and runs logit models to examine the effect of school quality on propensity to drop out. Students were in eighth grade in 1988, and 1990 follow-up data were used to measure dropout status. Explanatory variables include pupil-teacher ratio, salary expenditures per pupil, length of school year, enrollment, school programs (counseling, departmentalized instruction, and grade point average requirement for activities), dummy for private school, location	Change in probability of dropping out (standard deviation) Blacks: 0.012 (0.028) Whites: –0.067 (0.011)

Study	Description	Effect
	categories, student SES characteristics, and classroom racial and SES composition. Adjusts pupil-teacher ratio to measure average daily attendance per teacher, not total enrollment per teacher. Median sample size is 6,677.	Change in test score, scaled by race-specific standard deviation Blacks: 0.254 Whites: 0.123
Finn and Achilles (1990)	Reports results from a statewide experiment in Tennessee, in which students were randomly assigned to small or regular-size classes. Individual-level data on test scores in first grade are analyzed. School fixed effects are also employed as explanatory variables. Median sample size is 3,300.	
Boozer and Rouse (2001)	Finds that class size often varies within school due to compensatory class assignments that put gifted and regular students in larger classes than special needs and remedial students. With compensatory resource allocation, using school-level pupil-teacher ratios may bias coefficient estimates downward. Individual-level NELS data are used to estimate the effect of class size on test score gains.	Overall, seven-student decrease in class size increases test scores by 0.49 standard deviation. Class size does not statistically significantly vary by race.
Molnar and others (1999)	Evaluates Wisconsin's Student Achievement Guarantee in Education (SAGE) program, which reduced pupil-teacher ratio in selected schools. Only schools with student poverty rates of 30 percent or more were eligible to apply. Uses first grade CTBS test data for reading, math, and language arts. Presents differences between two cohorts of first grade students' scores in SAGE schools and comparison schools with similar characteristics. Sample size is 3,944.	Change in test score, scaled by comparison group standard deviation Blacks: 0.361 Whites: -0.127

Note: The studies are R. G. Ehrenberg and D. J. Brewer, "Do School and Teacher Characteristics Matter? Evidence from High School and Beyond," *Economics of Education Review*, vol. 13, no. 1 (1994), pp. 1–17; Charles R. Link and James G. Mulligan, "Classmates' Effects on Black Student Achievement in Public School Classrooms," *Economics of Education Review*, vol. 10, no. 4 (1991), pp. 299–310; P. Winkler, "Educational Achievement and School Peer Group Composition," *Journal of Human Resources*, vol. 10, no. 2 (1975), pp. 689–204; David Card and Alan B. Krueger, "School Quality and Black-White Relative Earnings: A Direct Assessment," *Quarterly Journal of Economics*, vol. 107, no. 1 (1992), pp. 151–200; J. K. Sengupta and R. E. Sfeir, "Production Frontier Estimates of School in Public Schools in California," *Economics of Education Review*, vol. 5, no. 3 (1986), pp. 297–307; B. M. Stecher and G. W. Bohrnstedt, *Class Size Reduction in California: The 1998–99 Evaluation Findings* (Sacramento, Calif.: California Department of Education, August 2000); Marie T. Mora, "Attendance, Schooling Quality, and the Demand for Education of Mexican Americans, African Americans, and Non-Hispanic Whites," *Economics of Education Review*, vol. 16, no. 4 (1997), pp. 407–18; Jeremy D. Finn and Charles M. Achilles, "Answers and Questions about Class Size: A Statewide Experiment," *American Educational Research Journal*, vol. 27 (Fall 1990), pp. 557–77; Michael Boozer and Cecilia Rouse, "Intraschool Variation in Class Size: Patterns and Implications," *Journal of Urban Economics*, vol. 50, no. 1 (July 2001), pp. 163–89; and Alex Molnar and others, "Evaluating the SAGE Program: A Pilot Program in Tarsetex Pupil-Teacher Reduction in Wisconsin," *Educational Evaluation and Policy Analysis*, vol. 21, no. 2 (Summer 1999), pp. 165–77. Logit coefficients in Mora, "Attendance," are transformed assuming the mean dropout probability equals 0.1.

Although the findings vary considerably from study to study, on the whole the results suggest that attending a smaller class has a more beneficial effect for minority students than for nonminority students. Stecher and Bohrnstedt provided a particularly relevant evaluation because they considered the effects of an actual, statewide class-size reduction initiative in California that could provide a model for other states.[20] In this enormous education reform, which was championed by then-governor Pete Wilson, California school districts that chose to participate received just over $800 for each K–3 student enrolled in a class of twenty or fewer students to encourage smaller classes. Because of the scale of this intervention, many implementation problems were encountered that do not arise in small-scale demonstration studies. For example, some higher income school districts reportedly raided teachers from lower income districts. In addition, many new classrooms had to be built to accommodate smaller classes, and temporary structures were often used. Nonetheless, Stecher and Bohrnstedt found that, after two years, the California class-size reduction initiative led to a 0.10 standard deviation increase in math scores and a 0.05 standard deviation increase in reading scores on the Stanford Achievement Test for third graders. Both of these effect sizes were statistically significant. They also found that schools with a larger share of minority students had larger effect sizes. The effect size was 0.10 standard deviation larger on the math exam in schools with 75 percent or more minority students compared with those with 25 percent or fewer minority students, for example, but this differential effect was not statistically significant.

Several other studies do not provide separate estimates by race, but they do examine the effect of reduced class size on low-income or low-achieving students. For example, Eric A. Hanushek, John F. Kain, and Steven G. Rivkin found a positive effect of smaller classes on math and reading achievement of low-income fourth- and fifth-grade students in Texas (37 percent of the sample), but insignificant (mostly positive) effects for other students.[21] Likewise, David W. Grissmer and others reported that the lowest socioeconomic status (SES) states with high pupil-teacher ratios (twenty-six students per teacher) gained 0.17 standard deviation on test scores from a three-student reduction in the pupil-teacher ratio.[22] The effect size diminishes as average pupil-teacher ratio decreases, or as SES increases. And Anita Summers and Barbara Wolfe found that low-achieving students perform worse when in larger classes, while high-achieving students perform better.[23] Thus, the literature suggests that disadvantaged students—minorities, low-SES, and low-achievers—gain the most from smaller classes. This conclusion is also reinforced by the findings from the Project STAR experiment.

Results from Project STAR

The Tennessee STAR experiment is the best-designed experiment available to evaluate the impact of class size in the early grades on student achievement. In Project STAR, a total of 11,600 students in kindergarten through third grade were randomly assigned to a small class (target of thirteen to seventeen students), regular-size class (target of twenty-two to twenty-five students), or regular-size class with a full-time teacher's aide, within seventy-nine Tennessee public schools.[24] The initial design called for students to remain in the same class type in grades K–3, although students were randomly reassigned between regular and regular with teacher's aide classes in first grade. New students entering Project STAR schools in grades one through three while this cohort was participating in the experiment were randomly assigned to a class type. Students who left the school or repeated a grade were dropped from the sample being tracked during the experiment, although data on their subsequent performance in many cases were added back to the sample after third grade, as other data sources were used. In fourth grade, all students were returned to regular classes.

Data are available for about sixty-two hundred students per year in grades K–3, and about seventy-seven hundred students per year in grade four through eight, after the experiment ended. The average student in the experiment who was assigned to a small class in the experiment spent 2.3 years in a small class. An important feature of the experiment is that teachers were also randomly assigned to class types. Alan B. Krueger evaluated some of the problems in the implementation and design of the STAR experiment, including high rates of attrition and possible nonrandom transitions between grade levels, and concluded that they did not materially alter the main results of the experiment.[25]

The small-class effects are measured by comparing students from different class types in the same schools. Because students were randomly assigned to a class type within schools, student characteristics—both measurable, such as free-lunch status, and unmeasurable, such as parental involvement in students' education—should be the same across class types, on average.

Standardized Test Scores, Grades K–8

Because students were randomly assigned to small and regular classes within schools, school effects must be controlled while estimating the treatment effect of being assigned to a small class. A simple estimator in this case is the balanced-sample estimator, which holds the distribution of students across schools constant. Specifically, for each school and grade we calculated the average percentile rank for students assigned to small classes and those assigned to normal-size classes.[26] (Because earlier research found that students in regular classes with and without a teacher's aide performed about equally well, we pool the aide and regular students together. We call this pooled group "normal-size classes.") We then calculated the weighted average of these school-level means, using as weights in each case the number of normal-size-class students in the school in that grade.[27] The difference between the two weighted means holds school effects constant. Intuitively, this arises because the difference could be calculated by first computing the difference in mean performance between small- and regular-class students within each school, and then taking the weighted mean of these school-level treatment effects.[28]

Class type in this analysis is based on the class the student attended in his or her initial year in Project STAR and does not vary over time. Using this categorization leads to what is commonly called an "intent to treat" estimator, as it was the intention to assign the students to their original class type. As a result, the estimated differences in means between small- and normal-class students are not subject to bias because of possible nonrandom transitions after the initial assignment. The estimates, however, will provide a lower bound estimate of the effect of actually attending a small class because some of the students assigned to a small class attended a normal-size class, and vice versa. This probably understates the effect of attending a small class by 10–15 percent.[29]

Figure 2-3 displays the weighted average percentile scores by class assignment for black students, and figure 2-4 displays the corresponding information for white students. In each case, the weights were the number of regular-class students of that race in the school. As studies by Finn and Achilles, Krueger, and Alan B. Krueger and Diane M. Whitmore found, the figure indicates that black students benefited comparatively more from being assigned to a small class.[30] In grades K–3, black students in small classes outperformed those in normal-size classes by 7–10 percentile points, on average, while white students in small classes had a 3–4 percentile-point advantage over their counterparts in normal-size classes.[31] For both racial groups, the small-class advantage remained roughly constant during the course of the experiment—that is, through third grade. In terms of standard deviation units (of the full sample), black students gained about 0.26 of a standard deviation from being assigned to a small class while white students gained about 0.13 standard deviation.

In fourth grade, the effect size falls about in half for both racial groups and remains roughly constant thereafter. The gain from having been

Figure 2-3. *Black Students' Average Test Scores Using the Balanced-Sample Estimator*

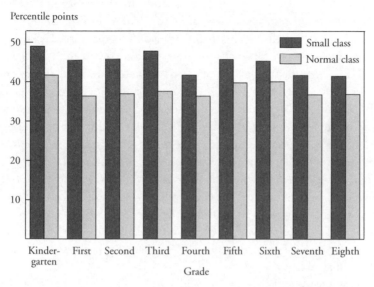

Figure 2-4. *White Students' Average Test Scores Using the Balanced-Sample Estimator*

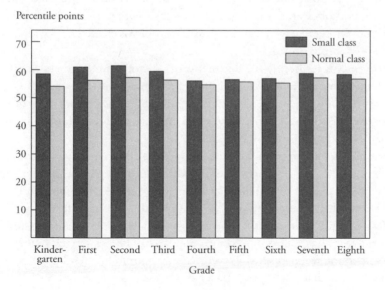

assigned to a small class is approximately 5 percentile points for black students in grades four through eight and 1.5 points for white students in grades four through eight. These effects are still statistically significant at conventional significance levels. The decline in the treatment effects in fourth grade could result from several factors. After third grade the experiment concluded and all students were enrolled in regular-size classes. Unfortunately, this also coincided with the time the assessment test was changed. In grades K–3, students took the Stanford Achievement Test, and in grades four through eight, they took the Comprehensive Test of Basic Skills (CTBS). Both tests are multiple-choice standardized tests that measure reading and math achievement, and they are taken by students at the end of the school year. We suspect the change in the test is not critical for the reduction in the treatment effect because the year-to-year correlations in students' percentile rankings are about the same between third and fourth grade (which encompass the different tests) and other adjacent grades (which use the same test). Another factor could be that the fourth-grade sample is a subset of the overall sample because Memphis schools administered the CTBS test only to about one-third of their students in 1990; in later years the test was universally administered.

The composition of the students underlying figures 2-3 and 2-4 is changing over time. The decline in the treatment effect in the first year after all students moved into regular-size classes is still apparent, however, if we use just the subsample of students with scores available in both third and fourth grade. It is also apparent if we use just the subset with scores available in both third and fifth grade, which avoids possible problems created by the omission of many Memphis fourth graders.

Although interpreting the decline in the treatment effect between third and fourth grade as a fading out of the gains achieved by the small-class students is tempting, peer effects could have increased the performance of students who had been in normal-size classes relative to those who had been in small classes after the experiment ended.

Another issue to bear in mind in interpreting the trends over time in figures 2-3 and 2-4 is that these tests are scaled according to percentile ranks and that percentile ranks are not a cardinal measure. A given percentile gap could, and likely does, correspond to a larger educational difference in later grades than in earlier grades.[32] The discrete decline in the small-class advantage the year all students moved into regular-size classes suggests, however, that something real happened. Nevertheless, a bottom line result from figures 2-3 and 2-4 is that assignment to a small class led to greater improvement in the relative position in the distribution of test scores for minority students than for white students—and it did so during the years when students were in small classes and subsequently.

The following calculation suggests that the effect of assignment to a small class on the racial test score gap is sizable. In third grade, for example, the black-white gap in the average percentile rank was 18.8 points in normal-size classes and 11.7 points in small classes. So according to these figures assigning all students to a class of fifteen students as opposed to twenty-two students for a couple of years in grammar school would lower the black-white gap by about 38 percent. Part of this beneficial effect appears to fade out over time. By eighth grade, assignment to a small class in the early grades appears to narrow the black-white test score gap by 15 percent. These figures are likely to understate the benefit of attending a small class because not everyone assigned to a small class attended one.

Lastly, we can also calculate the average treatment effect for white students using the school-level weights for black students to infer whether white students who attend the same mix of schools as black students have an average treatment effect that is close to that found for black students. For grades K–3, that is what the data suggest—the average treatment effect for white students, weighted by the number of black students in the school, is close to what figure 2-3 shows for black students. After grade three, however, this exercise produces an even smaller estimate for white students than what we found in figure 2-4, where the treatment effects for whites are weighted by the number of white students. If we do this exercise for black students (that is, weight their school-level treatment effects by the number of white students in normal classes in the school), the impact of being assigned to a small class is uniformly smaller in all grades.

College Entrance Exam–Taking Rates

Students who were assigned to a small class in grades K–3 were significantly more likely to take the SAT or ACT college entrance exam. Krueger and Whitmore reported initial results using data for students who graduated from high school in 1998.[33] That paper found that small-class attendance raised the likelihood that black students would take the ACT or SAT by a quarter—from 31.7 to 40.2 percent. As a result, the black-white gap in the test-taking rate was 54 percent smaller in small classes than in regular classes. This work, however, was limited by incomplete data on test scores.

UPDATED ACT DATA. To create the original longitudinal database with SAT and ACT information used by Krueger and Whitmore, in the summer of 1998 the ACT and Educational Testing Service (ETS) organizations matched

Project STAR student data to their national database of test records. The match was performed using student names, dates of birth, and Social Security numbers, or two of the three identifiers if one field was missing.[34] Because the test files are organized by graduating class, test data could be matched only for students who graduated in the class of 1998. As a result, any Project STAR student who repeated a grade (or skipped ahead) and did not graduate on schedule with the class of 1998 could not be matched. Based on data through eighth grade, nearly 20 percent of the Project STAR sample appeared to have been left behind a grade. Any student who had been left behind would be categorized as not having taken the ACT or SAT, even if the student had already taken the test during his or her junior year or took it a year later. The resulting misclassification tends to attenuate the effect of small classes on test-taking rates. To minimize the effects of misclassification, our earlier work presented most results limiting the sample to those who graduated on schedule.

For this paper we have obtained additional ACT data to augment the sample to include those students who did not graduate on schedule. The records that were not matched by ACT in our earlier data set were resubmitted, and ACT attempted to match them to their databases for the classes of 1997 through 2000. The SAT match was not updated, but this is probably inconsequential because based on the first match only 3.5 percent of Project STAR test takers took the SAT and not the ACT. Further, students who took only the SAT tended to have stronger academic records, so they are less likely to be behind a grade. As before, records were matched on student name, date of birth, and Social Security number. The match was done nationwide when all three variables were present. For cases that lacked a valid Social Security number (32 percent), the match was restricted to the state files of Kentucky, Mississippi, and Tennessee. These three states accounted for 95 percent of the ACT matches in the first round.

In the new match, an additional 10.7 percent of previously unmatched students were linked to ACT data.[35] Several checks indicate that the data were linked properly for students who were matched. For example, the correlation between the students' ACT score percentile rank and their eighth-grade CTBS percentile rank was 0.74, which is similar to the correlation between other percentile scores of tests given four years apart.[36] In addition, the sex of the student based on their Project STAR record matched their ACT-reported sex in 97.5 percent of the matches. These checks suggest that the Project STAR data were linked correctly, and they show that the new match is about the same quality as the previous match.

TEST-TAKING RATES. To examine whether assignment to a small class influences the college entrance exam test-taking rate, we again use a balanced-sample estimator to adjust for school effects.[37] For each school denoted j, racial group denoted r, and class type (small, regular, regular with teacher's aide) denoted c, we estimate the percentage of students who took either the ACT or SAT exam, denoted $\bar{Y}_{jr}^C$. We then calculate the weighted average of the school means, using as weights the number of regular-class students in each school (N^R).

$$\bar{\bar{Y}}_r^C = \frac{\sum_j \bar{Y}_{jr}^C N_{jr}^R}{\sum_j N_{jr}^R}.$$

The difference between the small-class and regular-class means ($\bar{\bar{Y}}_r^S - \bar{\bar{Y}}_r^R$) can be written as $\sum_j (\bar{Y}_{jr}^S - \bar{Y}_{jr}^R) \cdot w_{jr}$, where w_{jr} is the fraction of all students in the experiment of that race who were assigned to regular-size classes in that school. This shows that the difference between the means can be written as the weighted average of the school-level treatment effects, which makes transparent that school effects are held constant.

Our findings are illustrated in figure 2-5. This figure reports the percentage of students by race who took either the SAT or ACT, by the type of class they attended during their first year in Project STAR. For white students, 46.4 percent of those initially attending small classes took a college entrance exam, compared with 44.7 percent in regular classes and 45.3 percent in regular with teacher's aide classes. These differences in rates are not statistically significant. Black students were substantially more likely to take the SAT or ACT if they were assigned to a small instead of regular-size class: 41.3 percent of black students assigned to small classes took at least one of the college entrance exams, compared with 31.8 percent in regular classes and 35.7 percent in regular with teacher's aide classes. The chance of such a large difference in test-taking rates between the small and regular-class students occurring by chance is less than one in ten thousand.

The black-white gap in taking a college entrance exam was 12.9 percentage points for students in regular-size classes and 5.1 percentage points for students in small classes. Thus, assigning all students to a small class is estimated to reduce the black-white gap in the test-taking rate by an impressive 60 percent.

As before, we can also calculate the average treatment effect using different weights to infer whether white students who attend a similar mix of schools

Figure 2-5. *Percent of Students Taking the SAT or ACT, by Initial Class Type*

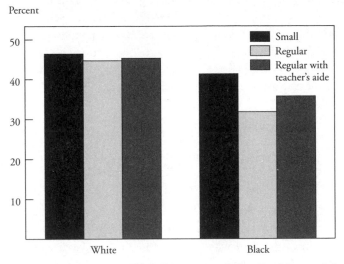

Percent

Legend:
- Small
- Regular
- Regular with teacher's aide

White   Black

Note: SAT = Scholastic Assessment Test; ACT = American College Test. Means are balanced within school using the balanced-sample estimator.

as black students have the same treatment effect as black students. That is, we have calculated the weighted average of the school-level treatment effects for whites using the number of black students in the school as weights. Remarkably, this indicated an even larger treatment effect for white students than was previously found for black students—about an 11 percentage-point higher rate of test taking for small-class students than normal-size-class students. Likewise, if we use the school-level treatment effects for the black students and the number of white regular students in the school as weights, the treatment effect for blacks shrinks to about that found for whites in figure 2-5.

These findings suggest that small classes matter for blacks because of something having to do with the schools they attend, not something inherent to individual black students per se. For example, black students could attend schools that have a disproportionately high number of disruptive students, or students with special needs, which distracts their teachers from instructional time.[38] In this case, white students in those schools would also benefit from smaller classes.

ACT TEST SCORES, WITH AND WITHOUT SELECTION ADJUSTMENT. For students who took the SAT but not the ACT exam, we converted their SAT score to an ACT-equivalent score using a concordance developed jointly by ACT and the College Board.[39] For any student who took the ACT exam we used the ACT score even if he or she also took the SAT. For students who took an exam more than once we used the first score. Any analysis of ACT and SAT scores can be performed only on the subset of students who took one of the exams. This creates a potential selection problem. Because a higher proportion of students from small classes took the SAT or ACT exam, the group from small classes likely contains a higher fraction of relatively weak students. That is, stronger students are likely to take an exam regardless of their class assignment, but marginal students who are induced to take the exam because they attended a small class are likely to be lower scoring students. Such a selection process would bias downward the effect of attending a small class on average test scores. The bias is also likely to be greater for black students, because a higher share of black students were induced to take the exam as a result of attending a small class.

To simplify the analysis, we compare students who initially attended small classes with the combined sample of those who initially attended either regular or regular with teacher's aide classes, and we control for school effects instead of school-by-entry-wave effects. Also, because we later implement a Heckman selection correction, we use raw ACT scores instead of percentile ranks for this analysis.[40] The raw ACT scores in our sample range from 9 to 36 and are approximately normally distributed.

The results are reported in table 2-3. For the sample of test takers, the average ACT score was virtually identical for students who were assigned to small and normal-size classes. The average white student in a small class scored 19.88, while the average white student in a regular class scored 19.87. Black students in small classes averaged 16.3, while black students in regular classes scored 16.1. The differences between small and normal-size classes are not statistically significant.

Past studies of state-level data have shown that average test scores tend to decline when more students take a college entrance exam, most likely because the marginal test takers are weaker students than the average student.[41] Project STAR had two confounding effects: selection and treatment. One might expect the treatment to result in small-class students scoring slightly higher on the ACT, as they did on previous tests through the eighth grade. But because a larger percentage of students assigned to small classes took the exam, a larger share of weaker students in small classes likely took the test. As a result, interpreting the score results is difficult because scores are only reported conditional on taking the exam, and the treatment appears to have affected the likelihood of taking the exam—particularly for black students. Columns 2 and 3 and columns 5 and 6 present two types of estimation results that attempt to adjust for this sample selection problem.

Table 2-3. *Effect of Class Size on ACT or SAT Score with and without Selection Correction*

	White students			Black students		
Explanatory variable	No correction (1)	Heckman correction (2)	Linear truncation (3)	No correction (4)	Heckman correction (5)	Linear truncation (6)
Intercept	20.233	16.386	20.242	17.073	7.443	17.164
	(0.138)	(0.524)	(0.138)	(0.275)	(3.610)	(0.274)
Small class	0.009	0.209	0.206	0.213	0.834	1.079
	(0.169)	(0.210)	(0.167)	(0.204)	(0.266)	(0.203)
Female (1 = yes)	0.056	1.787	0.021	0.522	2.229	0.378
	(0.156)	(0.197)	(0.156)	(0.190)	(0.237)	(0.191)
Free lunch (1 = yes)	-1.434	-4.859	-1.385	-1.715	-3.529	-1.725
	(0.180)	(0.241)	(0.179)	(0.265)	(0.332)	(0.263)
School fixed effects	Yes	Yes	Yes	Yes	Yes	Yes
Number of observations	3,198	7,124	3,173	1,427	4,117	1,357
Effect size	0.002	0.039	0.038	0.039	0.153	0.198

Note: Dependent variable equals American College Test (ACT) or ACT-equivalent score. Heteroskedasticity-adjusted standard errors are reported in parentheses for columns 1, 3, 4, and 6. If a student took only the Scholastic Assessment Test (SAT), that score is converted to its comparable ACT score. The mean (standard deviation) of the dependent variable is 19.9 (4.5) in column 1, 19.9 (4.4) in column 3, 16.1 (3.5) in column 4, and 16.3 (3.5) in column 6. The effect size is the coefficient on small class divided by the standard deviation of test scores among the full sample of students (5.4).

Columns 2 and 4 present results of a standard Heckman-correction procedure for white and black students. Identification in this model is based solely on the assumption of normal errors, as there is no exclusion restriction. We also calculate the effect size by dividing the coefficient on the small-class dummy by the standard deviation of ACT scores among all students who took the exam (equal to 5.4). The Heckman correction doubles the point estimate on the effect of attending a small class for white students, but the coefficient is still statistically insignificant and qualitatively small. For blacks, however, column 5 indicates that after adjusting for selection, students in small classes score 0.15 standard deviation higher than those in regular classes.

Columns 3 and 6 present results from a different approach for adjusting for selection. We have artificially truncated the sample of students from small classes so that the same proportion of students from small and regular-size classes is represented in the test-taking sample. Specifically, we drop from the sample the bottom X percent of students based on their test results, where X is determined so that the share of students from small classes who took the exam equals the share from regular-size classes. This approach is valid if all the additional small-class students induced to take the ACT are from the bottom of the distribution, and if attending a small class did not change the ranking of students in small classes. Although the former assumption is extreme, the results should provide an upper bound on the impact of selection bias and serve as a point of comparison to the Heckman-correction results.

Krueger and Whitmore provided some diagnostic information on these two selection-correction approaches by comparing the Heckman-correction procedure and the linear truncation model for eighth-grade students, when test scores were available for the full universe of students.[42] If the sample were artificially truncated to those who later took the ACT or SAT exam, the two selection-correction procedures bracketed the effect estimated by OLS for the full sample.[43]

The results in columns 3 and 6 are similar to the Heckman-correction results in columns 2 and 5. For white students, the linear truncation and Heckman selection-correction procedure indicate that students in small classes score insignificantly differently from students in normal-size classes, with a point estimate corresponding to a 0.04 standard deviation. For black students, the linear-truncation procedure yields an effect size of 0.20 standard deviation, somewhat larger than the 0.15 effect size from the Heckman-correction procedure.

THE EFFECT OF CLASS SIZE ON OTHER OUTCOMES. By raising economic and educational opportunities, smaller classes may also indirectly

Table 2-4. *Effects of Small Classes on Crime and Teen Pregnancy*

	White			Black		
	Small class	Regular class	Difference	Small class	Regular class	Difference
Dependent variable	(1)	(2)	(3)	(4)	(5)	(6)
(1) Ever convicted of a crime (males only)	0.023 (0.005)	0.022 (0.003)	0.001 (0.005)	0.025 (0.029)	0.031 (0.008)	−0.006 (0.030)
(2) Average sentence length in days (males only)	26.7 (5.4)	24.4 (3.6)	2.3 (6.5)	37.7 (7.4)	49.9 (11.8)	−12.2 (13.9)
(3) Birth rate (females only)	0.032 (0.006)	0.048 (0.004)	−0.016 (0.007)	0.059 (0.010)	0.044 (0.005)	0.015 (0.011)
(4) Fatherhood rate (males only)	0.020 (0.002)	0.016 (0.004)	0.004 (0.005)	0.015 (0.004)	0.025 (0.005)	−0.010 (0.006)

Note: Standard errors are in parentheses. Balanced within school estimator is used. Birth rates are limited to births in 1997 and 1998.

affect the frequency of negative social outcomes such as crime, welfare receipt, and teen pregnancy.

Criminal conviction data from Tennessee State Department of Corrections records were matched to Project STAR using student Social Security numbers. Crimes for which an individual was not convicted are not counted in the data set. Also, because the match was performed only in Tennessee, any crime committed by a student in another state is not included in the data set. This measurement problem would lead to a downward-biased estimate of the difference in criminal behavior by class assignment if the same proportion of participants from small and large classes moved out of state and if those students are just a random sample of the small- and large-class students. As long as small-class assignment did not increase the probability that a family moved away from Tennessee, the measurement error will likely attenuate the small-class impact.

Criminal convictions in this sample are rare. Only 1.6 percent of Project STAR students overall were reported as being convicted of a crime, and 2.6 percent of males were. Given that 88 percent of those convicted were males, for this analysis we restricted the sample to include only males. We employed the balanced-sample estimator described above and report the results in table 2-4. In the first row, we measure the rate of criminal activity of males by assigning a one to any student who was matched to the crime conviction data, and a zero otherwise. Columns 3 and 6 display the balanced-sample estimator. In column 6, black males in small classes are 0.6 percentage point less likely to be convicted of a crime than those in normal-size classes. This difference, however, is not close to being statistically significant.

Sentence length is measured as the maximum sentence (in days) faced by individuals for their specific crimes. Data are not available on length of actual sentence or time served, but maximum sentence length provides a measure of the severity of the crime committed. The sentences range from one year for minor theft and drug offenses to eight to twelve years for aggravated robbery and serious drug offenses. Students without convictions were assigned a zero sentence length. Column 6 indicates that black males in small classes on average committed crimes that carried twelve fewer days (or 24 percent) of maximum prison time than their peers in larger classes back in elementary school. Even though this effect is notable, it is not statistically significant with this size sample. Class size has a much smaller and opposite-signed effect on both crime rates and sentence length for white males.

Another important outcome to measure is the teen birth rate. Births to teens are highly correlated with female high school dropout rates and welfare utilization. Rebecca Maynard reported that roughly four-fifths of teen mothers end up on welfare, and their children are more likely to have low birth weight.[44] V. Joseph Hotz, Susan Williams McElroy, and Seth G. Sanders estimated that giving birth as a teen reduces the probability that a girl will graduate from high school by 15 to 16 percent.[45] The bottom portion of table 2-4 presents results on the effect of small-class assignment on the teen birth rate.

Birth records, like crime records, were matched in the state of Tennessee only. Records were matched by Social Security number of the mother and father reported on the birth certificate to Project STAR records, and then matches were confirmed by comparing student name.[46] If both of a newborn child's parents were STAR students, the birth record is counted for both the mother and the father. Birth records were only available by calendar year. We restricted our analysis to births during 1997 and 1998 because most students graduated high school in 1998.

The birth rates were constructed as follows: aggregate birth counts by class type, race, gender, and school were provided from Tennessee records. These were converted to rates by dividing by the total population in each cell. Row 3 in table 2-4 reports birth rates for females by race and class-assignment type. Small-class assignment is associated with a statistically significant 1.6 percentage points (or 33 percent) lower teen birth rate for white females. Row 4 has similar results for births in which a male STAR student was reported to be the father according to the birth records; the lower fatherhood rate for black males from small classes is on the margin of statistical significance. The effect of class assignment on the teen birth rate for white males and black females is not statistically significant.

Comparison with Voucher Results

The Project STAR class-size results for African Americans can be put in context by comparing them with other interventions. Here we compare the effect of attending a smaller class with the effect of private school vouchers, as estimated by William G. Howell and others.[47] They reported short-term test score gains estimated from privately funded voucher experiments conducted on low-income students in grades two through eight in Dayton, Ohio; New York City; and Washington, D.C. These experimental results indicated that after these students' first year in a private school, test scores increased by an average of 3.3 percentile points. By the end of the students' second year, black students who switched to a private school scored an average of 6.0 percentile points higher than their counterparts who did not switch, when the three sites are aggregated by weighting the site effects by their inverse sampling variances. For other ethnic groups, test scores declined on average if students switched to a private school, although the decline was not statistically significant. Howell and others also found that the test score effect for blacks did not vary by subject matter. Math and reading improved about the same amount.

To compare these voucher results with class-size reduction, we estimated a regression model for all black students who were in their second year after having been assigned to a small class, regardless of their grade level. Thus, the sample consists of students in their second year of Project STAR, whether that was grade one, two, or three. For this sample, we estimated an OLS regression in which the dependent variable was the average Stanford Achievement Test percentile score. The explanatory variables included a dummy variable for initial assignment to a small class, school-by-entry-wave dummies, current-grade dummies, free-lunch status, and sex. The effect of having been assigned to a small class in this model is 7.9 points (with a standard error equal to 1.1).

To further improve the comparability of the samples, we estimate the same model for black students who were initially on free or reduced-price lunch, as the voucher experiment was restricted primarily to those on free lunch. For this sample, assignment to a small class raised scores by an estimated 8.6 percentile points (standard error equal to 1.2) after two years.[48]

Our use of initial assignment to a small class understates the effect of attending a small class by about 15 percent because not everyone assigned to a small class actually attended one. Likewise, not every student randomly provided a voucher switched to a private school, but the estimates from Howell and others reported here adjust for incomplete take-up. Their intent-to-treat estimate in the second year after assignment is 3.5 percentile points.

We conclude from this comparison that, when comparable samples are considered, black students who attended a small class for two years in the STAR experiment improved their test performance by around 50 percent more than the gain experienced by black students who attended a private school as a result of receiving a voucher in the Dayton, New York, and Washington voucher experiments.[49]

Class Size and the Reduction in the Black-White Gap

Historically, black students attended schools with far larger pupil-teacher ratios than did white students. Horace Mann Bond eloquently summed up the situation this way: "Negro schools are financed from the fragments which fall from the budget made up for white children."[50] Throughout the twentieth century, the gap in school resources between white and black schools narrowed.[51] In 1915, for example, the pupil-teacher ratio was 61:1 in black schools in the segregated states and 38:1 in white schools; by 1953–54, on the eve of *Brown* v. *Board of Education*, it was 31.6:1 in black schools and 27.6:1 in white schools. By 1989, Michael Boozer, Alan Krueger, and Shari Wolkon estimated that the pupil-teacher ratio had converged in the schools the average black and white student attended, although Boozer and Rouse provided evidence that black students still attended larger classes within the same schools in the early 1990s.[52]

The black-white test score gap also narrowed over the last thirty years— and this trend probably began long before 1970, although consistent, nationally representative data are not available.[53] The pupil-teacher ratio fell over this period for both black and white students, and it fell slightly more for black students. Can the decline in the racial test score gap recorded in the NAEP be explained by the contemporaneous reduction in average class sizes, especially among black students?

To calculate the effect of reduced class sizes on the test score gap, we obtained the national average pupil-teacher ratio by year from the *Digest of Education Statistics*. Although average class size and the pupil-teacher ratio are not the same quantities, they should be closely related. Blacks were, on average, in larger classes than whites during most of the 1970s, but the gap closed by the late 1980s. To capture the relative difference in class-size reduction over this period, we crudely adjusted the national pupil-teacher ratio to derive separate estimates by race. For each year, we assigned the national pupil-teacher ratio to whites and inflated the pupil-teacher ratio by the inverse of the relative white-black pupil-teacher ratio reported by Boozer, Krueger, and Wolkon to obtain an estimate for blacks.[54]

To estimate the effect of a one-student reduction in class size, we use student-level data from STAR to estimate a 2SLS model by race. The dependent variable in the second-stage equation is a student's average scale score on the third-grade math and reading sections of the Stanford Achievement Test, and the key endogenous regressor is the student's actual third-grade class size. We also control for whether the student was assigned to a class with a teacher's aide, gender, free-lunch status, and school dummies. For class size, we use a dummy variable indicating whether the student was initially assigned to a small or normal-size class (as well as the other exogenous regressors). We then scale the estimated effect of a one-student change in class size by the standard deviation of test scores for all regular-size-class students in third grade. This yields an estimate that a one-student reduction in class size would lead to an increase in the third-grade test score by 0.02 standard deviation for whites and by 0.05 standard deviation for blacks. We use these estimates, together with the change in pupil-teacher ratios over time, to predict the gap in test scores by race.

Figures 2-6 and 2-7 display the actual (based on NAEP) and predicted black-white test score gap in math and reading, scaled by the subject-specific standard deviation in 1996. Figure 2-6 shows the decline in the math test score gap among nine-year-olds between 1973 and 1999. The actual score gap declined by 0.21 standard deviation, from 1.04 to 0.83 standard deviation, over these twenty-six years. During this period, average class sizes in elementary schools fell from 23.0 to 18.6 for whites, and from 25.4 to 18.6 for blacks. Based on our calculations, these changes in class sizes are predicted to reduce the black-white test score gap by 0.25 standard deviation, slightly more than the observed decline. Overall, however, the correspondence between the actual and predicted decline in the black-white gap is remarkably close. Figure 2-7 shows the analogous results for reading tests of nine-year-olds. Again, the predicted narrowing in the black-white achievement score gap is closely mirrored by our prediction based on changes in class size for black and white students over this period. Most of the predicted narrowing in the test score gap came about because of the decline in the pupil-teacher ratio generally—which has a larger effect on black students according to our estimates—than from the larger decline in the pupil-teacher ratio for black students relative to white students.

Figure 2-6. *Black-White Gap in Fourth-Grade Math Test Scores*

Standard deviation

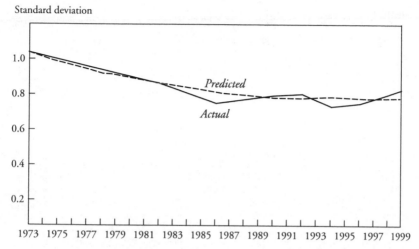

Note: Predicted gap is estimated using the change in average elementary school pupil-teacher ratio and black-white difference in pupil-teacher ratio from the *Digest of Education Statistics* and Michael Boozer, Alan Krueger, and Shari Wolkon, "Race and School Quality since *Brown* v. *Board of Education*," in Martin N. Baily and Clifford Winston, eds., *Brookings Papers on Economic Activity: Microeconomics* (Brookings, 1992), pp. 269–326, and estimates the effect of reduced class size on test scores based on Project STAR data.

We would not push these results too far, however, because other important determinants of student achievement scores have also changed since the 1970s, and because we can only crudely measure average class size for white and black students. Nevertheless, the results do suggest that the effect of class size on achievement by race as estimated from the STAR experiment are roughly consistent with the trends in test scores and pupil-teacher ratios that we have observed in the aggregate over time.

Conclusions

Our analysis of the STAR experiment indicates that students who attend smaller classes in the early grades tend to have higher test scores while they are enrolled in those grades than their counterparts who attend larger classes. The improvement in relative ranking on standardized tests that students obtain from having attended a small class is reduced when they move into regular-size classes, but an edge still remains. Moreover, black students tend to advance further up the distribution of test scores from attending a small class than do white students, both while they are in a small class and after-

Figure 2-7. *Black-White Gap in Fourth-Grade Reading Test Scores*

Standard deviation

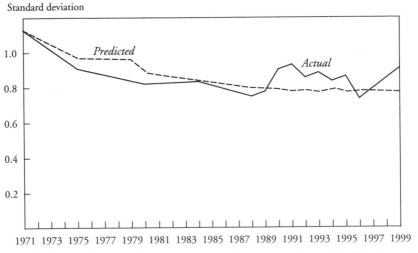

Note: Predicted gap is estimated using the change in average elementary school pupil-teacher ratio and black-white difference in pupil-teacher ratio from the *Digest of Education Statistics* and Michael Boozer, Alan Krueger, and Shari Wolkon, "Race and School Quality since *Brown* v. *Board of Education*," in Martin N. Baily and Clifford Winston, eds., *Brookings Papers on Economic Activity: Microeconomics* (Brookings, 1992), pp. 269–326, and estimates the effect of reduced class size on test scores based on Project STAR data.

ward. For black students, we also find that being assigned to a small class for an average of two years in grades K–3 is associated with an increased probability of subsequently taking the ACT or SAT college entrance exam and a 0.15–0.20 standard deviation higher average score on the exam. These findings are more or less consistent with most of the available literature.

Because black students' test scores appear to increase more from attending a small class than do white students', the decline in the pupil-teacher ratio nationwide over the last century should have led to a reduction in the black-white achievement gap. Moreover, the fact that the pupil-teacher ratio declined relatively more for black students should provide an added boost to the reduction in the achievement gap. Our calculations suggest that the decline in the pupil-teacher ratio for black and white students experienced since the early 1970s can account for most of the reduction in the black-white achievement score gap, although other factors surely were at work as well.

An important question is: Why do black students appear to gain more from attending a smaller class than white students? Although further research is needed, our analysis suggests that something about the schools that black students attend leads to a greater impact of smaller classes. That is, white students who attend the same mix of schools as black students appear to profit from smaller classes by about as much as black students do, and vice versa for black students who attend predominantly white schools. More generally, we find that students who attended schools with lower average test scores in the elementary grades benefit the most from attending smaller classes. One possible explanation for these findings is that teachers have to move very slowly through the curriculum if they have weak students—for example, because they are disrupted frequently or have to explain the material multiple times to the slower students. However, if they have smaller classes they can effectively teach more material. By contrast, teachers in schools with well-behaved, self-motivated students can move quickly through the material regardless of class size. This type of explanation might also partially explain why some countries, such as Japan, have high test scores despite having large classes. Regardless of the explanation, our findings suggest that class-size reductions will have the biggest bang for the buck if they are targeted to schools with relatively many minority students. But if such targeting is politically infeasible, then reducing class size generally would still lead to a closing of the black-white test score gap.

Notes

We thank Pat Turri and Jayne Zaharias for providing data, and David Card and Jens Ludwig for helpful discussions. They are not responsible for any mistakes we may have made.
    1. Christopher Jencks and Meredith Phillips, eds., *The Black-White Test Score Gap* (Brookings, 1998).
    2. Christopher Jencks, "Racial Bias in Testing," in Christopher Jencks and Meredith Phillips, eds., *The Black-White Test Score Gap* (Brookings, 1998), pp. 55–85.
    3. See, for example, Derek Neal and William Johnson, "The Role of Premarket Factors in Black-White Wage Differentials," *Journal of Political Economy*, vol. 104 (October 1996), pp. 869–95, for evidence on the impact of differential cognitive achievement on the black-white earnings gap.
    4. The early work is found in Eric A. Hanushek, "The Economics of Schooling: Production and Efficiency in Public Schools," *Journal of Economic Literature*, vol. 24 (September 1986), pp. 1141–77; and Eric A. Hanushek, "Assessing the Effects of School Resources on Student Performance: An Update," *Educational Evaluation and Policy Analysis*, vol. 19, no. 2 (1997), pp. 141–64. More recent evidence supporting the effect of smaller classes includes, for example, Larry V. Hedges, Richard Laine, and Rob Greenwald, "Does Money Matter? A Meta-Analysis of Studies of the Effects of Differential School Inputs on Student Outcomes," *Education Researcher*, vol. 23, no. 3 (1994), pp. 5–14; and Alan B. Krueger, "Economic Considerations and Class

Size," Working Paper 477 (Princeton University, Industrial Relations Section, September 2000).

5. Alan B. Krueger and Diane M. Whitmore, "The Effect of Attending a Small Class in the Early Grades on College-Test Taking and Middle School Test Results: Evidence from Project STAR," *Economic Journal*, vol. 111 (2001), pp. 1–28.

6. That is, we subtracted the 1996 national scale score average from each year's score and divided the resulting quantity by the 1996 cross-sectional standard deviation. Differences between whites and blacks, and over time, can therefore be interpreted as changes relative to the 1996 standard deviation.

7. Jencks and Phillips, *The Black-White Test Score Gap*.

8. SAT data by race for 1976–95 are from the *Condition of Education—1996*, supplemental table 22-2. Subsequent data are from various years of the College Board's *College-Bound Seniors National Profile Report*, available at www.collegeboard.org.

9. Krueger, "Economic Considerations and Class Size."

10. Hanushek, "Assessing the Effects of School Resources on Student Performance."

11. Charles R. Link and James G. Mulligan, "The Merits of a Longer School Day," *Economics of Education Review*, vol. 5, no. 4 (1986), pp. 373–81; and Charles R. Link and James G. Mulligan, "Classmates' Effects on Black Student Achievement in Public School Classrooms," *Economics of Education Review*, vol. 10, no. 4 (1991), pp. 297–310.

12. E. Cohn and S. D. Millman, *Input-Output Analysis in Public Education* (Cambridge, Mass.: Ballinger, 1975).

13. Anita Summers and Barbara Wolfe, "Do Schools Make a Difference?" *American Economic Review*, vol. 67, no. 4 (1977), pp. 649–52.

14. Summers and Wolfe, "Do Schools Make a Difference?" table 1.

15. See Summers and Wolfe, "Do Schools Make a Difference?" table 3.

16. These criticisms should not necessarily be interpreted as a critique of the underlying studies. Many of the studies were not about class size and were only conditioned on class size as an ancillary variable.

17. Hanushek has argued that studies that use a value-added specification are of the highest quality, but a number of authors have highlighted problems with the value-added specification. See, for example, Jens Ludwig and Laurie Bassi, "The Puzzling Case of School Resources and Student Achievement," *Educational Evaluation and Policy Analysis*, vol. 21, no. 4 (1999), pp. 385–403; John Cawley, James Heckman, and Edward Vytlacil, "On Policies to Reward the Value Added by Educators," *Review of Economics and Statistics*, vol. 81, no. 4 (1999), pp. 720–27; and Mikael Lindahl, "Home versus School Learning: A New Approach to Estimating the Effect of Class Size on Achievement," in Swedish Institute for Social Research, *Studies of Causal Effects in Empirical Labor Economics*, vol. 43 (University of Stockholm, 2000).

18. B. M. Stecher and G. W. Bohrnstedt, eds., *Class Size Reduction in California: The 1998-99 Evaluation Findings* (Sacramento, Calif.: California Department of Education, August 2000); Jeremy D. Finn and Charles M. Achilles, "Answers and Questions about Class Size: A Statewide Experiment," *American Educational Research*

Journal, vol. 27 (Fall 1990), pp. 557–77; Alex Molnar and others, "Evaluating the SAGE Program: A Pilot Program in Targeted Pupil-Teacher Reduction in Wisconsin," *Educational Evaluation and Policy Analysis,* vol. 21, no. 2 (Summer 1999), pp. 165–77; Marie T. Mora, "Attendance, Schooling Quality, and the Demand for Education of Mexican Americans, African Americans, and Non-Hispanic Whites," *Economics of Education Review,* vol. 16, no. 4 (1997), pp. 407–18; and Michael Boozer and Cecilia Rouse, "Intraschool Variation in Class Size: Patterns and Implications," *Journal of Urban Economics,* vol. 50, no. 1 (July 2001), pp. 163–89.

19. Link and Mulligan, "Classmates' Effects on Black Student Achievement in Public School Classrooms."

20. Stecher and Bohrnstedt, *Class Size Reduction in California.*

21. Eric A. Hanushek, John F. Kain, and Steven G. Rivkin, "Teachers, Schools, and Academic Achievement," Working Paper 6691 (Cambridge, Mass.: National Bureau of Economic Research, August 1998).

22. David W. Grissmer and others, "Improving Student Achievement: What State NAEP Test Scores Tell Us," Issue Paper 924 (Santa Monica, Calif.: RAND, July 2000).

23. Summers and Wolfe, "Do Schools Make a Difference?"

24. For more detail on the experiment, see E. Word and others, *The State of Tennessee's Student/Teacher Achievement Ratio (STAR) Project: Technical Report 1985–1990* (Tennessee State Department of Education, 1990); Barbara Nye and others, *The Lasting Benefits Study: A Continuing Analysis of the Effect of Small Class Size in Kindergarten through Third Grade on Student Achievement Test Scores in Subsequent Grade Levels,* seventh-grade technical report (Tennessee State University, Center of Excellence for Research in Basic Skills, 1994); C. Achilles, *Let's Put Kids First, Finally: Getting Class Size Right* (Thousand Oaks, Calif.: Corwin Press, 1999); or Alan B. Krueger, "Experimental Estimates of Educational Production Functions," *Quarterly Journal of Economics,* vol. 114, no. 2 (1999), pp. 497–532.

25. Krueger, "Experimental Estimates of Educational Production Functions."

26. The percentiles were derived in grades K–8 by using the distribution of raw scores for students in regular and regular with teacher's aide classes, as described in Krueger, "Experimental Estimates of Educational Production Functions." We use the average percentile score of the math and reading exams. If a student repeated a grade, we used his or her first test score for that grade level.

27. For regular students, the resulting average is just the unweighted average score in the sample of regular students.

28. Regressions of test scores on a dummy indicating initial assignment to a small class and school fixed effects yielded qualitatively similar results. See Krueger and Whitmore, "The Effect of Attending a Small Class in the Early Grades on College-Test Taking and Middle School Test Results."

29. We derive this figure by regressing a dummy indicating whether students actually attend a small class on a dummy indicating whether they were initially assigned to a small class and school-by-wave dummies.

30. Finn and Achilles, "Answers and Questions about Class Size"; Krueger,

"Experimental Estimates of Educational Production Functions"; and Krueger and Whitmore, "The Effect of Attending a Small Class in the Early Grades on College-Test Taking and Middle School Test Results."

31. The estimated intent-to-treat effects are unlikely to have occurred by chance. In grades K–3, the standard error of the small-regular difference is around 1.2 for black students and 0.9 for white students. In grades four to eight the standard errors fall to around 1.2 for black students and 0.8 for white students.

32. Jeremy D. Finn and others, "Short- and Long-Term Effects of Small Classes," mimeo (State University of New York at Buffalo, 1999), presents evidence that—when grade-equivalent scores are used to scale the tests—the gap between students in small and regular-size classes expands from kindergarten to grade three and from grades four to eight.

33. Krueger and Whitmore, "The Effect of Attending a Small Class in the Early Grades on College-Test Taking and Middle School Test Results."

34. See Krueger and Whitmore, "The Effect of Attending a Small Class in the Early Grades on College-Test Taking and Middle School Test Results," for a more complete description. After the records were merged, student names, dates of birth, and Social Security numbers were concealed to preserve confidentiality.

35. Many of the students appear to have been held back a grade: 48.7 percent of students matched reported that they graduated high school in 1999 or 2000, one or two years late. Another 10.8 percent graduated in 1997—a year ahead of normal progress. The class of 1998, which should have been matched in the original data, accounted for 38.9 percent of the new match. Of the new class of 1998 matches, 43 percent took the test after graduating high school, while the remaining 57 percent appear to have been missed in the first round, in part reflecting better information on Social Security numbers that we obtained in the meantime.

36. The correlation between the third-grade Stanford Achievement Test and seventh-grade Comprehensive Test of Basic Skills (CTBS) is .75, and the correlation between the CTBS in fourth and eighth grade is .80.

37. We note that nominally, beginning in the spring of 1998, Tennessee required high school students to take an exit exam as part of statewide curriculum changes introduced by the Education Improvement Act. Students completing the university-track diploma were required to take the SAT or American College Test (ACT). Students opting for a technical diploma could take the SAT, ACT, or Work Keys. Despite this new requirement, however, the share of Tennessee high school students taking the ACT did not increase in 1998, according to ACT records. Moreover, students who were not college-bound would be likely to take the Work Keys test, which we do not code as taking a college entrance exam. Thus, we suspect our measure provides a meaningful indication of whether students were college-bound, despite this requirement.

38. See Edward P. Lazear, "Educational Production," Working Paper 7349 (Cambridge, Mass.: National Bureau of Economic Research, 1999), for a formal economic model that predicts that smaller classes lead to higher achievement by reducing the number of disruptions in a class.

39. See www.collegeboard.org for the concordance. The concordance maps re-centered SAT I scores (verbal plus math) into ACT composite scores. One hundred twenty-one students, or 2.6 percent of the test-taking sample, took the SAT and not the ACT. For the 378 students in our sample who took both tests, the correlation between their SAT and ACT scores is .89.

40. James Heckman, "The Common Structure of Statistical Models of Truncation, Sample Selection, and Limited Dependent Variables and a Simple Estimator for Such Models," *Annals of Economic and Social Measurement*, vol. 5 (1976), pp. 475–92.

41. See, for example, David Card and Abigail Payne, "School Finance Reform, the Distribution of School Spending, and the Distribution of SAT Scores," Working Paper (University of California at Berkeley, Center for Labor Economics, 1998).

42. Krueger and Whitmore, "The Effect of Attending a Small Class in the Early Grades on College-Test Taking and Middle School Test Results."

43. In principle, the Heckman procedure provides an estimate of the effect of attending a small class on test scores for the entire population of students (including those who did not take the test), whereas the linear-truncation approach provides an estimate of the effect of attending a small class on scores for students from regular classes who otherwise would have taken the ACT. If there is a homogeneous treatment effect, the two parameters would be equal.

44. Rebecca Maynard, *Kids Having Kids* (Washington: Urban Institute Press, 1997).

45. V. Joseph Hotz, Susan Williams McElroy, and Seth G. Sanders, "Teenage Childbearing and Its Life Cycle Consequences: Exploiting a Natural Experiment," Working Paper 7397 (Cambridge, Mass.: National Bureau of Economic Research, October 1999).

46. Individual data were then aggregated by initial school, class type, race, and gender. We do not have access to the microdata.

47. William G. Howell and others, "Test-Score Effects of School Vouchers in Dayton, Ohio, New York City, and Washington, D.C.: Evidence from Randomized Field Trials," research paper (Harvard University, Program on Education Policy and Governance, August 2000).

48. Math and reading are impacted by the same magnitude if the equation is estimated separately.

49. We note that some of the gain for students who attended a private school may result from the fact that, at least in New York City, participating private schools had two to three fewer students per class than public schools, on average.

50. Horace Mann Bond, *The Education of the Negro in the American Social Order* (New York: Prentice Hall, 1934).

51. See, for example, Michael Boozer, Alan Krueger, and Shari Wolkon, "Race and School Quality since *Brown* v. *Board of Education*," in Martin N. Baily and Clifford Winston, eds., *Brookings Papers on Economic Activity: Microeconomics* (Brookings, 1992), pp. 269–326.

52. Boozer, Krueger, and Wolkon, "Race and School Quality since *Brown* v. *Board of Education*"; and Boozer and Rouse, "Intraschool Variation in Class Size."

53. Michael Cook and William Evans, "Families or Schools? Explaining the Convergence in White and Black Academic Performance," *Journal of Labor Economics*, vol. 18, no. 4 (October 2000), pp. 729–54, in a careful decomposition of the narrowing of the black-white National Assessment of Educational Progress test score gap between 1970 and 1988, find that at least three quarters of the reduction in the gap occurred within schools and no more than one quarter occurred because of relative changes in parental education. The fact that black students appear to benefit more from smaller classes than white students—combined with the general decline in class size—could account for the large within-school effect that they find.

54. Boozer, Krueger, and Wolkon, "Race and School Quality since *Brown* v. *Board of Education*."

3

Voucher Programs and the Effect of Ethnicity on Test Scores

PAUL E. PETERSON AND WILLIAM G. HOWELL

J ust ten years ago, the only data available related to school vouchers came from a flawed public choice program conducted during the 1960s in Alum Rock, California. But the early and mid-1990s brought new privately and publicly funded voucher programs to cities such as Cleveland, Ohio; Dayton, Ohio; Indianapolis, Indiana; Milwaukee, Wisconsin; New York City; San Antonio, Texas; and Washington, D.C.[1] With them came a wealth of new research opportunities.

Three privately funded voucher programs were particularly advantageous. The programs in Dayton, New York City, and the District of Columbia awarded vouchers by lottery, thus creating ideal conditions for a randomized field trial. Before the lotteries were conducted, our evaluation team collected data on student test scores and family background characteristics. As of mid-2000, students had been reevaluated one and two years later. Because the abilities and family backgrounds of the test and control groups were, on average, similar before they entered the lottery, subsequent differences observed between the lottery winners and losers may be attributed to the effects of a voucher. Because of their design, our evaluations of the Dayton, New York City, and Washington, D.C., voucher programs have yielded the best available information on students' test score outcomes and parental assessments of public and private schools.

Elsewhere in 2000 we, with our colleagues, reported the impact of vouchers on student test score performance in all three cities, finding positive effects of vouchers on African American test scores but no effects on the test scores of students from other ethnic backgrounds.[2] In this paper we summarize these findings, then examine parental responses in New York City to try to explain why vouchers seem to have differential effects depending on the students' ethnic background.

Prior Research

The first indication that private school effects are concentrated among African American students came from the High School and Beyond data collected by the U.S. Department of Education in 1980 and 1982. By surveying and testing a national sample of public and private schools in two waves, the Department of Education generated data on the determinants of academic gains in high school between a student's sophomore and senior years. In a 1985 issue of *Sociology of Education,* three particularly trenchant essays analyzed and interpreted the data.[3]

The authors of these essays noted serious disagreements about aggregate private school impacts. Thomas Hoffer, Andrew Greeley, and James Coleman found substantial, positive private school effects on student test performance, while Douglas Wilms found trivial effects, if any. Christopher Jencks mediated the conflict, reaching judicious conclusions somewhere in the middle.

Few observers, however, noticed in the *Sociology of Education* disputation the discussion of the effects of private schools on minority students. Hoffer, Greeley, and Coleman found especially strong positive effects on low-income, minority students, whose test scores increased by 4.4 answers, as compared to 1.6 answers for students generally.[4] Jencks showed that Wilms's data, despite their exclusion of dropouts, also contained positive (though not statistically significant) effects of attending a Catholic school on African Americans' reading scores. Taking all of the evidence from both studies into account, Jencks concluded that "the evidence that Catholic schools are especially helpful for initially disadvantaged students is quite suggestive, though not conclusive."[5] While overall impacts remained contested, those on minorities appeared more robust.

Subsequent studies tended to reaffirm Hoffer, Greeley, and Coleman's findings. In an analysis of the National Longitudinal Survey of Youth, Derek Neal concluded that students who attend Catholic schools are more likely to graduate from high school and college. The effects, Neal noted, are the greatest among urban minorities. Catholic schools also have a significant, positive effect on black earnings potential, but not whites'.[6] In separate studies, David

Figlio and Joseph Stone and William N. Evans and Robert M. Schwab generated consistent findings for African Americans.[7]

Because they draw upon national data sets, all of these studies are of particular interest. One cannot rule out the possibility, however, that the observed positive effects were due to selection bias, a problem that arises when a population differentiates itself by freely choosing a treatment—in this case, attending a private school. This problem may be serious if those families with children in private schools looked very different from those with children remaining in public schools. Most of these studies adjusted for observable family background characteristics, such as mother's education, family income, and other demographic factors. Still, one cannot be sure that the adjustments adequately account for an intangible factor—the willingness of a family to pay for their child's tuition, and all that this implies about the importance it places on education. Others performed two-stage regression models that reduce potential selection bias. But as the disagreements between Neal and Figlio and Stone attest to, instrumental variables that are correlated with the type of school students attended but unrelated to the error term in the second-stage equation are sparse.

The best solution to the self-selection problem is the random assignment of students to test and control groups. Until recently, most evaluations of voucher programs have not utilized a random-assignment research design and therefore cannot rule out possible selection problems. Privately funded programs in Indianapolis and San Antonio admitted students on a first-come, first-served basis. And in the state-funded program in Cleveland, though scholarship winners were initially selected by means of a lottery, eventually all applicants were offered a scholarship, thereby precluding the conduct of a randomized experiment. The public Milwaukee program did award vouchers by a lottery, but data collection was incomplete.[8]

As a consequence, the programs in Dayton, New York, and Washington, D.C., provide unique opportunities to examine the effects of school vouchers on students from low-income families who live in central cities. In contrast to prior studies, the evaluation team conducted the lotteries in all three cities. Follow-up test score information was obtained from about one-half to two-thirds of the students who participated in the lottery, and baseline data provided information that allowed the analysts to adjust for nonresponse.

The Programs

In several key respects, the three voucher programs followed similar designs. All were privately funded; all were targeted at students from low-income families, most of whom lived in the inner city; all provided only partial vouchers that the families were expected to supplement; and all of the students in the evaluations of these three programs previously had been attending public schools.

In the spring of 1998, Parents Advancing Choice in Education (PACE) offered low-income students in grades K–12 the opportunity to win a scholarship to attend private school in Dayton, Ohio. For the 1998–99 school year, PACE offered scholarships to 515 students who were in public schools and to 250 who were already enrolled in private schools in the Dayton metropolitan area. During the program's first year, the PACE scholarships covered 50 percent of tuition at a private school, up to $1,200. Support was guaranteed for at least four years, with a possibility of continuing through high school, provided funds remained available. Of those students offered scholarships, 51 percent enrolled in a private school during the second year of the program.[9]

The School Choice Scholarships Foundation (SCSF) in New York City offered thirteen hundred scholarships worth up to $1,400 annually toward tuition at a private school for at least three years. To qualify for a scholarship, children had to be entering grades one through four, live in New York City, attend a public school at the time of application, and come from families with incomes low enough to qualify for the U.S. government's free school lunch program. More than twenty thousand students applied between February and late April 1997. By the end of the scholarship program's second year, 74 percent of the lottery-winning students were attending a private school.

The Washington Scholarship Fund (WSF), established in 1993, is the oldest of the three programs. By the fall of 1997, the WSF was serving approximately 460 children at twenty-two private schools. After receiving a large infusion of new funds from two philanthropists, the WSF announced a major expansion in October 1997.

To qualify, applicants had to reside in Washington, D.C., and be entering grades K–8 in the fall of 1998. Families with incomes at or below the poverty line received vouchers that equaled 60 percent of tuition, or $1,700, whichever was less. Families with incomes above the poverty line received smaller scholarships. Families with incomes higher than two-and-a-half times the poverty line were ineligible. The WSF claims that it will maintain tuition support for at least three years and, if funds remain available, until students complete high school. In April 1998, the WSF awarded more than one thousand scholarships by lottery, with the majority going to students previously attending a public school. Of those students offered scholarships, 48 percent were still using them to attend a private school in the second year of the program.

Evaluation Procedures

The evaluation procedures used in all three studies conform to those in randomized field trials. Our evaluation team collected baseline test score and family background information before the lottery, administered the lottery, and collected follow-up information one and two years later.

Students took the Iowa Test of Basic Skills (ITBS) in reading and mathematics. Students who were entering grades one through four in New York City and grades two through eight in Dayton (and other parts of Montgomery County, Ohio) and Washington, D.C., were included in the evaluations. Parents filled out surveys on their satisfaction with their children's schools, their involvement in their children's education, and their demographic characteristics. Students in grades four and higher completed similar surveys. In all three cities, the follow-up procedures replicated the pre-lottery procedures: students again took the ITBS in reading and math; parents and older students filled out surveys regarding their backgrounds and educational experiences.

In Dayton, 1,440 students were tested pre-lottery, 803 of whom were attending public schools at the time. More than five thousand students participated in pre-lottery testing in New York City. Of the students who did not win the lottery, approximately one thousand were selected at random to compose a control group representing approximately 960 families. All of these students were attending public schools at the time. In Washington, D.C., 2,023 students were tested pre-lottery, of whom 1,582 were attending a public school. Because only public school children were eligible to apply for a scholarship in New York, separate public and private lotteries did not have to be held there. Separate lotteries were held in Dayton and Washington for students who were enrolled in public and private schools. Only those students who were in public schools at the time of the lotteries are included in this study.

In Dayton, 47 percent of the students participating in the second year of the evaluation were African Americans; in New York City, 42 percent; and in Washington, 94 percent. Hispanic students accounted for 2 percent of the Dayton population, 51 percent of New York City's, and 4 percent of Washington's. Whites accounted for 24 percent of Dayton's evaluation group, versus 5 percent in New York City and 1 percent in Washington. The remaining students came from a variety of other ethnic backgrounds.

In Dayton, 56 percent of the students included in the evaluation attended the first-year testing sessions; 49 percent attended the second-year sessions. In New York City, 82 percent of families attended follow-up sessions after one year, and 66 percent after two years. In Washington, the response rate after one year was 63 percent; after two years, 50 percent.

We are reasonably confident that these modest response rates do not undermine the integrity of our findings. First, with the exception of the second year in New York, response rates were similar for treatment and control groups after one and two years in all three cities. Second, comparisons of baseline test scores and background characteristics revealed only minor differences between the second-year respondents and nonrespondents in all three cities. Finally, to account for the minor differences between respondents and nonrespondents that we did observe, the test scores of children who, based on their demographic characteristics, were more likely to attend follow-up sessions were weighted less heavily, while the test scores of children who were less likely to attend follow-up sessions, but nevertheless did, were weighted more heavily. Given the slight differences between respondents and nonrespondents, however, the weights do not change the results substantially.

The randomized lottery ensured that lottery winners as a group were not significantly different from the control group (those who did not win a scholarship). In all three cities, the demographic characteristics and pre-lottery test scores of scholarship winners and losers (the treatment and control groups, respectively) were identical to one another. Only in Dayton were minor differences in the pre-lottery test scores observed: those offered a voucher scored 6.5 percentile points lower in math and 3.1 points lower in reading than those not offered a scholarship, a statistically significant difference.

To measure the impact on children's test scores of switching to a private school, we estimated a statistical model that takes into account whether a child attended a public or private school, as well as baseline reading and math test scores. Baseline test scores were included to adjust for the minor baseline differences between the treatment and control groups on the achievement tests and to increase the precision of the estimated impacts of switching from a public to a private school.

The lottery generated two groups: those who were offered a voucher and those who were not. In this paper, we are less interested in the effect of being offered a voucher than the effect of using a voucher to attend a private school. A simple comparison between public and private school students, however, is inappropriate because certain students may be more likely to take advantage of a voucher offered them. Their parents might place greater value on education, have greater resources to supplement the voucher, or may live in a neighborhood with a broader selection of private schools. If these children differ from students who won a voucher but failed to use it in ways that are related to student achievement, it could bias our findings.

To solve this problem, we performed a two-stage regression model. In the first stage of the model, we predicted the probability that each individual would attend a private school based upon whether or not he or she was offered a voucher. With these predicted values, we then recovered estimates of the impact of switching from a public to a private school. This two-stage technique was first used in medical research and is now commonplace in econometric studies of educational interventions.[10]

Test Score Results

This chapter reports the impacts of vouchers on student test scores after one and two years in Dayton, New York City, and Washington. Impacts are different from levels or trends. Levels refer to the absolute standards at which students perform at a given time; trends refer to changes in levels experienced by a single group over time. Impacts, by contrast, refer to the differences in test scores between those students who received treatment and those who did not. Consequently, positive impacts imply that those who attended a private school scored higher than comparable students who remained in public schools; and negative impacts suggest that members of the treatment group scored lower than they otherwise would have.

Our findings varied systematically according to the student's ethnicity. In all three cities, no significant differences were found between the test score performance of non–African American students who switched from a public to a private school and the performance of students in the control group—either after one or two years (see table 3-1).[11] For African American students, however, vouchers made a substantial difference. In the three cities combined, African American students who switched from public to private schools scored, after one year, 3.9 percentile points higher on the combined math and reading tests (expressed as national percentile ranking [NPR] points, which run from 0 to 100 with a national median of 50). After two years, African American students who used a voucher to enroll in a private school scored 6.3 percentile points higher than their public school peers.

The data in table 3-1 also show that the largest voucher impacts for African American students were observed in the Washington, D.C., program. African American students who attended D.C. private schools for two years scored 9.2 percentile points higher than students in the control group. The smallest differences after two years were observed in New York City, where African American students attending private schools scored 4.3 percentile points higher than the control group. In Dayton, the difference between test and control groups was 6.5 percentile points.

Table 3-1. *Impact of Switching to a Private School on Test Score Performance*

Ethnic group	Year one		Year two	
	Percentile	Number	Percentile	Number
African Americans				
Dayton, Ohio	3.3	296	6.5*	273
New York City	5.4***	622	4.3**	497
Washington, D.C.	–0.9	891	9.2***	668
Average private school impact	3.9*		6.3***	
All others				
Dayton, Ohio	1.0	108	–0.2	96
New York City	–2.2	812	–1.5	699
Washington, D.C.	7.4	39	–0.1	42
Average private school impact	–1.0		–1.4	

* Significant at the 0.10 level on a two-tailed test.
** Significant at the 0.05 level on a two-tailed test.
*** Significant at the 0.01 level on a two-tailed test.

Note: Weighted two-stage least squares regressions performed; treatment status used as instrument. Impacts expressed in terms of national percentile rankings. In Dayton, 2.0 percent of the African American control group in the year-two models attended a private school in the second but not the first year; in New York City, 2.8 percent of the African American control group in the year-two models attended a private school for one of two years; and in Washington, D.C., 3.7 percent of the African American control group in the year-two models attended a private school in the second year but not the first year.

The average impact of vouchers on the test scores of African Americans was moderately large. After one year, black students who switched to private schools scored 0.18 of a standard deviation higher than the students in the control group. After two years, the difference grew to 0.28 of a standard deviation, roughly one-third of the test score gap between blacks and whites.

The magnitude of the effects can be further assessed by comparing them to those effects observed in an evaluation of a class-size reduction intervention conducted in Tennessee, the only other major education reform to be evaluated with a randomized field trial. The effects on African Americans of attendance at a private school shown here are comparable to the estimated effect of a seven-student reduction in class size. According to a recent reanalysis of data from Tennessee, the class-size reduction effect for African Americans after two years was, on average, between 7.9 and 8.6 percentile points, slightly higher than the 6.3 percentile effect of switching to a private school.[12]

The size of the effects of the voucher intervention can also be compared with the size of the effects reported in the RAND study entitled *Improving*

School Achievement released in August 2000.[13] Identifying the most successful states, North Carolina and Texas, which have introduced rigorous accountability systems that involve statewide testing, the study finds what it says are "remarkable" one-year gains [in math scores] of "as much as 0.06 to 0.07 standard deviation per year"—or 0.12 to 0.14 over two years. The two-year effects of the school voucher intervention on African American students observed here are roughly twice as large.

Controlling for Demographics

Most research on the impact of private schools attempts to control for differences in family income and other background characteristics among students attending public and private schools. When a lottery is used to separate research subjects into experimental and control groups, however, such statistical adjustments are generally unnecessary, given that the two groups being compared are virtually identical to one another.

Nonetheless, a number of analysts have expressed concern at the apparent absence of controls for family background characteristics. Bruce Fuller and his colleagues at the University of California at Berkeley, for instance, argued that "the experimental group may have been biased as some of the most disadvantaged voucher winners did not switch to a private school, and therefore were excluded from the group (possibly boosting mean achievement levels artificially)."[14] An interest group, People for the American Way, lodged a similar complaint: "The . . . study's key finding improperly compares two dramatically different groups and may well reflect private-school screening-out of the most at-risk students."[15]

In the three cities, approximately half the students took the voucher that was offered to them (the takers) and about half did not (the decliners). However, the decliners remained a part of the evaluation, contrary to the suggestions made by Fuller and by People for the American Way. All those offered a voucher and all members of the control group were invited to follow-up testing sessions, and all the participating students are included in the analysis. The analysis does not provide a simple, raw comparison between those who took the voucher and the members of the control group who did not win the lottery. Instead, as previously discussed, the fact that the vouchers were awarded randomly is used to create an instrumental variable that permits one to recover a consistent estimate of the effect of switching to a private school.

Given this analytical strategy, results are unlikely to vary, if one controls for family background characteristics. The use of a randomized lottery ensures that the background characteristics of lottery winners and losers will not differ significantly. To show this, we recalculate the impact of attending a private school on test scores, this time including explicit controls for the mother's educational level, her employment status, family size, and whether the family received welfare. As expected, the difference in combined reading and math test scores of African Americans after two years in all three cities remains exactly the same—6.3 NPR points, a statistically significant impact.

The Sore Loser Hypothesis

Since releasing our study in 2000, some have suggested that the observed differences between public and private school parents may be due to the frustrations of members of the control group. *New York Times* columnist Richard Rothstein, for example, iterates a hypothesis first made by Stanford University professor Martin Carnoy:

> Volunteers for vouchers . . . may have their hopes raised, then dashed when they were not selected for a voucher. Sorely disappointed, they may then demand less of their children in public school.[16]

To explore this hypothesis, we examined the control group's satisfaction levels at baseline, after one year, and after two years. On each of these occasions, parents were asked: "How satisfied are you with the following aspects of your child's current school?" Items included teaching, school safety, parental involvement, class size, school facility, student respect for teachers, communication regarding student progress, freedom to observe religious traditions, and the school's location.[17] Parents then were given four response options, "very satisfied," "satisfied," "dissatisfied," and "very dissatisfied." Indexes of satisfaction were constructed from all individual satisfaction items and range from 1 ("very dissatisfied") to 4 ("very satisfied"). The results presented here come from New York City.

In all cases, those not receiving the voucher reported slightly higher levels of satisfaction one year after having been denied a scholarship than at baseline. At baseline, members of the control group scored, on average, 2.7 on the satisfaction scale; one year later, they scored 2.8; and then after two years, 2.7. Overall, no evidence shows that upon learning that children of members of the control group had not won a voucher, satisfaction rates among the parents declined significantly.

Parental responses to questions about their relationships with their children cast further doubt on the hypothesis that the frustration associated with losing the voucher lottery lead control-group parents to care less about the education of their children. Parents were asked how often they helped their child with homework, talked with their child about school, attended school

Table 3-2. *Impacts of Switching to a Private School on Measures of Parental Involvement of African Americans and Latinos in New York City*

| | African Americans | | Latinos | | Difference |
Parental involvement	Percentile	Number	Percentile	Number	in impacts
With child's education					
Year-one impact	−0.04	531	−0.11	568	—
Year-two impact	−0.06	470	−0.15	529	—
With child's school					
Year-one impact	−0.15	518	0.04	553	—
Year-two impact	−0.23*	470	−0.08	529	—

* Significant at the 0.10 level on a two-tailed test.
— Not statistically significant.
Note: The last column denotes whether the difference in the estimated impacts for African Americans and Latinos is statistically significant. Weighted two-stage least squares regressions performed; treatment status used as instrument. All models control for lottery indicators. Impacts expressed in terms of effect sizes.

activities, and worked on school projects. In every case, the answers given by parents with children in the public school control group after both one and two years remained roughly constant, and they closely resembled the responses of parents in the treatment group (see table 3-2).[18]

These data lend little support for the claim that control-group parents were sore losers. Given that parents knew their children had only about a one in twenty chance of winning the lottery, their initial expectations probably were not unduly high. It is hard to imagine, then, that whatever disappointment parents felt when their children lost the lottery led to their children's systematic underachievement when tested one and two years later.

Hawthorne Effects

As a corollary to the sore loser hypothesis, Carnoy suggested that our findings might represent Hawthorne effects. If so, then the observed gains for African Americans may have little to do with vouchers per se, but rather the surge of enthusiasm associated with winning a lottery. Upon learning that their children could now attend a private school, the interest and involvement of treatment-group parents in their children's education may have been reinvigorated. A year later, such enthusiasm might wane and children could lose the family support they need to excel academically.

To ascertain whether Hawthorne effects explain the pattern of results, we revisited our measures of parental satisfaction, again focusing on New York

Table 3-3. *Impacts of Switching to a Private School on Measures of Satisfaction for African Americans and Latinos in New York City*

Satisfaction index	African Americans		Latinos		Difference in impacts
	Percentile	Number	Percentile	Number	
Year-one impact	1.18***	533	0.99***	567	**
Year-two impact	1.00***	466	1.12***	529	—

** Significant at the 0.05 level on a two-tailed test.
*** Significant at the 0.01 level on a two-tailed test.
— Not statistically significant.
Note: The last column denotes whether the difference in the estimated impacts for African Americans and Latinos is statistically significant. Weighted two-stage least squares regressions performed; treatment status used as instrument. All models control for lottery indicators. Impacts expressed in terms of effect sizes.

City. The parental satisfaction indexes were standardized to have a standard deviation of 1.0.

When comparing the impact of attending a private school on parental satisfaction in years one and two, we find some support for the Hawthorne hypothesis. The effect size of attending a private school on the parental satisfaction of African Americans in year one was fully 1.2 standard deviations (see table 3-3). The effect size attenuates somewhat in year two, dropping to 1.0 standard deviation.

Other facts, however, cast doubt on Carnoy's intuition. First, the impact of attending a private school on parental satisfaction remains very large in both years one and two. Even after two years, the effect size for parental satisfaction hovers around a full standard deviation. The 0.2 diminution of satisfaction among African American parents that occurred between year one and year two was modest when compared with the striking differences in satisfaction with private and public schools that remained after two years.

Second, the impacts on satisfaction rates of Latino and African American parents were comparable in year one, and by year two the impact for Latinos was slightly higher. If all it takes to elevate test scores is to enhance parental satisfaction with a school, then why haven't Latinos posted significant test score gains?

Finally, while they may inform parental satisfaction rates, Hawthorne effects are less likely to drive student achievement. Students participating in voucher experiments are being asked to change schools, form new friendships, adjust to new rules and expectations, and acquire new study habits. In Washington, D.C., for instance, older students who transferred to private schools indicated intense resentment with these changes, which in turn was reflected in their first-year test scores.[19] Instead of leveling off, then, observed impacts may increase as students have a greater amount of time to adjust to their new schools and the educational expectations laid upon them.

Explaining Ethnic Differences in Voucher Impacts

Neither the absence of background controls, nor the disappointment of losing a voucher, nor Hawthorne effects appear to explain away the observed gains for African Americans, at least after two years. An important puzzle, therefore, arises. Why should vouchers have a positive impact on the test scores of African American students, but not anybody else? This finding is particularly curious in New York, where African American students posted positive and significant test score gains, but Latinos did not. As poor, minority residents of inner cities, both groups presumably face a common set of educational obstacles. One would think, then, that an intervention that successfully improves the test scores of one group would have a similar impact on the other.

The remainder of this chapter draws upon parental survey data from New York City to assess a broad array of possible explanations for the observed differential race effects: language, school disruptions, class size, school size, parental communications, and a kitchen-sink model that simultaneously controls for a multiplicity of factors. We first test the impact of vouchers for African Americans and Latinos on each of these aspects of a student's education. Using these results, we then select a subset of factors to include in the original test score models to see whether or not they reduce the positive effect of vouchers experienced by African Americans. Unfortunately, they do not, either singularly or additively. Ultimately, and perhaps unfortunately, we are better able to rule out possible explanations than draw positive conclusions.

Language Needs

The fact that African Americans appear to benefit from vouchers, but Latinos do not, may have nothing to do with race per se, and everything to do with language. Private schools may be poorly equipped to deal with students who do not speak English as their primary language; public schools, meanwhile, often have well-established English as a Second Language (ESL) programs and specially trained personnel to deal with the particular cultural and linguistic needs of minority populations. The gains associated with a private education may transfer only to those students who can function in all-English classrooms.

Table 3-4. *Impact of Switching to a Private School on Test Score Performance in New York for Latinos Who Speak English as a Primary and Secondary Language*

Impact	English primary		English secondary	
	Percentile	Number	Percentile	Number
Year one	−2.6	399	2.3	305
Year two	−1.6	342	3.1	290

Note: Weighted two-stage least squares regressions performed; treatment status used as instrument. All models control for baseline test scores and lottery indicators. In no year are the estimated impacts for the two groups of Latinos statistically significantly different from one another.

To test this hypothesis, we compared the impact of switching to a private school on the test scores of Latino students whose primary language (according to their parents) was English with the impact on those for whom English was a secondary language. As can be seen in table 3-4, the results, if anything, run directly contrary to expectation. Non–English speaking Latinos post slightly positive impacts, while Latinos for whom English is the primary language post slightly negative effects. Neither the positive nor negative impacts, nor the slightly larger differences in impacts, are statistically significant.

These findings do not provide much of a basis on which to judge the ways in which public and private schools deal with students with language needs. They probably rule out language, however, as an explanation for why African Americans appear to benefit from vouchers, while Latinos do not.

Parental Perceptions of Public and Private Schools

Parents accompanied children to follow-up testing sessions. Because the testing took over an hour, parents had time to complete fairly lengthy questionnaires about the schools their children were attending. In previous papers, we reported the results from these surveys for all parents regardless of their ethnic background.[20] These results provide information concerning the impact of switching to a private school on parental perceptions of numerous aspects of school life. Generally speaking, in Dayton, New York, and Washington, D.C., we found that

—Private schools have stricter dress codes.

—Hallways in public schools are more closely monitored—students are more likely to need passes to leave the classroom and visitors are more likely to have to get permission slips.

—School disruptions—fighting, cheating, property disruption, student misbehavior, truancy, tardiness, and so forth—are more extensive in public schools.

—Suspension rates are similar in the two sectors.

—Public schools have more physical resources—cafeteria, nurse's office, gymnasium, and so forth.

—Public schools have a greater variety of academic programs—special education, advanced education, bilingual education, and so forth.

—Private schools communicate more with parents by means of teacher-parent conferences, parental participation in school, and so forth.

—Students in private schools do more homework.

—Private schools have fewer students and smaller classes.

—Although results differ from city to city, on the whole the degree of segregation is similar in the two education sectors.

—Parents in both sectors are equally involved in their child's education.

—Parents in both sectors volunteer and participate equally in their child's school.

The observed impacts of vouchers on some of these school characteristics may vary for different ethnic groups, and therefore may explain why African Americans appear to benefit from vouchers, while Latinos do not. To explore this possibility, we estimated the impact of attending a private school in New York City separately for African Americans and Latinos.

Some aspects of school life—class size, school size, amount of time spent on homework, degree of ethnic segregation, and suspension rates—could be easily measured by using responses parents gave to a single question. When possible, though, we constructed indexes from multiple survey questions that measured the same school characteristic. Appendix 3A reports questions used to generate each index.

We estimated the impact of switching to a private school on each aspect of school life in the same way that we estimated the impacts on test scores, except that we did not control for baseline test scores. The results of this investigation are reported in table 3-5; for parental involvement items, see table 3-2.

For African Americans, the impacts of switching to a private school on parental perceptions of most aspects of school life were fairly stable from the first to the second year. In both years, African American parents with children in private schools reported significantly fewer school disruptions (fighting, cheating, property destruction, and so forth) than parents with children in public schools. They also reported significantly more demanding dress codes, less hallway monitoring, fewer school resources, greater parental communication with the school, more homework, smaller schools, and slightly less involvement in school activities (though this final difference is statistically significant only in year two). In year one, African American parents

Table 3-5. *Impacts of Switching to a Private School on Characteristics of Schools Attended by African Americans and Latinos in New York City*

Characteristic	African Americans		Latinos		Difference in impacts
	Percentile	Number	Percentile	Number	
School disruptions					
Year-one impact	−0.46***	524	−0.02	564	**
Year-two impact	−0.27**	465	−0.16	523	—
Suspensions					
Year-one impact	0.01	514	−0.13	547	—
Year-two impact	0.02	463	0.09	526	—
Dress rules					
Year-one impact	1.47***	525	1.30***	559	**
Year-two impact	1.06***	461	0.90***	512	—
Hallway monitors					
Year-one impact	−0.62***	516	−0.55***	556	—
Year-two impact	−0.67***	464	−0.10	519	***
School facilities					
Year-one impact	−0.24*	529	−0.15	567	—
Year-two impact	−0.49***	468	−0.08	526	**
School programs					
Year-one impact	0.22*	527	0.05	564	—
Year-two impact	−0.16	462	−0.04	522	—
School communication with parents					
Year-one impact	0.71***	532	0.30**	564	***
Year-two impact	0.78***	469	0.43***	528	**
Amount of homework					
Year-one impact	0.64***	527	0.49***	565	—
Year-two impact	0.48***	470	0.33**	527	—
Class size					
Year-one impact	−0.61***	515	−0.04	540	***
Year-two impact	−0.21	460	0.01	512	—
School size					
Year-one impact	−0.88***	366	−0.47***	364	**
Year-two impact	−0.82***	353	−0.54***	408	*
Racial segregation					
Year-one impact	−0.02	517	−0.07	553	—
Year-two impact	−0.16	457	−0.11*	513	—

* Significant at the 0.10 level on a two-tailed test.
** Significant at the 0.05 level on a two-tailed test.
*** Significant at the 0.01 level on a two-tailed test.
— Not statistically significant.
Note: The last column denotes whether the difference in the estimated impacts for African Americans and Latinos is statistically significant. Weighted two-stage least squares regressions performed; treatment status used as instrument. All models control for lottery indicators. Impacts expressed in terms of effect sizes.

with children in private schools reported that their child was in a significantly smaller class, but not in year two. African American parents with children in private schools, as compared with those in public schools, also reported no differences in suspension rates, in their involvement with their child's education, in the likelihood that their child attended a segregated school, and the number of specific programs (bilingual education, special education, advanced education, and so forth) at their child's school.

In some respects, the results for Latino parents revealed similar trends. Latino parents with children in private schools reported stricter dress codes, more communication with their schools, more homework, and smaller schools. They also reported no difference between the two sectors in suspension rates, the range of school programs, and their own involvement with their child's education.

In several other respects, however, school vouchers appeared to have very different effects on the education of Latino students. Latino parents whose children attended private schools, for instance, did not report a reduction in the number of school disruptions. Nor did they report smaller classes or fewer school resources than the control group in either year. Only after one year did Latino parents with children in private schools report less hallway monitoring and less racial segregation in the private sector.

The last column of tables 3-2 and 3-5 identifies whether or not the observed impacts for African Americans and Latinos are statistically significantly different from one another. Those items with asterisks represent plausible components of an explanation for why African Americans appear to benefit from vouchers, but Latinos do not. Four aspects of school life stand out: school size, parental communications, class size, and school disruptions. In both years, vouchers had a smaller impact on the size of the private schools and classrooms attended by Latino students than they did on those attended by African Americans. Also, while vouchers had a large and positive impact on the communication levels of African Americans, they had a relatively small impact on those of Latinos. And perhaps most striking, the magnitude of the impacts on school disruptions varied dramatically for Latinos and African Americans.

Other differences are evident in one of the two years. In year two the negative impact of attending a private school on hallway monitoring was significantly smaller for Latinos than it was for African Americans. The year-two impact on school resources, meanwhile, was larger. Given the sign of these differences, however, they probably do not explain why African American voucher students log the only test score gains. Could it be that African American students in private schools benefit from the fact that their hallways are less closely monitored? Do black students in private schools benefit because

Table 3-6. *Impact of Switching to a New York City Private School on African Americans' Test Scores Controlling for Likely Suspects*

Characteristic	Year one		Year two	
	(1)	(2)	(3)	(4)
Attend private school	5.4***	5.7***	4.3**	5.2**
School disruptions	—	–0.3	—	–2.1***
Communication	—	–0.4	—	–0.9
School size	—	–0.1	—	1.0
Class size	—	0.3	—	–0.2
Baseline math score	0.4***	0.4***	0.4***	0.4***
Baseline reading score	0.4***	0.4***	0.3***	0.3***
Constant	–2.9	–2.2	0.5	3.4
N	622	622	497	497
Adjusted R^2	.52	.51	.45	.43

   ** Significant at the 0.05 level on a two-tailed test.
   *** Significant at the 0.01 level on a two-tailed test.
   — Item not included in this model.
   Note: Weighted least squares regressions performed. Impacts expressed in terms of national percentile rankings. All models control for baseline test scores and lottery indicators. Missing values for school covariates imputed by best subset regression.

they have fewer school resources than their public school peers, while Latinos in private schools have comparable levels? Probably not.

Note that from these impacts we cannot infer whether African Americans are coming from a particularly poor lot of public schools or are gaining access to a particularly effective group of private schools. All that we know is that along some dimensions, the impact of the switch from public to private school for African Americans was greater than that for Latinos.

School Characteristics and Voucher Effects

We added to our test score model measures of class size, school disruptions, school size, and school communications. If these four school characteristics explain the differential impact of attending a private school on the two ethnic groups, the voucher impact on African Americans should diminish or entirely disappear once they are included in the model.

The results for African Americans are reported in table 3-6. Column 1 reports the impact on African American test scores of attending a private school in New York City after one year: 5.4 percentile points. Column 3 shows the same effect after two years: 4.3 percentile points.

In columns 2 and 4, we report the effects of attending a private school in years one and two, respectively, after controlling for parental reports on

Table 3-7. *Impact of Switching to a New York City Private School on Latinos' Test Scores Controlling for Likely Suspects*

Characteristic	Year one		Year two	
	(1)	(2)	(3)	(4)
Attend private school	−1.4	−1.4	−0.9	−1.0
School disruptions	—	−2.2***	—	−0.9
Communication	—	1.5*	—	−0.3
School size	—	1.0	—	0.9
Class size	—	1.3*	—	2.5***
Baseline math score	0.4***	0.4***	0.4***	0.4***
Baseline reading score	0.4***	0.4***	0.3***	0.3***
Constant	20.2*	11.6	11.5	4.9
N	704	704	612	612
Adjusted R^2	.44	.46	.45	.46

* Significant at the 0.10 level on a two-tailed test.
*** Significant at the 0.01 level on a two-tailed test.
Note: Weighted least squares regressions performed. Impacts expressed in terms of national percentile rankings. All models control for baseline test scores and lottery indicators. Missing values for school covariates imputed by best subset regression.

school disruptions, school communications, class size, and school size. If these factors drive African American test score gains, then the effect of a voucher should diminish or disappear once they are added to the model. Unfortunately, this does not happen. The size of the impact remains essentially constant. Neither separately nor combined, these four factors do not explain why African Americans perform better on tests when given an opportunity to attend a private school. Parenthetically, only one of the four items in either year—the school disruption index in year two—has a significant and direct impact on African Americans' test scores. The others do not appear to have any causal impact at all.

Table 3-7 reports the results for Latino students from equivalent regressions. The offer of a voucher has no impact on student performance either before or after additional items are included in the equation. Furthermore, school disruptions appear to have a negative direct impact on student performance, especially after one year. Class size also has an effect, but its sign is perverse: Latinos do better in larger classes. This correlation could be caused, however, by the assignment of Latino students with language or learning difficulties to smaller classes.

Perhaps the factors that impact African American test scores are not the same ones that distinguish the impact of vouchers on the perceptions of

African American and Latino parents. Instead, some other factor or all factors combined may account for the differential race effects on test scores that we observe. To examine this possibility, we conducted a kitchen-sink analysis, one that included every survey item in a single model, along with all relevant interaction terms. Such a model is not a very good way of estimating the impact of any particular aspect of school life on student test score performance. Because few of the indexes measure distinct school characteristics, the estimated impact of each is partially estimated by others. However, this approach allows us to ascertain whether measurable aspects of school life help explain the private school advantage for African Americans.

Again, they appear not to. Even when we include all items—not only school disruptions, school communications, school size, and class size but also suspensions, dress rules, hallway monitoring, school resources, homework, segregation, parental involvement with child, and parental involvement with the school—in the equation, the impact of attending a private school on African American test scores remains statistically significant, while that for Latinos does not. In both years one and two, the impacts for African Americans in the comprehensive models register a statistically significant 6.3 NPR points. For Latinos, the impacts for years one and two were –1.8 and –1.5, respectively.

Discussion

If African Americans learn more in New York City private schools than they do in public schools, and if the private school impact is not due to school size, class size, school disruptions, school communications, desegregation, dress rules, hallway monitoring, school resources, homework, level of parental involvement with child's education, or their involvement with the school, then what does explain the difference?

Parental perceptions are not always as precise as one might like, and so these school characteristics should not be prematurely ruled out as possible explanations for the differential race effects that vouchers seem to generate. Still, though, we remain impressed by the similar patterns of parental response from one year to the next and one city to another. If parents were responding to questions more or less randomly, then we should observe different patterns that vary across city and over time. Instead, the pattern of parental responses is remarkably stable.

The voucher impacts could derive not from these items considered separately or additively, but through some complex interaction among some or all of the variables. Perhaps it is the interaction between school disruptions and school size that counts? Or the interaction between parental-school communications and class size? Different aspects of school life may come together in different ways for African Americans and Latinos, generating contrasting test scores outcomes for the two groups.

Private school impacts also could stem from instructional factors that none of the items in our parental survey adequately measures. Perhaps the disparities between the quality of teachers for African American students in public and private schools are much wider than those for Latino students. Perhaps African American students are particularly and uniquely receptive to teaching techniques that are more prevalent in private schools. Recent research has shown that teacher effectiveness can have a large impact on student test score performance.[21] Our models, however, do not include any measures of curriculum, teaching techniques, the expectations that teachers place on their students, or teacher quality. Such factors might be the key to understanding why African Americans benefit from choice, but Latinos do not.

Finally, the effects may have nothing to do with the characteristics of public and private schools that African Americans and Latinos attend. They may instead derive from the quality of the peer groups at these schools. Richard Rothstein, for instance, has suggested that positive effects arise when voucher recipients "are surrounded by pupils with higher academic expectations."[22] If African Americans attend private schools with a particularly elite group of classmates, while the peer groups of Latinos who switch from public to private school change very little, then peer effects may lie at the heart of the story we are trying to uncover.

We still do not know what makes private schools successful, at least for African Americans. And without an answer, it remains unclear how, or even whether, public schools can introduce appropriate reforms that benefit African American students. Future pilot studies that contain a larger number of subjects, proceed for longer periods of time, and collect a broader array of information may unearth some of the reasons that at least some students appear to benefit from choice.

Appendix 3A

Depending upon which year the surveys were administered, indexes were constructed from all or a subset of the items that follow. Response categories are available upon request.

School disruptions. "How serious are the following problems at this child's school? Very serious, somewhat serious, or not serious?: Kids destroying property; kids being late for schools; kids missing classes; fighting; cheating; racial conflict; guns or other weapons; drugs or alcohol."

Suspensions. "During this past year, was this child ever suspended for disciplinary reasons?"

Dress rules. "Are students required to wear a uniform?" "Are certain forms of dress forbidden?"

Hallway monitors. "Are visitors required to sign in at main office?" "Are hall passes required to leave class?"

School resources. "At the school this child attends, which of the following programs or facilities are available to students?: A computer lab; a library; a gym; a cafeteria; child counselors; a nurses' office."

School programs. "At the school this child attends, which of the following programs or facilities are available to students?: Special programs for non–English speakers; individual tutors; special programs for students with learning problems; special programs for advanced learners; a music program; an arts program; an after-school program."

School communication with parents. "Do the following practices exist in this child's school?: Parents informed about student grades halfway through the grading period; parents notified when student are sent to the office the first time for disruptive behavior; parents speak to classes about their jobs; parents participate in instruction; parent open-house or back-to-school night held at school; regular parent-teacher conferences held; parents receive notes about this student from this child's teachers; parents receive a newsletter about what is going on in this child's school or classroom."

Amount of homework. "Approximately how much homework is assigned on an average day?"

Class size. "Approximately how many students are in this child's class?"

School size. "Approximately how large is the school this child attends?"

Racial segregation. "What proportion of students in this child's classroom is minority?" Percent responding "everyone" or "90–100 percent."

Parental involvement with child's education. "In the past month, how often did you do the following?: Help this child with his or her homework; help this child with reading or math that was not part of his or her homework; talk with this child about his or her experiences at school; attend school activities; work on school projects."

Parental involvement with child's school. "How many parent-teacher conferences did you attend this school year?" "How many hours have you volunteered in this child's school this past month?" "Are you a member of a PTA [Parent-Teacher Association] or other similar organization (Parent's Council, for example)?"

Satisfaction index. "How satisfied are you with the following aspects of this child's current school?: Location of school; school safety; teaching; how much school involves parents; class sizes; school facilities; student respect of teachers; how much teachers inform parents of students' progress; how much students can observe religious traditions; parental support for the school; discipline; clarity of school goals; teamwork among staff; teaching values; academic quality; the sports program; what is taught in the school."

Notes

We wish to thank the principals, teachers, and staff at the private schools in Dayton, Ohio; New York City; and Washington, D.C., who assisted in the administration of tests and questionnaires. We also wish to thank the School Choice Scholarships Foundation (SCSF), Parents Advancing Choice in Education (PACE), and the Washington Scholarship Fund (WSF) for cooperating fully with these evaluations. Kristin Kearns Jordan, Tom Carroll, and other members of the SCSF staff assisted with data collection in New York City. John Blakeslee, Leslie Curry, Douglas Dewey, Laura Elliot, Heather Hamilton, Tracey Johnson, John McCardell, and Patrick Purtill of the Washington Scholarship Fund provided similar cooperation. T. J. Wallace and Mary Lynn Naughton, staff members of Parents Advancing Choice in Education, provided valuable assistance with the Dayton evaluation. Chester E. Finn, Bruno Manno, Gregg Vanourek, and Marci Kanstoroom of the Fordham Foundation, Edward P. St. John of Indiana University, and Thomas Lasley of the University of Dayton provided valuable suggestions throughout various stages of the research design and data collection. We wish to thank especially David Myers of Mathematica Policy Research, who is a principal investigator of the evaluation of the New York School Choice Scholarship Program; his work on the New York evaluation has influenced in many important ways the design of the Washington and Dayton evaluations. We thank William McCready, Robin Bebel, Kirk Miller, and other members of the staff of the Public Opinion Laboratory at Northern Illinois University for their assistance with data collection, data processing, conduct of the lottery, and preparation of baseline and year-one follow-up data. We are particularly grateful to Tina Elacqua and Matthew Charles for their key roles in coordinating data collection efforts.

We received helpful advice from Paul Hill, Christopher Jencks, Donald Rock, and Donald Rubin. Daniel Mayer and Julia Chou were instrumental in preparing the New York City survey and test score data and in executing many of the analyses reported in the paper. Patrick Wolf and David Campbell oversaw the collection of the Washington, D.C., and Dayton data. Additional research assistance was provided by Rachel Deyette, Jennifer Hill, and Martin West; Shelley Weiner, Lilia Halpern, and Micki Morris provided staff assistance.

These evaluations have been supported by grants from the following foundations: Achelis Foundation, Bodman Foundation, Lynde and Harry Bradley Foundation,

William Donner Foundation, Thomas B. Fordham Foundation, Milton and Rose D. Friedman Foundation, John M. Olin Foundation, David and Lucile Packard Foundation, Smith-Richardson Foundation, Spencer Foundation, and Walton Family Foundation. The methodology, analyses of data, reported findings, and interpretations of findings are our sole responsibility and are not subject to the approval of SCSF, WSF, PACE, or of any foundation providing support for this research.

1. Disparate findings have emerged from these studies. For example, one analysis of the Milwaukee, Wisconsin, choice experiment found test score gains in reading and math, particularly after students had been enrolled for three or more years, while another study found gains only in math, and a third found gains in neither subject. Jay P. Greene, Paul E. Peterson, and Jiangtao Du, "School Choice in Milwaukee: A Randomized Experiment," in Paul E. Peterson and Bryan C. Hassel, eds., *Learning from School Choice* (Brookings, 1998), pp. 335–56; Cecilia Rouse, "Private School Vouchers and Student Achievement: An Evaluation of the Milwaukee Parental Choice Program," Princeton University, Department of Economics, 1997; and John F. Witte, "Achievement Effects of the Milwaukee Voucher Program," paper presented at the 1997 annual meeting of the American Economics Association. On the Cleveland, Ohio, program, see Jay P. Greene, William G. Howell, and Paul E. Peterson, "Lessons from the Cleveland Scholarship Program," in Paul E. Peterson and Bryan C. Hassel, eds., *Learning from School Choice* (Brookings, 1998), pp. 357–92; and Kim K. Metcalf and others, "A Comparative Evaluation of the Cleveland Scholarship and Tutoring Grant Program: Year One: 1996–97," Indiana University, School of Education, Smith Research Center, March 1998. Greene, Peterson, and Du, "School Choice in Milwaukee," reports results from analyses of experimental data; the other studies are based upon analyses of nonexperimental data.

2. Since this paper was prepared, further information has been gathered and is reported in William Howell and Paul E. Peterson, with Patrick Wolf and David Campbell, *The Education Gap: Vouchers and Urban Schools* (Brookings, 2002). See also William G. Howell and others, "School Vouchers and Academic Performance: Results from Three Randomized Field Trials," *Journal of Policy Analysis and Management,* vol. 21, no. 2 (2002), pp. 191–218.

Other papers that report results from the evaluations include William G. Howell and Paul E. Peterson, "School Choice in Dayton, Ohio: An Evaluation after One Year," paper prepared for the Conference on Charters, Vouchers, and Public Education, 2000, sponsored by Harvard University, John F. Kennedy School of Government, Taubman Center on State and Local Government, Program on Education Policy and Governance, Cambridge, Mass., available at www.ksg.harvard.edu/pepg/; and Patrick J. Wolf, William G. Howell, and Paul E. Peterson, "School Choice in Washington, D.C.: An Evaluation after One Year," paper prepared for the Conference on Charters, Vouchers, and Public Education, 2000, sponsored by Harvard University, John F. Kennedy School of Government, Taubman Center on State and Local Government, Program on Education Policy and Governance, Cambridge, Mass., available at www.ksg.harvard.edu/pepg/. First-year results from the New York City evaluation are reported in Paul E. Peterson and others, "The Effects of School Choice in New York City," in Susan B. Mayer and Paul E. Peterson, eds., *Earning and Learning: How Schools Matter* (Brookings, 1999), chapter 12. For results from the second-year evaluation of New York City's voucher program, see David Myers and others, "School Choice in New York City after Two Years: An Evaluation of the School Choice Scholarships Program," Occasional Paper (Harvard University, John F. Kennedy School of Government, Taubman Center on State and Local Government, Program on Education Policy and Governance, September 2000), available at www.ksg.harvard.edu/pepg/.

3. Thomas Hoffer, Andrew Greeley, and James Coleman, "Achievement Growth in Public and Catholic Schools," *Sociology of Education*, vol. 58 (April 1985), pp. 74–97; Douglas Wilms, "Catholic School Effects on Academic Achievement: New Evidence from the High School and Beyond Follow-up Study," *Sociology of Education*, vol. 58 (April 1985), pp. 98–114; and Christopher Jencks, "How Much Do High School Students Learn?" *Sociology of Education*, vol. 58 (April 1985), pp. 128–35.

4. Hoffer, Greeley, and Coleman, "Achievement Growth in Public and Catholic Schools," tables 1.7 and 1.8., pp. 80–81; these are the estimates of effects when controlling for background characteristics and years in Catholic school.

5. Jencks, "How Much Do High School Students Learn?" p. 134.

6. Derek Neal, "The Effects of Catholic Secondary Schooling on Educational Achievement," *Journal of Labor Economics*, vol. 15, no. 1 (1997), part 1, pp. 98–123.

7. William N. Evans and Robert M. Schwab, "Who Benefits from Private Education? Evidence from Quantile Regressions," University of Maryland, Department of Economics, 1993; and David Figlio and Joe Stone, "School Choice and Student Performance: Are Private Schools Really Better?" University of Wisconsin, Institute for Research on Poverty, 1977. Other studies finding positive educational benefits from attending private schools include James S. Coleman, Thomas Hoffer, and Sally Kilgore, *High School Achievement* (Basic Books, 1982); and John E. Chubb and Terry M. Moe, *Politics, Markets, and America's Schools* (Brookings, 1990). Critiques of these studies have been prepared by Arthur S. Goldberger and Glen G. Cain, "The Causal Analysis of Cognitive Outcomes in the Coleman, Hoffer, and Kilgore Report," *Sociology of Education*, vol. 55 (April-July 1982), pp. 103–22.

8. Results from these evaluations are reported in Paul E. Peterson and Bryan C. Hassel, eds., *Learning from School Choice* (Brookings, 1998).

9. Take-up rates are the percentage of those offered vouchers who attend private schools. The rates reported here are for those who participated in the evaluations in years one and two. Take-up rates are somewhat lower when calculated for those who did not participate in the evaluation.

10. More precisely, the notation for the two-stage models is as follows:

$$P = \alpha_1 + \beta_1 V + \beta_2 Y_{0R} + \beta_3 Y_{0M} + \mu_1$$
$$Y_t = \alpha_2 + \beta_4 P + \beta_5 Y_{0R} + \beta_6 Y_{0M} + \mu_2$$

P is an indicator variable for attendance at a private school. β_2 represents the estimated impact of switching from a public to a private school on student test scores. Y_t is each student's total achievement score on the Iowa Test of Basic Skills expressed in national percentile ranking (NPR) points, where the subscript t denotes the year the student completed the follow-up test (either 1 or 2). The total achievement score is a simple average of the math and reading components. Because it is based upon a larger number of test items, the total achievement score is likely to generate more stable estimates than are reading and math scores estimated separately. (See Alan B. Krueger, "Experimental Estimation of Production Function," *Quarterly Journal of Economics* [May 1999], pp. 497–537.) V is an indicator variable for whether or not an individual was offered a voucher. Y_{0R} and Y_{0M} are the baseline reading and math scores.

11. In this paper we focus on overall or combined test score results, which simply represent the average of the math and reading components. When we use one-hour testing sessions to gauge student performance, their combined reading and math scores serve as a better indicator of student achievement than either subcomponent separately. Theoretically, the more test items used, the more likely performance is accurately measured. As Jencks, "How Much Do High School Students Learn?" p. 131, points out with respect to Douglas Wilms's findings in "Catholic School Effects on Academic Achievement," "some of the apparent 'noise' in Wilms's Table 7 might have disappeared had he collapsed different sophomore tests into a single composite."

12. See chapter 2 in this volume, Alan B. Krueger and Diane M. Whitmore, "Would Smaller Classes Help Close the Black-White Achievement Gap?"

13. See also Ann Flanagan, Jennifer Kawata, and Stephanie Williamson, *Improving Student Achievement: What NAEP Test Scores Tell Us* (Santa Monica, Calif.: RAND Corporation, 2000), p. 59.

14. Bruce Fuller, Luis Huerta, and David Ruenzel, *A Costly Gamble or Serious Reform? California's School Voucher Initiative—Proposition 38* (University of California at Berkeley and Stanford University, Policy Analysis for California Education, 2000), p. 10.

15. *Deception by the Numbers: Ten Reasons to Doubt the Latest Claims for Vouchers*, report available at www.pfaw.org.

16. Richard Rothstein, "Judging Vouchers' Merits Proves to be Difficult Task," *New York Times*, December 13, 2000, p. A25; and Martin Carnoy, "Do School Vouchers Improve Student Performance?" *American Prospect*, vol. 12, no. 1 (January 2001), available at www.prospect.org.

17. Items listed in the previous section include only those that formed part of the baseline survey. Later surveys added more items.

18. Howell and Peterson, with Wolf and Campbell, *The Education Gap*, chapter 5.

19. Wolf, Howell, and Peterson, "School Choice in Washington, D.C."

20. See Howell and others, "Test-Score Effects of School Vouchers"; Howell and Peterson, "School Choice in Dayton, Ohio"; Wolf, Howell, and Peterson, "School

Choice in Washington, D.C."; Peterson and others, "The Effects of School Choice in New York City"; and Myers and others, "School Choice in New York City after Two Years."

21. Steven G. Rivkin, Eric A. Hanushek, and John F. Kain, "Teachers, Schools and Academic Achievement," April 2000.

22. Rothstein, "Judging Vouchers' Merits Proves to Be Difficult Task," p. A25.

4

"Success for All" and African American and Latino Student Achievement

ROBERT E. SLAVIN AND NANCY A. MADDEN

The gap in academic achievement between African American and Latino children and their white peers is arguably the most important of all educational problems. This gap, which appears early in elementary school, grows in absolute terms over the school years. On several scales of the National Assessment of Educational Progress (NAEP), African American and Latino seventeen-year-olds perform at the level of white thirteen-year-olds.[1] These differences translate directly into differences in high school graduation rates, in college attendance and completion, and, ultimately, in income and socioeconomic status that underlie the country's most critical social problems. If African American, Latino, and other minority students performed in school at the same level as whites, the broad social impact would be profound, almost certainly affecting the socioeconomic status of minority individuals, college admissions, and ultimately segregation, prejudice, and racial tension.

In 1954, when the U.S. Supreme Court decision in *Brown* v. *Board of Education* began the process of school desegregation, social scientists confidently predicted that the racial gap in academic performance would soon be eliminated. Sadly, this did not occur. According to scores on NAEP, the reading achievement of white fourth graders is virtually unchanged since the earliest national assessments in 1971 (see figure 4-1).[2] During the 1970s, African American and Latino students made significant progress on NAEP

Figure 4-1. *National Assessment of Educational Progress Reading Scale Scores at Age Nine, by Ethnicity, 1971–99*

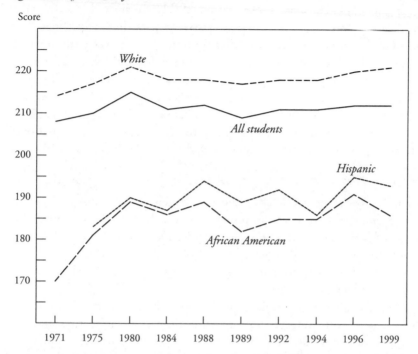

Source: Based on data from J. R. Campbell, C. M. Hombo, and J. Mazzeo, *NAEP 1999: Trends in Academic Progress*, Report 2000–469 (U.S. Department of Education, National Center for Education Statistics, 2000).

reading, but little further change has been evident since the early 1980s. In subjects other than reading, similar patterns have also been seen, and significant gaps in performance still exist today and are no longer diminishing.

The gap reduction seen in the 1970s is important in demonstrating that the achievement gap is not immutable but can be changed on a national scale. Many explanations for this period of progress have been advanced, but the greatest likelihood is simply that schooling for African American and Latino children went from abysmal to merely terrible. This was the period when the country saw the first fruits of the Johnson administration's Great Society programs, such as Title I, desegregation, and other improvements in basic schooling of African American and Latino students. Significantly, the greatest advances were seen among African American children in the South, where the most dramatic social and educational changes took place in the civil rights era.

Since 1980, according to NAEP, achievement for all ethnic groups has virtually stagnated, and therefore the gap has remained unchanged. African Americans and Latinos, on average, attend schools that are far less well funded than those attended by whites, their teachers are less highly qualified, and their families are more likely to suffer from the ills of poverty, all of which have direct bearing on children's success in school. Some theorists suggest that educational equality will not be achieved until economic and social equality is achieved, but given the dependence of socioeconomic status on educational attainment, economic success seems unlikely to precede academic success, at least in the near term. If it is possible, direct intervention in the quality of education provided to African American and Latino children is essential.

Educational Approaches to Gap Reduction

Many approaches to accelerating the achievement of African American and Latino children have been proposed. Some researchers have argued that schools fail to take advantage of the cultural and personal assets of African American students, and innovative schools and laboratory research have shown that culturally consistent instruction can be beneficial to African American students.[3]

Another approach to reducing the achievement gap is simply to improve the quality of instruction provided to African American and Latino students. In this regard, several lines of research suggest that the achievement of African American students is particularly susceptible to improvements in educational quality. For example, the famous Tennessee class-size study found significant positive effects for all children of reducing class sizes from an average of twenty-two to an average of fifteen.[4] However, the impact of class-size reduction was much greater for African American students than for white students. Longitudinal follow-up studies have shown lasting benefits of class-size reduction in grades K–3, but, again, African American students continue to show the most significant benefits. The 2000 evaluations of voucher experiments in four cities have been highly controversial, as are vouchers themselves.[5] However, critics as well as defenders of the study agree that if any group of children benefited from the opportunity to attend private schools, it was African American students alone who showed achievement gains. Sociological studies have often shown that the payoffs of educational attainment are greater for African Americans than for other groups. It is not entirely clear why African American students would be particularly responsive to improvements in educational quality, but the phenomenon has been demonstrated often enough to be taken seriously by policymakers as well as social scientists.

For Latino students, reductions in achievement gaps are complicated by issues of language. A component of the achievement gap between Latino and Anglo students is certainly limited English proficiency among a significant minority of Latino students, especially those in the first generation. (Note that students at the lowest levels of English proficiency are excluded from the NAEP, meaning that the true gap is even larger than it appears.) However, studies also find lower academic attainment for second- and third-generation Latino students, so recent immigration or limited English language proficiency cannot be responsible for the entire gap. Improvements are clearly necessary in the schooling of all Latino students, both fully English proficient and limited English proficient.

Success for All and the Achievement Gap

One educational innovation that is having a widespread and disproportionate impact on African American and Latino students is Success for All, a comprehensive reform model for elementary schools developed and piloted in inner-city Baltimore in 1987. Today, Success for All is used in about sixteen hundred schools in forty-eight states, serving about one million children. Overwhelmingly, these schools are high-poverty, Title I schoolwide projects, and about two-thirds of all Success for All children are African American or Latino. Success for All is the most widely used set of whole-school reform models, which focus on changing all aspects of school functioning—from curriculum and instruction to parent involvement, provisions for children experiencing difficulties, and assessment. These comprehensive reform models, especially James Comer's School Development Project and Direct Instruction, are primarily used in Title I schoolwide projects and disproportionately serve African American and Latino students.[6]

Success for All, which focuses primarily on reading, provides schools with research-based curriculum materials, instructional strategies, and extensive professional development and follow-up. It provides one-to-one tutoring for young children struggling in reading, as well as active parent involvement programs. Box 4-1 summarizes the program's main elements.

Success for All (and other comprehensive reforms) might be expected to affect the achievement gap between African American and Latino students and their white counterparts in two ways. First, because it is so often adopted by schools that are majority African American or Latino, the program could affect the gap simply by giving these children more effective instruction. Second, even in integrated schools, Success for All could have a differential positive effect on the achievement of African American or Latino students. Evidence supports both means.

Box 4-1. Major Elements of Success for All

Success for All, a schoolwide program for children in prekindergarten to grade five, organizes educational resources to attempt to ensure that virtually every student will reach the third grade on time with adequate basic skills and will build on this foundation throughout the elementary grades. The goal is for no student to fall between the cracks. The main elements of the program are as follows.

A schoolwide curriculum. During reading periods, students are regrouped across age lines so that each reading class is at one reading level. Use of tutors as reading teachers during reading time reduces the size of most reading classes to about twenty students. The reading program in grades K–1 emphasizes language and comprehension skills, phonics, sound blending, and use of shared stories that students read to one another in pairs. The shared stories combine teacher-read material with phonetically regular student material to teach decoding and comprehension in the context of meaningful, engaging stories. In grades two to six, students use novels or basals but not workbooks. This program emphasizes cooperative learning activities built around partner reading, identification of characters, settings, problems, and problem solutions in narratives, story summarization, writing, and direct instruction in reading comprehension skills. At all levels, students are required to read books of their own choice for twenty minutes at home each evening. Classroom libraries of trade books are provided for this purpose. Cooperative learning programs in writing or language arts are used in grades K–6.

Tutors. In grades one to three, specially trained certified teachers and paraprofessionals work one-to-one with any students who are failing to keep up with their classmates in reading. Tutorial instruction is closely coordinated with regular classroom instruction. It takes place twenty minutes daily during times other than reading periods.

Preschool and kindergarten. The preschool and kindergarten programs in Success for All emphasize language development, readiness, and self-concept. Preschools and kindergartens use thematic units, language development activities, and a program called Story Telling and Retelling (STaR).

Eight-week assessments. Students in grades one to six are assessed every eight weeks to determine whether they are making adequate progress in reading. This information is used to suggest alternate teaching strategies in the regular classroom, changes in reading group placement, provision of tutoring services, or other means of meeting students' needs.

Family support team. A family support team works in each school to help parents in ensuring the success of their children, focusing on parent education, parent involvement, attendance, and student behavior. This team is composed of existing or additional staff such as parent liaisons, social workers, counselors, and vice principals.

Facilitator. A program facilitator works with teachers to help them implement the reading program, manages the eight-week assessments, assists the family support team, makes sure that all staff are communicating with each other, and helps the staff as a whole make certain that every child is making adequate progress.

Research on the Achievement Effects of Success for All

From the beginning, Success for All focused on research and evaluation, and most of the studies of this model have involved African American or Latino students. Longitudinal evaluations of Success for All emphasizing individually administered measures of reading were begun in its earliest sites, six schools in Baltimore and Philadelphia. Later, third-party evaluators at the University of Memphis (Steven Ross, Lana Smith, and their colleagues) added studies in Memphis, Tennessee; Houston, Texas; Charleston, South Carolina; Montgomery, Alabama; Ft. Wayne, Indiana; Caldwell, Idaho; Tucson, Arizona; Clover Park, Washington; Little Rock, Arkansas; and Clarke County, Georgia. Each of these evaluations has compared Success for All schools with matched comparison schools using either traditional methods or alternative reform models on measures of reading performance, starting with cohorts in kindergarten or in first grade and continuing to follow these students as long as possible. Other studies have compared Success for All with a variety of alternative reform models, have compared full and partial implementations of Success for All, and have made other comparisons. Several studies have also examined the impact of Success for All on state accountability measures, compared with gains made in the state as a whole or with other comparison groups.[7]

Comparing Success for All to Matched Control Groups

The largest number of studies has compared the achievement of students in Success for All schools with that of children in matched comparison schools using traditional methods, including locally developed Title I reforms. These studies primarily used individually administered, standardized measures of reading.

A total of thirty-five schools in thirteen districts have been involved in studies using individually administered reading measures. Twenty-one of these schools were majority African American, and seven more had populations that were 25 percent to 50 percent African American. Four were majority Latino, and three more had Latino minorities of 20–25 percent.

A common evaluation design, with variations resulting from local circumstances, has been used in the Success for All studies carried out by researchers at Johns Hopkins University, the University of Memphis, and WestEd. Each Success for All school involved in a formal evaluation was matched with a control school that was similar in poverty level (percent of students qualifying for free lunch), historical achievement level, ethnicity, and other factors.

Figure 4-2. *Comparison of Success for All and Control Schools in Mean Reading Grade Equivalents and Effect Sizes, 1988–99*

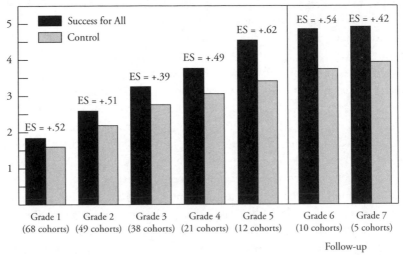

Grade equivalents

Note: Effect size (ES) is the proportion of a standard deviation by which Success for All students exceeded controls. Includes approximately six thousand children in Success for All or control schools since first grade.

Schools were also matched on district-administered standardized test scores given in kindergarten or on Peabody Picture Vocabulary Test (PPVT) scores given by the evaluators in the fall of kindergarten or first grade. The measures used in the evaluations were three scales from the Woodcock Reading Mastery Test (Word Identification, Word Attack, and Passage Comprehension, kindergarten to grade six), the Durrell Oral Reading Scale (grades one to three), and the Gray Oral Reading Test (grades four to seven). Analyses of covariance with pretests as covariates were used to compare raw scores in all evaluations. Results for all experimental-control comparisons in all evaluation years are averaged and summarized in figure 4-2 using a method called multisite replicated experiment.[8]

Reading Outcomes

The results of the multisite replicated experiment evaluating Success for All are summarized in figure 4-2 for each grade level, one through five, and for follow-up measures into grades six and seven. The analyses compare cohort means for experimental and control schools. A cohort is all students at a given grade level in a given year. For example, the first-grade graph compares sixty-eight experimental with sixty-eight control cohorts, with the cohort (50–150 students) as the unit of analysis. In other words, each first-grade bar is a mean of scores from about six thousand students. Grade equivalents are based on the means and are only presented for their informational value. No analyses were done using grade equivalents.

Statistically significant (p = .05 or better) positive effects of Success for All (compared with controls) were found on every measure at every grade level, one to five, using the cohort as the unit of analysis. For students in general, the effect size (ES) averaged around a half standard deviation at all grade levels. Consistently, effect sizes for students in the lowest 25 percent of their grades were particularly positive, ranging from ES = +1.03 in first grade to ES = +1.68 in fourth grade. Again, cohort-level analyses found statistically significant differences favoring low achievers in Success for All on every measure at every grade level. A follow-up study of African American students in five Baltimore schools found that similar positive program effects for the full sample of students continued into grade six (ES = +0.54) and grade seven (ES = +0.42), when students were in middle schools.

Ft. Wayne Study of Achievement Gap Reduction

One of the studies included in figure 4-2 took place in two experimental and two control schools in Ft. Wayne, Indiana. In this study, the authors found significant gaps between African American and white students at pretest on individually administered reading measures.[9] At posttest, the achievement gaps had grown in the control group but had diminished in the Success for All schools, so that the gap was no longer statistically or educationally significant.

Effects on District-Administered Standardized Tests

The formal evaluations of Success for All have relied primarily on individually administered assessments of reading. The Woodcock and Durrell scales used in these assessments are far more accurate than district-administered tests, and they are much more sensitive to real reading gains. They allow testers to hear children reading material of increasing difficulty and responding to questions about what they have read. The Woodcock and Durrell scales are nationally standardized tests and produce norms (for example, percentiles, normal curve equivalents [NCEs], and grade equivalents) just like any other standardized measure.

However, educators usually want to know the effects of innovative programs on the kinds of group-administered standardized tests for which they are usually held accountable. District test score data can produce valid evaluations of educational programs if comparison groups are available. To obtain this information, researchers have often analyzed standardized or state criterion-referenced test data comparing students in experimental and control schools.

Memphis, Tennessee

One of the most important independent evaluations of Success for All is a study carried out by researchers at the University of Tennessee at Knoxville for the Memphis city schools.[10] William Sanders, who was the architect of the Tennessee Value-Added Assessment System (TVAAS) and who was not familiar with any of the developers of the programs he evaluated, carried out the analysis. The TVAAS gives each school an expected gain, independent of school poverty levels, and compares it with actual scores on the Tennessee Comprehensive Assessment Program (TCAP). TVAAS scores above 100 indicate gains in excess of expectations; those below 100 indicate the opposite. Sanders compared TVAAS scores in twenty-two Memphis Success for All schools with those in other reform designs, in matched comparison schools, and in all Memphis schools. Almost all of the children in the Success for All schools, and most of those in the other Memphis schools, were African American.

Figure 4-3 summarizes the results for all subjects assessed. At pretest, the Success for All schools were lower than all three comparison groups on TVAAS. However, after two to four years of implementation, they performed significantly better than comparison schools, in all subjects.

Success for All schools averaged the greatest gains and highest levels on the TVAAS of the six restructuring designs (Co-nect, Accelerated Schools, Audrey Cohen College, ATLAS, and Expeditionary Learning), as well as exceeding controls, averaging across all subjects. However, as a group, all of the schools implementing reform designs scored better on TVAAS than students in comparison groups.

The importance of the Memphis study lies in several directions. First, it is an independent evaluation that involved state assessment scores of the kind used in most state accountability systems. While the article reporting the analysis was prepared by University of Memphis researchers long associated with Success for All, the analyses themselves were carried out by William Sanders and S. Paul Wright, researchers with no connection to the project. Second, it shows carryover effects of a program focused on reading, writing, and language arts into science and social studies outcomes.

An earlier study of Success for All schools in Memphis also showed positive effects on the TCAP.[11] This was a longitudinal study of three Success for All and three control schools. On average, Success for All schools exceeded

Figure 4-3. *Memphis City Schools Scores on Tennessee Value-Added Assessment System, Success for All, Other Comprehensive School Reform Designs, and Control Schools*

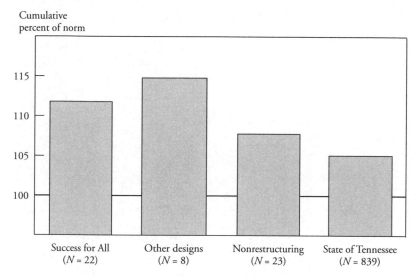

Cumulative
percent of norm

| | Success for All (N = 22) | Other designs (N = 8) | Nonrestructuring (N = 23) | State of Tennessee (N = 839) |

Source: Data from W. L. Sanders and others, *Value-Added Achievement Results for Three Cohorts of Roots & Wings Schools in Memphis: 1995–1999 Outcomes* (University of Memphis, Center for Research in Educational Policy, 2000).

controls on TCAP reading by an effect size of +0.38 in first grade and +0.45 in second grade.

Bilingual and ESL Adaptations of Success for All

Several studies have examined the effects of Success for All on the achievement of limited English proficient students taught in Spanish or English.[12] Three studies of the bilingual Spanish adaptation of Success for All found positive effects for Spanish-dominant children also taught in Spanish in comparison to those in control schools. Further, Spanish-dominant English language learners gained more than matched controls in two studies of the English as a Second Language (ESL) adaptation of Success for All. These findings provide important evidence to support the observation that Latino students, like African American students, gain outstandingly from Success for All.

State of Texas

The largest study ever done to evaluate achievement outcomes of Success for All was completed in 2001 by E. Hurley and others.[13] This study also pro-

Figure 4-4. *Texas Assessment of Academic Skills Reading Score from Preimplementation Year to 1998, All Students, Grades Three to Five*

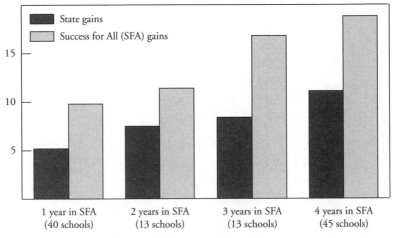

vides the best evidence regarding reductions in achievement gaps between African American and Latino students and white students. Using data available on the Internet, Hurley and others compared every school that ever used Success for All anywhere in the state of Texas during the period 1994–98 ($N = 111$ schools). Gains in these schools on the percent of students passing the Texas Assessment of Academic Skills (TAAS) reading measures were compared for grades three to five in the Success for All schools and for the state as a whole. In each case, gains from the year before program inception to 1998 were compared. (Changes in testing procedures made 1999 scores noncomparable.) Figure 4-4 shows the overall results, which indicate greater gains for Success for All schools than for the rest of the state for every cohort. Analyzing school means, the differences are highly significant ($p < .001$; ES = +0.60).

Combining across cohorts, scores of African American students gained significantly more in Success for All schools than in the state ($p < .05$), as did scores of Latino students ($p < .05$).

The TAAS has been criticized for having a ceiling effect, giving the appearance of significantly reducing the gap between minority and white students.[14] The Success for All analysis regarding Texas may reflect this problem, as Success for All schools are far more impoverished than the state average (students receiving free lunches are 85 percent of those in Success for All

Figure 4-5. *Texas Assessment of Academic Skills Reading Score Gains from Preimplementation Year to 1998, African American Students, Grades Three to Five*

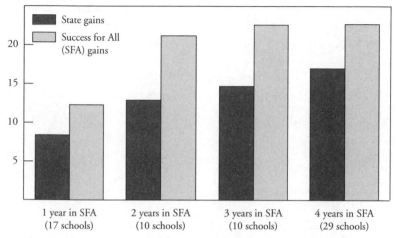

Gain in percent meeting minimum expectations

State gains

Success for All (SFA) gains

1 year in SFA (17 schools) 2 years in SFA (10 schools) 3 years in SFA (10 schools) 4 years in SFA (29 schools)

schools and 45 percent in the state as a whole). However, if there is a ceiling effect, it exists primarily among white students, who averaged 94.1 percent passing in 1998. In contrast, African American students across the state averaged 81.8 percent passing, and Hispanic students averaged 79.6 percent passing, making ceiling effects less likely. Hurley and others compared scores for African American and Hispanic students in Success for All schools and those for similar students in the state as a whole for 1995–98 (years when state scores were available by ethnicity).

As figure 4-5 shows, African American students in Success for All schools were closing the gap with white students much faster than were other African American students. For example, Success for All African American students advanced from 63.3 percent passing in 1995 to 86.2 percent passing in 1998, while other African American students only gained from 64.2 percent passing to 78.9 percent passing.

The Texas data are presented in a different form in figure 4-6. It shows the score gap between African American and white students for the Success for All schools and for other African American students in Texas, for each cohort, 1994–97, at pretest and at posttest (1998). The figure shows that, while the gap diminished for African American students throughout Texas, it diminished more for students in the Success for All schools in every cohort.

Figure 4-6. *Changes in African American–White Gaps in Percent of Students Passing Texas Assessment of Academic Skills in Reading, Grades Three to Five, 1994–98*

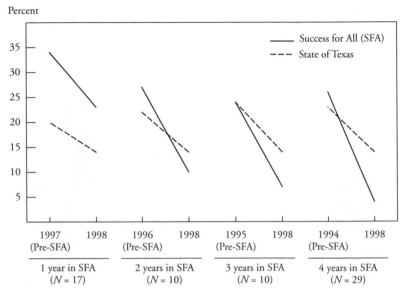

Percent

The overall gap reduction may be due in part to a ceiling effect for white students but does not explain the relative gap reduction, especially in the three cohorts in which initial gaps were nearly identical for African American students in Success for All schools and those in the rest of Texas.

Combining across all four cohorts (N = 66 schools), the achievement gap diminished by 15 points (from 28 to 13) in the Success for All classes, but only diminished by 8 points (from 22 to 14) in the state as a whole. This difference (in school-level change scores) is statistically significant (p < .01).

Similar patterns were found for gaps between Latino and white students; gaps diminished more in Success for All schools than in other Texas schools in three of four cohorts.[15] These results are summarized in figures 4-7 and 4-8. Combining across the four cohorts (N = 95 schools), the gap in Success for All schools dropped 11 percentage points, from 22 to 11, while the gap among the Texas Latino students changed only 6 percentage points, from 16 to 10.

What is particularly important about the Texas analyses is that they involve all 111 schools that ever used Success for All in Texas during 1994–98. There is no cherry picking; that is, selection of schools that happened to have made gains. Further, although the analyses were carried out by

Figure 4-7. *Texas Assessment of Academic Skills Reading Score Gains from Preimplementation Year to 1998, Hispanic Students, Grades Three to Five*

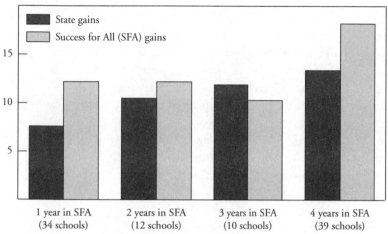

Gain in percent meeting
minimum expectations

Figure 4-8. *Changes in Latino-White Gaps in Percent of Students Passing Texas Assessment of Academic Skills in Reading, Grades Three to Five, 1994–98*

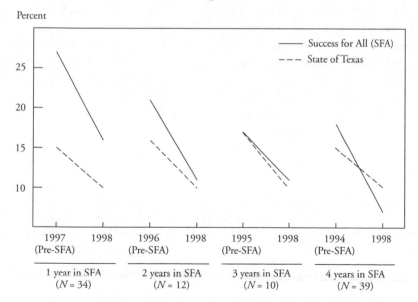

Percent

researchers at the Success for All Foundation, they used data that are readily available on the Internet, so anyone with an Internet account and a list of schools can replicate them.

Conclusion

The data evaluating Success for All show the potential of one form of comprehensive school reform to reduce the gap between African American and Latino students and white students in reading performance in the elementary grades. The evidence supports two mechanisms by which Success for All might reduce the achievement gap. First, the clear, powerful, and widely replicated effects of the program imply that if Success for All were disproportionately applied to schools serving many African American and Latino students, students in these schools would close the gap with other students. Second, some evidence (from the Ft. Wayne and Texas statewide studies) suggests that Success for All may have a differential effect on student achievement, affecting the performance of African American and Latino students more than it affects the performance of white students.

Research on Success for All demonstrates that the reading achievement of children in high-poverty Title I schools is not immutable but can be changed on a substantial scale. Quality of implementation and other factors make a difference in the outcomes obtained, but even averaging across better and worse implementations, outcomes are still strong and positive. If programs such as Success for All were widely applied to Title I schools, especially to Title I schoolwide projects (schools in which at least 50 percent of students qualify for free lunches), the average reading performance of all of America's children likely would advance, and the gap between African American and Latino students and white students likely would be significantly smaller than it is today. This must be an essential goal of research, development, and policy in the new millennium.

Notes

This paper was written under funding from the U.S. Department of Education, Office of Educational Research and Improvement (R–117–40005). Any opinions expressed are ours and do not necessarily represent the positions or policies of our funders.

For additional articles and other information on Success for All, see the website at www.successforall.net or call 1-800-548-4998. Success for All is disseminated by the Success for All Foundation, a nonprofit organization in Baltimore, Maryland.

1. J. R. Campbell, C. M. Hombo, and J. Mazzeo, *NAEP 1999: Trends in Academic Progress*, Report 2000–469 (U.S. Department of Education, National Center on Education Statistics, 2000).

2. P. L. Donahue and others, *NAEP 1998 Reading Report Card for the Nation* (U.S. Department of Education, National Center for Education Statistics, 1999).

3. For example, A. W. Boykin, "A Talent Development Approach to School Reform," paper presented at the annual meetings of the American Educational Research Association, New York, April 1996.

4. C. M. Achilles, J. D. Finn, and H. P. Bain, "Using Class Size to Reduce the Equity Gap," *Educational Leadership*, vol. 55, no. 4 (1997–98), pp. 40–43.

5. W. G. Howell and others, "Test-Score Effects of School Vouchers in Dayton, Ohio, New York City, and Washington, D.C.: Evidence from Randomized Field Trials," paper presented at the annual meeting of the American Political Science Association, Washington, D.C., September 2000.

6. James Comer, "Educating Poor Minority Children," *Scientific American*, vol. 259 (1988), pp. 42–48; and G. L. Adams and S. Engelmann, *Research on Direct Instruction: 25 Years beyond DISTAR* (Seattle, Wash.: Educational Achievement Systems, 1996).

7. For comprehensive reviews of the research, see R. E. Slavin and N. A. Madden, "Effects of Bilingual and English as a Second Language Adaptations of Success for All on the Reading Achievement of Students Acquiring English," *Journal of Education for Students Placed at Risk*, vol. 4, no. 4 (1999), pp. 393–416; R. E. Slavin and N. A. Madden, *Success for All/Roots & Wings: 1999 Summary of Research on Achievement Outcomes* (Johns Hopkins University, Center for Research on the Education of Students Placed at Risk, 1999); R. E. Slavin and N. A. Madden, "Research on Achievement Outcomes of Success for All: A Summary and Response to Critics," *Phi Delta Kappan*, vol. 82, no. 1 (2000), pp. 38–40, 59–66; and R. E. Slavin and N. A. Madden, *One Million Children: Success for All* (Thousand Oaks, Calif.: Corwin, 2000. For third-party reviews, see R. Herman, *An Educator's Guide to Schoolwide Reform* (Arlington, Va: Educational Research Service, 1999); J. Traub, *Better by Design? A Consumer's Guide to Schoolwide Reform* (Washington: Thomas Fordham Foundation, 1999); or Ohio Department of Education, *Choosing a Reading Program: A Consumer's Guide* (Columbus, Ohio, 2001).

8. See Slavin and Madden, *One Million Children*.

9. S. M. Ross, L. J. Smith, and J. P. Casey, *1994–1995 Success for All Program in Ft. Wayne, IN: Final Report* (University of Memphis, Center for Research in Educational Policy, 1995).

10. W. L. Sanders and others, *Value-Added Achievement Results for Three Cohorts of Roots & Wings Schools in Memphis: 1995–1999 Outcomes* (University of Memphis, Center for Research in Educational Policy, 2000).

11. Ross, Smith, and Casey, *1994-1995 Success for All Program in Ft. Wayne, IN*.

12. See Slavin and Madden, "Effects of Bilingual and English as a Second Language Adaptations of Success for All on the Reading Achievement of Students

Acquiring English"; and R. E. Slavin and M. Calderón, eds., *Effective Programs for Latino Students* (Mahwah, N.J.: Erlbaum, 2001).

13. E. Hurley, and others, "Effects of Success for All on TAAS Reading: A Texas Statewide Evaluation," *Phi Delta Kappan,* vol. 82, no. 10 (2001), pp. 750–56.

14. B. M. Specher and others, *What Do Test Scores in Texas Tell Us?* (Santa Monica, Calif.: RAND, 2000).

15. See Hurley and others, "Effects of Success for All on TAAS Reading."

5

Wisconsin's SAGE Program and Achievement through Small Classes

ALEX MOLNAR, JOHN ZAHORIK, PHIL SMITH,
ANKE HALBACH, AND KAREN EHRLE

To promote academic achievement of students in kindergarten through third-grade classrooms in selected Wisconsin schools serving low-income children, the Student Achievement Guarantee in Education (SAGE) program was established in 1995. The program, available for schools with at least 30 percent of their children below the poverty level from districts with a total enrollment at least 50 percent below the poverty level, consists of four interventions. In exchange for $2,000 from the Wisconsin Department of Public Instruction for each low-income student, schools were required to (1) reduce the student-teacher ratio within a classroom to fifteen students per teacher beginning with kindergarten and first grade in 1996–97, adding second grade in 1997–98, and then adding third grade in 1998–99, (2) establish "lighted schoolhouses" open from early morning until late in the evening, (3) develop a rigorous curriculum, and (4) create a system of staff development and professional accountability. Originally SAGE consisted of thirty schools in twenty-one districts throughout the state. As a result of two expansions of the program, SAGE classrooms were in 566 schools as of 2001–02.

Of the four interventions, student-teacher ratio within a classroom became the primary change in participating schools. All schools immediately reduced class size to fifteen students, but because most schools already had a curriculum in place that they would label "rigorous," some form of "lighted schoolhouse" schedule, and a staff development program, changes in these areas varied considerably. Although the class-size change was immediate, it was not uniform. Four distinct class-size configurations were used by schools to meet the student-teacher ratio requirement. The most commonly used configuration was the 15:1 student-teacher ratio classroom, termed the regular type of reduced-size classroom. The other types were the shared-space classroom, consisting of two 15:1 student-teacher ratio classes occupying one room fitted with a temporary room divider; the teamed classroom, in which two teachers collaboratively taught thirty students; and the floating teacher classroom, where one teacher taught thirty students except during reading, language arts, and mathematics, when another teacher joined the class to reduce the ratio to 15:1.

A longitudinal evaluation of the SAGE program begun during the first year of program implementation has focused on two general areas: (1) the effects of the program on student academic achievement in reading, language arts, and mathematics at the first-, second-, and third-grade levels, and (2) the classroom events resulting from reducing class size to a 15:1 student-teacher ratio that may account for any program effects on student learning.[1] The purpose of this paper is to report on the reduced class size effects on achievement of low-income, African American students in two cohorts of SAGE students.

Achievement of low-income, African American students and other low-income students has declined in comparison to white students since about 1990, according to K. Haycock, although the gap had been closing between 1970 and 1990.[2] Haycock's recommendations for reversing this trend among African American students are to establish high standards and ask more of students; implement a rigorous, challenging curriculum to accompany the standards; provide extra help for students in need; and employ trained, experienced teachers who are knowledgeable in the subjects they teach.

Research has shown that classroom environment in the form of reduced class size has promise for making an important contribution to narrowing the achievement gap between minority and white students. The Tennessee Project STAR study, by E. Word and others, found that minority students in small classrooms outperformed minority students in large classes in reading and mathematics. A. Krueger and A. Krueger and D. Whitmore found that lower achieving, minority, and poor students benefit most from attending smaller classes. C. Bingham concluded, from a review of the minority-white achievement gap issue, that small class size in the early grades is an effective preventive measure. The positive influence of reduced class size on achievement of minority students is not found in all reduced class-size programs, however. M. Snow's data show no differences in achievement between minority or low-income students and white students.[3]

The focus of the present study is low-income, African American students as opposed to minority students in general. The purpose is to bring more clarity to the issue regarding the importance of reduced class size in narrowing the achievement difference between African American students and white students in reading and mathematics in the primary grade.

Evaluation Design

Because students and teachers could not be randomly assigned to classrooms, classrooms could not be kept intact from year to year, and actual classroom size could not be controlled, a quasi-experimental, comparative change design was used to determine the impact of SAGE student-teacher class reductions on student achievement. SAGE classes were compared with classes from a set of comparison schools with normal class size from SAGE-participating districts. The comparison schools, which over time varied in number from seventeen to fourteen, are similar to the SAGE schools in race, gender, income, and other factors as can be seen in table 5-1. Approximately 25 percent of both the SAGE and comparison students are African Americans.

Cohort One consists of students who were enrolled in SAGE at the first-grade level in 1996–97 and remained in the program through second grade in 1997–98 and third grade in 1998–99. Cohort Two consists of students who were enrolled in SAGE at the first-grade level in 1997–98 and remained in the program through second grade in 1998–99 and third grade in 1999–2000. Total SAGE and comparison school enrollments are presented in table 5-2.

To determine student achievement, the Comprehensive Test of Basic Skills (CTBS) complete battery, Terra Nova edition, was administered at each grade level in participating SAGE and comparison schools. Level 10 was administered in the fall as a pretest and in the spring as a posttest in 1996–97. In 1997–98 level 11 was administered in the spring as the first-grade posttest. At the second grade, level 12 was administered as the posttest in spring, and at the third grade, level 13 was administered as the posttest in spring. For second and third grade, the posttest administered in the preceding year served as the pretest. The complete battery includes subtests in reading, language arts, and mathematics. CTBS was selected because it is derived from an Item Response Theory model that allows comparison of performance across time and it minimizes items biased against minorities and edu-

Table 5-1. *Characteristics of Students in SAGE and Comparison Schools, 1996–97, 1997–98, 1998–99, and 1999–2000*
Percent

Characteristic	Students in SAGE schools				Students in comparison schools			
	1996–97	1997–98	1998–99	1999–2000	1996–97	1997–98	1998–99	1999–2000
Gender								
Female	48.6	48.4	48.6	48.6	49.4	48.5	48.7	48.2
Male	51.4	51.6	51.4	51.3	50.6	51.5	51.3	51.8
Race or ethnicity								
African American	24.8	26.3	22.4	25.3	32.9	24.7	19.7	27.4
Asian	5.7	5.2	4.8	5.2	5.5	5.6	5.9	6.5
Hispanic	6.6	6.5	6.4	7.8	8.0	10.0	9.5	12.5
Native American	11.7	10.3	10.9	10.4	1.4	1.5	1.5	1.3
White	48.8	43.8	44.2	46.9	49.0	52.2	53.4	48.5
Other	1.6	2.0	1.8	1.4	2.7	2.3	2.3	2.4
Subsidized lunch eligibility								
Free	57.7	54.0	52.7	53.1	49.4	43.4	40.7	48.4
Reduced	10.9	10.6	11.5	12.3	9.9	8.9	10.4	11.2
Not eligible	31.4	35.4	35.8	31.6	40.7	47.7	48.8	38.6
Repeating grade	3.2	2.7	2.0	1.6	2.6	2.0	1.5	1.0
English as second language	8.2	7.9	7.5	7.0	4.9	6.4	6.7	9.2
Referred to M-Team	13.6	9.6	12.7	13.2	9.2	6.8	9.1	11.3
Exceptional education need	13.1	10.0	12.7	13.7	9.7	7.1	1.3	11.1

Note: SAGE = Student Achievement Guarantee in Education. M-Team = multidisciplinary team that meets to determine if a child has exceptional education needs.
Percentages may not always total 100 percent because of incomplete reports submitted by some schools.

Table 5-2. *Number of Students in SAGE and Comparison Schools, by Grade and School Year*

Number

Grade	Students in SAGE schools				Students in comparison schools			
	1996–97	1997–98	1998–99	1999–2000	1996–97	1997–98	1998–99	1999–2000
Kindergarten	1,494	1,524	1,416	n.a.	820	676	887	n.a.
First grade	1,723	1,567	1,525	n.a.	1,001	985	983	n.a.
Second grade	n.a.	1,541	1,446	1,636	n.a.	868	1,047	991
Third grade	n.a.	n.a.	1,531	1,611	n.a.	n.a.	1,041	1,045
Total	3,217	4,632	5,918	3,247	1,821	2,529	3,958	2,036

Note: SAGE = Student Achievement Guarantee in Education. n.a. = Not available. The number of comparison schools participating in the study since 1996 has fluctuated from fourteen to seventeen. Student numbers for comparison schools reflect this fluctuation.

cationally disadvantaged students. Statistical analysis concerning achievement of African American students enrolled in SAGE and comparison schools consisted of determining the significance of difference in means.

Results

Two types of results are presented regarding African American student achievement for each cohort. First, achievement of African American students in SAGE schools is compared with African American students in comparison schools on subtests and total scale scores. Then, achievement of African American students is compared with achievement of white students in both SAGE and comparison schools on total scale scores. Data analyses were based on third-grade students in each cohort who had valid test scores. Test score differences were based on those students who had valid test scores for both times included in the test score differences. Table 5-3 shows the number of third-grade students with valid third-grade test scores. Table 5-4 shows the number of students with valid test scores at both times when score differences were computed.

Cohort One

Tables 5-5, 5-6, and 5-7 present the findings comparing achievement of African American students in SAGE reduced-size classes with achievement of African American students in comparison school, normal-size classes from Cohort One.

As shown in table 5-5, African American first-grade students scored higher than comparison school first-grade students on the posttest in all areas and on the total test. Except for mathematics, the differences are not significant, however. Change scores also favor SAGE students, but here the differences are statistically significant. The change score results mean that at the first-grade level African American SAGE students scored lower on the CTBS pretest than African American comparison school students, but they made significantly larger gains than comparison school students from pretest to posttest and surpassed African American comparison school students on the posttest.

Table 5-6 presents results for second-grade SAGE and comparison school African American students. When using the first-grade pretest as the baseline score, statistically significant change scores are found on all scores except reading. However, using the first-grade posttest as the baseline score shows no statistically significant differences between SAGE and comparison schools.

Table 5-3. *Number of Students with Valid Third-Grade Total Scale Scores*
Number of students

Cohort	SAGE schools	Comparison schools
1996–99		
African American	286	219
White	595	402
1997–2000		
African American	213	138
White	501	409

Note: SAGE = Student Achievement Guarantee in Education.

Table 5-4. *Number of Students with Valid Difference Total Scale Scores*
Number of students

Difference	Cohort	SAGE schools	Comparison schools
First-grade pretest to third-grade posttest	*1996–99*		
	African American	161	109
	White	458	158
	1997–2000		
	African American	160	103
	White	421	200
First-grade posttest to third-grade posttest	*1996–99*		
	African American	165	119
	White	477	160
	1997–2000		
	African American	155	112
	White	430	212
Second-grade posttest to third-grade posttest	*1996–99*		
	African American	233	165
	White	546	190
	1997–2000		
	African American	196	131
	White	478	404

Note: SAGE = Student Achievement Guarantee in Education.

Table 5-5. *African American First-Grade Test and Change Scores,*
by SAGE and Comparison Schools, 1996–97, Cohort One

Subject	SAGE schools	Comparison schools	Difference
Language arts			
Mean posttest	563.2	560.4	2.80
Mean change, pretest to posttest	54.0	41.0	13.00*
Reading			
Mean posttest	569.0	565.3	3.70
Mean change, pretest to posttest	52.2	44.8	7.40*
Mathematics			
Mean posttest	524.0	518.6	5.40
Mean change, pretest to posttest	54.9	43.0	11.90*
Total			
Mean posttest	553.0	548.1	4.91
Mean change, pretest to posttest	54.1	42.5	11.60*

* Significant at the 0.05 level.
Note: SAGE = Student Achievement Guarantee in Education.

The results provided in table 5-7 show that the differences between mean changes for African American third-grade SAGE students and African American comparison third-grade students are statistically significant. When using the first-grade pretest as the baseline score, statistically significant changes are found on all scores. Using the first-grade posttest as the baseline score shows statistically significant differences between African American SAGE students and African American comparison students on the mathematics subtest and total score. When using the second-grade test as the baseline score, the reading and mathematics subtests and total scores show statistically significant change scores. African American SAGE student change was greater than African American comparison students, although the differences were not significant in language arts from the first-grade posttest and the second-grade test to the third-grade test and in reading from the first-grade posttest to the third-grade test.

Taken as a whole, data portrayed in tables 5-5, 5-6, and 5-7 show that Cohort One African American students in reduced-size classes gain, maintain, and, in some cases, improve an achievement advantage over African American students in normal-size classes. Table 5-8 provides data on how the achievement of African American students compares with the achievement of white students. African American students scored lower than white students on total scale scores at each grade level. This result is statistically significant

Table 5-6. *African American Second-Grade Change Scores, by SAGE and Comparison Schools, 1997–98, Cohort One*

Subject	SAGE schools	Comparison schools	Difference
Language arts			
Mean change from first-grade pretest to second grade	74.11	62.59	11.52*
Mean change from first-grade posttest to second grade	19.95	21.53	−1.58
Reading			
Mean change from first-grade pretest to second grade	72.59	68.39	4.20
Mean change from first-grade posttest to second grade	18.67	22.54	−3.86
Mathematics			
Mean change from first-grade pretest to second grade	73.10	58.49	14.61*
Mean change from first-grade posttest to second grade	16.21	20.47	−4.26
Total			
Mean change from first-grade pretest to second grade	72.97	65.20	7.76*
Mean change from first-grade posttest to second grade	17.77	21.58	−3.81

* Significant at the 0.05 level.
Note: SAGE = Student Achievement Guarantee in Education.

for both SAGE and comparison schools, though the gap between African Americans and whites is larger in the SAGE schools. The change from the first-grade posttest to the third-grade test shows that the SAGE African American students kept pace with white students but did not further close the achievement gap in second grade. The change from the second-grade to the third-grade test shows SAGE African American students gaining significantly more than SAGE white students, closing the achievement gap further. A similar result was not found for comparison students.

Cohort Two

The findings comparing African American student achievement in reduced-sized SAGE classes with achievement of African American students in normal-size comparison classes are reported in tables 5-9, 5-10, and 5-11 for Cohort Two.

Table 5-7. *African American Third-Grade Change Scores,*
by SAGE and Comparison Schools, 1998–99, Cohort One

Subject	SAGE schools	Comparison schools	Difference
Language arts			
Mean change from first-grade pretest to third grade	104.43	89.77	14.66*
Mean change from first-grade posttest to third grade	48.68	44.06	4.62
Mean change from second-grade test to third grade	27.80	24.85	2.95
Reading			
Mean change from first-grade pretest to third grade	105.12	92.41	12.71*
Mean change from first-grade posttest to third grade	50.10	44.04	6.06
Mean change from second-grade test to third grade	29.78	19.20	10.58*
Mathematics			
Mean change from first-grade pretest to third grade	123.28	93.67	29.61*
Mean change from first-grade posttest to third grade	70.05	48.75	21.30*
Mean change from second-grade test to third grade	48.16	29.98	18.18*
Total			
Mean change from first-grade pretest to third grade	110.93	92.67	18.26*
Mean change from first-grade posttest to third grade	55.86	46.76	9.10*
Mean change from second-grade test to third grade	35.51	24.42	11.09*

*Significant at the 0.05 level.
Note: SAGE = Student Achievement Guarantee in Education.

Table 5-8. African American and White Achievement on Total Scale, 1996–99, Cohort Two

Schools	First-grade pretest	First-grade posttest	Second-grade test	Third-grade test	Change from first-grade pretest to third grade	Change from first-grade posttest to third grade	Change from second grade to third grade
SAGE							
African American	505.41	559.63	579.90	615.41	110.00	55.78	35.51
White	535.07	583.27	608.28	634.04	99.76	51.37	25.76
Difference	−29.66*	−23.64*	−28.38*	−18.63*	10.24*	4.41	9.75*
Comparison							
African American	511.77	556.84	575.94	600.36	88.59	43.52	24.42
White	533.45	580.19	603.14	628.03	94.58	47.84	24.89
Difference	−21.68*	−23.35*	−27.20*	−27.67*	−5.99	−4.32	−0.60

*Significant at the 0.05 level.
Note: SAGE = Student Achievement Guarantee in Education.

Table 5-9. *African American First-Grade Change Scores, by SAGE and Comparison Schools, 1997–98, Cohort Two*

Subject	SAGE schools	Comparison schools	Difference
Language arts			
Mean posttest	574.23	559.74	14.49*
Mean change pretest to posttest	57.88	36.52	21.36*
Reading			
Mean posttest	572.90	554.60	18.30*
Mean change pretest to posttest	50.09	24.89	25.20*
Mathematics			
Mean posttest	523.46	511.07	12.39*
Mean change pretest to posttest	50.02	26.96	23.06*
Total			
Mean posttest	557.34	544.52	12.82*
Mean change pretest to posttest	53.03	32.08	20.95*

* Significant at the 0.05 level.
Note: SAGE = Student Achievement Guarantee in Education.

The data in table 5-9 show that on the posttest at the first-grade level African American SAGE students scored higher than African American comparison school students on every subtest and on the total scale score. The differences between SAGE and comparison schools on posttest scores are all statistically significant. In addition, the differences between SAGE and comparison schools on mean change scores from pretest to posttest scores are statistically significant. In other words, African American SAGE students scored lower on the CTBS pretest than African American comparison school students but made significantly larger gains than comparison school students from pretest to posttest and surpassed African American comparison school students on the posttest.

This evidence of the positive effect of reduced-size class on the achievement of African American students at the first-grade level in Cohort Two in comparison to Cohort One may be a result of the using CTBS level 10 as a posttest with Cohort One. Using level 10 instead of level 11, which was used with Cohort Two, created a ceiling effect that compressed posttest scores. Level 11 did not impose a ceiling on posttest scores.

Table 5-10 shows that the differences in change scores between African American SAGE students and African American comparison students on the second-grade test scores are statistically significant. When using the first-grade pretest as the baseline score, statistically significant change scores are

Table 5-10. *African American Second-Grade Change Scores, by SAGE and Comparison Schools, 1998–99, Cohort Two*

Subject	SAGE schools	Comparison schools	Difference
Language arts			
Mean change from first-grade pretest to second grade	74.50	54.54	19.96*
Mean change from first-grade posttest to second grade	20.73	18.06	2.67
Reading			
Mean change from first-grade pretest to second grade	73.08	55.17	17.91*
Mean change from first-grade posttest to second grade	22.46	25.09	−2.63
Mathematics			
Mean change from first-grade pretest to second grade	73.66	44.55	29.11*
Mean change from first-grade posttest to second grade	27.60	19.57	8.04*
Total			
Mean change from first-grade pretest to second grade	73.27	51.91	21.36*
Mean change from first-grade posttest to second grade	24.09	20.80	3.29

* Significant at the 0.05 level.
Note: SAGE = Student Achievement Guarantee in Education.

found in all areas. Using the first-grade posttest as the baseline score shows statistically significant differences between SAGE and comparison schools on the mathematics subtest only. Comparison school students made a larger gain on the reading subtest, but the gain is not statistically significant.

The differences between African American SAGE students and African American comparison school students can be seen in table 5-11. The differences on the mathematics and language subscales and the total scale scores are statistically significant. When using the first-grade pretest as the baseline score, statistically significant change scores are found in all areas, with African American SAGE students again outperforming African American comparison students. Using the first-grade posttest as the baseline score shows African American SAGE students continuing to make statistically significant gains on the mathematics subtest. However, using the second grade test as the baseline score shows that further gains in achievement between SAGE and comparison African American students are not significant.

Table 5-11. *African American Third-Grade Change Scores, by SAGE and Comparison Schools, 1999–2000, Cohort Two*

Subject	SAGE schools	Comparison schools	Difference
Language arts			
Mean change from first-grade pretest to third grade	92.48	75.89	16.59*
Mean change from first-grade posttest to third grade	41.40	39.69	1.71
Mean change from second-grade test to third grade	20.33	23.87	−3.54
Reading			
Mean change from first-grade pretest to third grade	91.88	76.67	15.21*
Mean change from first-grade posttest to third grade	44.01	50.35	−6.34
Mean change from second-grade test to third grade	18.93	19.78	−0.85
Mathematics			
Mean change from first-grade pretest to third grade	113.81	82.00	31.81*
Mean change from first-grade posttest to third grade	66.04	57.24	8.80*
Mean change from second-grade test to third grade	36.41	35.76	0.65
Total			
Mean change from first-grade pretest to third grade	99.42	77.98	21.44*
Mean change from first-grade posttest to third grade	50.08	49.45	0.63
Mean change from second-grade test to third grade	25.53	26.56	−1.03

* Significant at the 0.05 level.
Note: SAGE = Student Achievement Guarantee in Education.

Consistent with the results for Cohort One regarding the achievement of African American students in reduced-size SAGE classes and normal-size comparison classes, African American students in reduced-size classes gain, maintain, and, in some cases, improve an achievement advantage over African American students in normal-size classes. A comparison of African American and white SAGE and comparison students from Cohort Two is displayed in table 5-12. African American students, as a group, scored lower than white students on the total scale scores at each grade level. This result is statistically significant for both SAGE and comparison schools. African American students continued to score significantly lower than white students on total scale scores and on all subtests, regardless of whether they were SAGE or comparison school students. However, gains made by African American versus white students were better in SAGE schools from the beginning of first grade to the end of third grade and significantly better in SAGE schools from second grade to third grade. African American SAGE students improved more than white students, thus reducing the African American–white achievement gap. The significant change difference between the first-grade pretest and the third-grade test in comparison schools shows that the gap has widened for comparison school African American students.

Discussion

These longitudinal findings from two cohorts of students provide support for the conclusion that reducing class size to fifteen students can result in improved performance in reading, language arts, and mathematics for African American students in the primary grades. They have higher achievement gains than African American students in normal-size classes, and, although their achievement test scores remain lower than the achievement test scores of white students, they achieve at a faster rate than their white counterparts. Reduced class size results in a narrowing of the difference in achievement between low-income African American and white students.

The question of why reduced class size benefits low-income African American students invites discussion. They probably outperform African American students in normal-size classes for the same reasons that all students in reduced-size classes outperform students in normal-size classes. The SAGE research on classroom events has revealed that in reduced-size classes teachers individualize their instruction to a considerable degree.[4] They adjust their teaching to the needs of each student. Through one-to-one tutoring, small groups teaching, and total class teaching, individual student understandings are repeatedly elicited, critiqued, and corrected or extended. All students are

Table 5-12. Third-Grade African American and White Achievement on Total Scale, 1997–2000, Cohort Two

Schools	First-grade pretest	First-grade posttest	Second-grade test	Third-grade test	Change from first-grade pretest to third grade	Change from first-grade posttest to third grade	Change from second grade to third grade
SAGE							
African American	510.14	560.83	585.45	610.98	99.42	50.08	25.53
White	536.87	584.06	611.22	632.76	95.15	48.55	21.54
Difference	−26.73*	−23.23*	−25.77*	−21.78*	4.27	1.53	3.99*
Comparison							
African American	519.69	550.95	573.51	600.07	80.38	49.12	26.56
White	536.07	578.90	600.77	627.01	90.94	48.11	26.24
Difference	−16.38*	−27.95*	−27.26*	−26.94	−10.56*	1.01	0.32

* Significant at the 0.05 level.
Note: SAGE = Student Achievement Guarantee in Education.

expected to learn the same content, but the teacher varies his or her instructional procedures with the student.

This increased use of individualization in reduced-size classes is a result of increased knowledge of students; less discipline, which makes more time available for instruction; and greater teacher enthusiasm. Because the class is small it takes on a family-like atmosphere. The teacher knows each student's strengths, weaknesses, personality, interests, and other characteristics. A small class reduces the need for discipline because transgressions are immediately observed and can be immediately dealt with before they become intractable. With less time devoted to class management, teachers devote more time to teaching and students spend more time engaged in learning tasks. The outcome for the teacher is more satisfaction and a willingness to be of service to students. The individualization that increased student knowledge, less discipline, and more teacher enthusiasm produce results in greater and deeper content understanding and, ultimately, greater student learning as evidenced by higher achievement scores.

The question of why African American students in reduced-size classes achieved at a faster rate than white students in reduced-size classes has not been researched, but a plausible speculation can be made based on the SAGE classroom events data. African American students in reduced-size classes may receive more individualized attention than their white counterparts in reduced-size classes. For classes that are racially integrated, African American students may receive more individualized attention than white students because, as the SAGE pretests at the first-grade level reveal, they are the students in greatest need. As a group, their scores are consistently and significantly below the scores of white students. The squeaky-wheel phenomenon that operates to some degree in all classrooms is a major force in reduced-size classrooms. Teachers tend to concentrate on students who are the farthest behind. When the class becomes small, the students that are the farthest behind became more visible and teachers spend more time with them identifying their misunderstandings, structuring personal learning opportunities, checking on progress, and reteaching when necessary. Improving the learning of the students who are the farthest behind results in higher mean achievement scores for the total group of students. Thus, low-income African American students, students often the farthest behind, close the achievement gap with white students. This suggestion incorporates Haycock's recommendation for extra help.[5]

In classes that are totally or largely African American the same squeaky-wheel phenomenon operates. Here the farthest behind African American students in the total class of African American students get special attention, again resulting in increased mean achievement test scores. Individualization also might be increased in African American classrooms that have been reduced in size because they typically are urban schools whose normal class size approached thirty students in comparison to integrated or white classes in small nonurban districts where normal class sizes were smaller. Boozer and Rouse found that schools that are largely African American are likely to have significantly larger class sizes than other schools, often three or four students more per class.[6] The class-size reduction, therefore, can be greater for African American classes, and greater class size reduction results in greater individualization compared with the reduction and individualization in nonurban schools.

Notes

1. A. Molnar, P. Smith, and J. Zahorik, *1999–2000 Evaluation Results of the Student Achievement Guarantee in Education (SAGE) Program* (University of Wisconsin at Milwaukee, Center for Education, Research, Analysis, and Innovation, 1999).

2. K. Haycock, "Closing the Achievement Gap," *Educational Leadership*, vol. 58 (2001), pp. 6–11.

3. E. Word and others, *Student/Teacher Achievement Ratio (STAR) Tennessee's K–3 Class Size Study*, final summary report 1985–90 (Nashville: Tennessee Department of Education, 1990); A. Krueger, "Experimental Estimates of Education Production Functions," Working Paper 379 (Princeton University, Industrial Relations Section, 1997); A. Krueger and D. Whitmore, "Would Smaller Classes Help Close the Black-White Achievement Gap?" paper prepared for the Closing the Gap: Promising Approaches to Reducing the Achievement Gap conference, Brookings Institution and Edison Schools Inc., 2001; C. Bingham, *White-Minority Achievement Gap Reduction and Small Class Size: A Research and Literature Review* (Nashville, Tenn.: Center of Excellence for Research and Policy on Basic Skills, 1993); and M. Snow, *An Evaluation of the Class Size Reduction Program* (Carson City, Nev.: Nevada Department of Education, 1998).

4. Molnar, Smith, and Zahorik, *1999–2000 Evaluation Results of the Student Achievement Guarantee in Education (SAGE) Program*; and J. Zahorik and others, "Small Class, Better Teaching? Effective Teaching in Reduced Size Classes," in S. Laire and J. Ward, eds., *Using What We Know: A Review of Research in Implementing Class-Size Reduction Initiatives for State and Local Policy Makers* (Oak Brook, Ill.: North Central Regional Educational Laboratory, 2000).

5. Haycock, "Closing the Achievement Gap."

6. M. Boozer and C. Rouse, "Intraschool Variation in Class Size: Patterns and Implications," Working Paper 344 (Princeton University, Industrial Relations Section, 1995).

6

High-Stakes Testing, Accountability, and Student Achievement in Texas and Houston

LAURENCE A. TOENJES, A. GARY DWORKIN,
JON LORENCE, AND ANTWANETTE N. HILL

According to *Education Week*'s most recent *Quality Counts 2000* report, forty-one states have some form of test-based educational accountability system to help ensure that their public school students receive a quality education, and forty-nine states have adopted specific academic standards.[1] Accountability systems are still controversial, despite their widespread adoption. For example, some critics believe that accountability systems result in an unacceptable degree of state authority over local schools. Others claim that educational accountability systems, especially if based upon a statewide system of standardized tests, narrow curricula and remove opportunities for teachers to utilize fully their extensive classroom experience and to teach creatively in challenging all students. Still others contend that such systems place certain student groups, especially ethnic or racial minorities, at a distinct disadvantage and reduce their chances for academic success. However, proponents of state accountability systems maintain that they have finally given some direction and coherence to public education by holding teachers and administrators responsible for the academic progress of all students—and are already having a positive effect.

Texas's accountability system should be viewed as a work in progress. It reflects years of dedication and effort by many individuals and groups. Although aspects of it need improvement, some of which are in the process of being addressed already, our overall evaluation is that the positive aspects of Texas's accountability system outweigh any negative features. It should continue to receive strong public support as well as constructive criticism.

A Brief History

When the National Commission on Excellence in Education published *A Nation at Risk* in 1983, confidence in public education had reached a nadir. Business and government leaders were concerned that public schools were creating an uneducated and unprepared work force that threatened U.S. economic competitiveness. In their annual poll of public opinion about schooling that year, the Gallup organization reported that merely 31 percent gave high marks of "A" or "B" to their local schools, compared with 48 percent a decade earlier. As had been the case since the first Gallup Poll, far fewer respondents rated the nation's schools that well.[2] The commission called for strengthening graduation requirements, lengthening the amount of time students spend learning, raising the standards for preparation of teachers, and committing schools to adopt measurable standards for student academic performance.

State governments responded to *A Nation at Risk* by instituting a variety of reforms. In Texas, Governor Mark White empanelled a commission headed by Dallas billionaire H. Ross Perot, which recommended sweeping reforms to the state education code. In 1984 those reforms were passed by the legislature under the title of House Bill 72. The 122-page bill established the minimum passing score (70 percent) on tests and courses; created the "No Pass-No Play" rule, which prohibited students who failed courses from participating in extracurricular activities; and created minimum competency tests for teachers. Legislation that followed House Bill 72 created an accountability system tied to student passage of a standardized test. One hallmark of that accountability system was the requirement that campus and district ratings depended upon each major ethnic or racial and economic group passing a state test. Most other states do not disaggregate passing rates in determining the accountability ratings of school districts or campuses. During site visits to school districts across Texas, we confirmed that teachers and administrators are now concerned about the academic performance of all students, even those who had been overlooked in the past.

Central to the Texas accountability system has been the use of a standardized test to assess student achievement. Results of the test affect high school graduation and the assessment of campuses and districts. Initially the test assessed basic skills, but by the end of the 1980s the legislature mandated that the test assess both problem solving and critical thinking skills. The result was the Texas Assessment of Academic Skills (TAAS), a criterion-referenced test based on essential educational elements in the curriculum. The legislature in 1997 enhanced the standards with the Texas Essential Knowledge and Skills (TEKS), an even more rigorous curriculum. Beginning in the 1993–94 school year, tests in reading and mathematics have been administered to students in grades three through eight, and a writing test has been given to students in grades four and eight. In addition, tenth-grade students must pass reading, mathematics, and writing sections of the TAAS before graduating from high school.[3] The TAAS is also administered in Spanish in grades three through six for students in bilingual programs. Students in English as a Second Language programs must take the English version of the TAAS.

The passing standard for the exit-level TAAS has been maintained at a level equivalent to correctly answering 70 percent of the items that appeared on the October 1990 exit-level test. Raw scores are adjusted so that this level of proficiency corresponds to a Texas Learning Index (TLI) score of 70. Beginning in 1994, test results in reading and math in grades three through eight were also scaled in a manner that aligns the passing standard in these grades with a TLI score of 70 on the exit-level test. Because of variations in test difficulty from year to year, and from grade to grade for the same subject, the raw percentage needed to pass varies somewhat. For example, on the year 2000 reading test in grade eight, a passing TLI score of 70 corresponded to a percent correct score of 64.6, whereas in mathematics only 60 percent correct was required to obtain a TLI of 70.

Individual schools and school districts are given a performance rating each year, which is based primarily upon the percentage of students passing the TAAS tests. Dropout and attendance rates also figure into the ratings.[4] The accountability system is a combination of the following elements: TAAS criterion-referenced tests based on a statewide curriculum, district and campus ratings, and recognition for high performance and significant increases in performance, as well as sanctions for poor performance.[5] Mandatory public reporting of school and district performance is an integral part of the state's accountability system. The Texas Education Agency (TEA) has made voluminous amounts of data available on its website. The availability of such data has helped to ensure that academically underachieving schools or districts are compared with those with superior performance.

During the period that statewide testing and the accountability system were being implemented, Texas was undergoing major changes to its school funding system. A 1995 state court decision resulted in an influx of new revenues for less wealthy school districts.[6] The additional funds directed to poorer school districts made the imposition of the new academic require-

Figure 6-1. *Percentage Passing All Texas Assessment of Academic Skills Tests Taken, 1994–99*

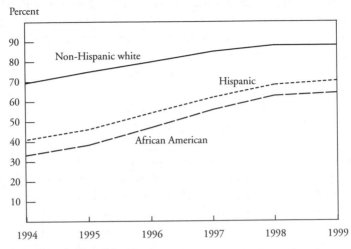

Source: Data from the Texas Education Agency.
Note: Results for 1999 include special education and Spanish, grades three and four, reading and math.

ments more palatable to administrators and teachers and increased the likelihood that the new standards might be met.

Trends on the TAAS, 1994 to 1999

In 1994, 55.6 percent of the students tested for accountability purposes passed all tests. By 1999 this passing rate had risen to 78.3 percent. This pattern of improvement is shown in figure 6-1 for the state's three major ethnic groups—African Americans, Hispanics, and non-Hispanic whites. The passing rates increased dramatically for all three ethnic groups, and the passing rates of African American and Hispanic students increased the most rapidly. While a flattening of the trend lines is noticeable between 1998 and 1999, the percentage of students tested for accountability purposes increased from 76.0 in 1998 to 84.2 in 1999.[7]

To some extent, these increases in passage rates have been a function of the nature of the TAAS exam and the minimum score needed to pass. The TAAS is a criterion-referenced test designed in such a manner that the majority of students, if sufficiently motivated and properly instructed, are expected to pass. Although the data in figure 6-1 reveal that non-Hispanic white students are more likely to pass the TAAS than African American and Hispanic students, only 69.4 percent of non-Hispanic white students managed to pass all subjects in 1994. The state attempted to establish a passing level that was a challenge to most students, yet not so difficult that it would have been demoralizing to historically low-performing groups. By 1999 the average passing rates on reading, math, and writing exceeded 85 percent for all ethnic groups combined.[8]

The substantial increases in passing rates may have resulted from the existence of large numbers of students in the early years of TAAS testing whose TLI scores were only marginally below the minimum passing level of 70. For such students, modest increases in TLI scores would have allowed them to pass. If progress is measured by improvements in the average TLI itself, instead of by the percentage of students who passed, then the increases appear less dramatic. However, they still tell the same story of gains for all ethnic groups and a reduction of the gap between non–Hispanic white students and African American or Hispanic students. For each grade and subject, the TLI gain achieved by African American and Hispanic students exceeded that of non–Hispanic white students, reducing the interethnic performance gap.

A more detailed analysis of TAAS trends is presented in table 6-1, which shows the TLI scores of major ethnic or racial groups in 1994 and 1999. Over the five-year period, among all students, the average reading score increased by more than 6 points while the mean score in mathematics increased by almost 11 points. Asian American and non-Hispanic white students had higher reading and mathematics scores than African American, Hispanic, and Native American students. These comparisons do not account for potential differences in the characteristics of students in each of the broad groups. We adjusted statistically for differences in grade level, gender, Limited English Proficiency (LEP) status, special education classification, and economic disadvantage (that is, whether students were on free or reduced-price lunch) to gauge more accurately differences in TLI scores across the five broad ethnic or racial groups. The adjusted mean TLI scores of pupils in grades three through eight increased slightly for minority students while the means for the non-Hispanic white pupils decreased. These findings indicate that social characteristics of students affect achievement among the ethnic or racial groups.

In addition to examining statewide test results, we examined the scores of one of the state's largest urban school districts, the Houston Independent School District (HISD). Table 6-2 reveals a pattern similar to the entire state. Although non-Hispanic white students made up only 15 and 12 percent of HISD pupils with test scores in 1994 and 1999, respectively, these students obtained significantly higher reading and mathematics TLI scores than did

Table 6-1. *Observed and Adjusted Texas Learning Index for Major Groups, by Subject Matter and Year, Texas Students, Grades Three to Eight*

Ethnic or racial group	Reading 1994			Reading 1999			Mathematics 1994			Mathematics 1999		
	N	Mean	Adjusted mean[a]	N	Mean	Adjusted mean[a]	N	Mean	Adjusted mean[b]	N	Mean	Adjusted mean[b]
Non-Hispanic white	725,852	82.3	80.6	720,383	87.9	86.1	725,852	74.3	72.9	720,383	83.7	82.6
Hispanic	420,134	72.8	75.4	499,119	80.3	82.9	420,134	65.5	67.7	499,119	78.6	80.2
African American	184,846	70.8	71.3	195,476	78.9	79.1	184,846	62.0	62.5	195,476	75.0	75.2
Asian American	21,013	83.7	83.1	25,392	88.8	88.1	21,013	79.0	78.2	25,392	86.2	85.5
Native American	345	74.9	74.7	238	80.9	80.9	345	66.2	66.0	238	77.4	77.5
Total	1,352,190	77.8		1,440,608	84.1		1,352,190	70.0		1,440,608	80.8	

Note: The total of the means is the sum of the individual means weighted by the number of cases per category.

a. Means are adjusted for differences across groups with respect to grade, gender, limited English proficiency, special education, and economic disadvantage.

b. Means are adjusted for differences across groups with respect to grade, gender, limited English proficiency, special education, economic disadvantage, and overage status.

Table 6-2. Observed and Adjusted Texas Learning Index for Major Groups, by Subject Matter and Year, Houston Students, Grades Three to Eight

Ethnic or racial group	Reading 1994			Reading 1999			Mathematics 1994			Mathematics 1999		
	N	Mean	Adjusted mean[a]	N	Mean	Adjusted mean[a]	N	Mean	Adjusted mean	N	Mean	Adjusted mean
Non-Hispanic white	9,465	84.5	81.5	8,582	89.0	85.1	9,465	77.4	74.8	8,577	83.6	81.4
Hispanic	25,607	71.7	73.8	32,289	77.0	79.6	25,607	65.2	66.7	32,289	75.7	77.1
African American	25,798	71.7	70.8	25,548	78.4	76.5	25,798	63.2	62.7	25,548	73.2	72.2
Asian American	1,797	82.5	81.8	2,246	86.2	85.4	1,797	78.8	77.9	2,246	84.4	83.6
Native American	60	72.2	71.1	127	81.6	77.7	60	64.8	64.0	127	75.2	73.3
Total	62,727	74.0		68,792	79.3		62,727	66.6		68,792	76.0	

Note: The total of the means is the sum of the individual means weighted by the number of cases per category.

a. Means are adjusted for differences across groups with respect to grade, gender, limited English proficiency, special education, economic disadvantage, and overage status.

Table 6-3. *Mean Differences in Texas Assessment of Academic Skills Test Performance between Non-Hispanic White and Minority Students*

Students	Reading		Mathematics	
	1994	1999	1994	1999
Texas				
Non-Hispanic white and				
Hispanic students				
Mean	9.5	7.6	8.8	5.1
Adjusted mean	5.2	3.2	5.2	2.4
Non-Hispanic white and				
African American students				
Mean	11.5	9.0	12.3	10.4
Adjusted mean	9.0	7.0	8.7	7.4
Houston Independent School District				
Non-Hispanic white and				
Hispanic students				
Mean	12.8	12.0	12.2	7.9
Adjusted mean	7.7	5.5	8.1	4.3
Non-Hispanic white and				
African American students				
Mean	12.8	10.6	14.2	10.4
Adjusted mean	10.7	8.6	12.1	9.2

Hispanic and African American pupils. However, the differences between non-Hispanic whites and the two largest racial or ethnic minority groups decreased.

Table 6-3 shows that the gap between non-Hispanic whites and Hispanics shrank from 9.5 to 7.6 TLI points from 1994 to 1999. The gap between the adjusted means, which control for major social differences among pupils, declined from 5.2 to 3.2 TLI points. The mean difference on the TAAS mathematics test decreased even more between the two ethnic groups over the five-year period. Non-Hispanic whites scored almost 9 points higher than Hispanic pupils in 1994, but by 1999 the difference was only 5 points. Comparing the difference between the adjusted means shows that the gap decreased by over 50 percent, from 5.2 TLI points in 1994 to 2.4 TLI points in 1999. The difference in TAAS performance between non-Hispanic whites and African American students throughout the entire state also narrowed over the period.

In Houston, Hispanic and African American students closed the reading score gap with non-Hispanic white pupils by about 2 TLI points. The test score gap decreased even further, by approximately 4 points, on the mathematics test of the TAAS. Overall, the test scores of ethnic or racial minorities are becoming more comparable to those of non-Hispanic white students.[9]

Comparing all student test scores from one year with scores in subsequent years does not control for the differences among cohorts—students who begin school during a particular year. School administrators often claim that a particular class is "smarter" or "had more trouble with the coursework" than previous classes. The optimal strategy for analysis, which we utilized, includes only students who took the 1994 TAAS as third graders, the 1995 TAAS as fourth graders, the 1996 TAAS as fifth graders, and so forth through the 1999 TAAS as eighth graders. Omitted are students who repeated a grade or students who were not tested each year. The average TAAS TLI score of the same 136,709 students taking the test each year is shown in table 6-4.

The gain for this group of students was 6.6 TLI points in reading and 10.0 TLI points in mathematics. The gains for the panel are numerically similar to the gains in previous panels of data, suggesting that testing effects, that is, gains from repeated exposure to the TAAS, may play a smaller role in score improvement than changes in teaching and curriculum. In both reading and math, the differences between non-Hispanic whites and African Americans, non–Hispanic whites and Hispanics, and nonpoor and poor have narrowed. Space limitations do not permit us to present a comparable cohort analysis table for the Houston Independent School District; however, the district data closely parallel those of the statewide results.

Test Exemptions, Ninth-Grade Pileup, and Increased Dropouts

The charge that the TAAS exit test has somehow caused an increase in the numbers of students who remain in the ninth grade an extra year, which results in their dropping out before taking the exit test, has been developed most extensively by Walter Haney.[10] Haney has charged that the much publicized improvement in TAAS pass rates is a myth; that the high school dropout rate in Texas is among the nation's highest; and that the high dropout rate, in large part a response to the tenth-grade exit test, results in a "boost" in exit-level test scores.[11] While Haney acknowledges that the percent of students passing all tests (reading, math, and writing) increased from 52 in 1994 to 72 in 1998, he has referred to this 20-point improvement as a miracle, a myth, or "an outright fraud."[12]

Haney demonstrates that the 20-point improvement in the tenth-grade passing rate is overstated by focusing upon the potential impact of increases in the percentage of tenth-grade students classified as special education stu-

Table 6-4. Texas Student Cohort Mean TLI Scores, by Race and Economic Group

Subject and student cohort	1994 Grade three	1995 Grade four	1996 Grade five	1997 Grade six	1998 Grade seven	1999 Grade eight	Change from 1994 to 1999
Reading							
Non-Hispanic white	83.5	84.9	86.7	89.1	88.3	89.1	5.6
Hispanic	76.8	78.7	80.0	82.6	82.5	84.7	7.9
African American	74.8	75.4	77.2	79.9	79.6	82.5	7.7
Asian American	84.2	85.8	88.6	91.3	90.4	91.7	7.5
Low income	75.6	77.2	78.4	81.3	81.2	83.4	7.8
Not low income	82.7	84.2	86.0	88.4	87.6	88.8	6.1
Total	80.4	81.9	83.6	86.0	85.5	87.0	6.6
Mathematics							
Non-Hispanic white	75.9	79.4	81.7	83.5	84.3	84.6	8.7
Hispanic	68.9	73.5	77.0	79.0	79.5	80.7	11.8
African American	65.6	69.4	72.2	75.4	75.5	77.5	11.9
Asian American	78.5	82.5	85.3	86.3	87.1	87.5	9.0
Low income	67.7	72.1	75.5	77.9	78.3	79.7	12.0
Not low income	74.9	78.6	81.0	82.8	83.5	84.0	9.1
Total	72.6	76.5	79.2	81.2	81.8	82.6	10.0

Note: TLI = Texas Learning Index. N = 136,709. The total of the means is the sum of the individual means weighted by the number of cases per category.

dents, and therefore excluded from having to take the tests, and increases in the number of high school students who drop out before being required to take the exit test for the first time in the second half of their sophomore year.

The effect of increases in the special education classification among tenth graders was estimated by Haney to account for 2 percent of the 20-point gain in TAAS passing rates from 1994 to 1998. This was based on a documented increase in tenth-grade special education students from 3.9 percent in 1994 to 6.3 percent in 1998.[13] Assuming that none of the new special education students would have passed the exit exams, and given that about 80 percent of the students were tested, the increase in exempted special education students caused the pass rate to increase by approximately 1.7 percent, close to Haney's figure of 2 percent.

The 18 percent gain that remains unexplained must therefore be due to the alleged increase in students who dropped out before taking the tenth-grade exit test. Haney initially estimated the number of dropouts by examining the ratio of ninth graders to twelfth graders over time.[14] This ratio has grown significantly since the early 1980s.[15] The implication is that schools were playing a cynical game of retaining ninth graders who were unlikely to pass the tenth-grade exit exam.[16] These retained students would later drop out of school. Many of the lower performing retained students would never take the exit exam, leading to higher passing rates among those who were tested.

In setting about to calculate the impact of this process on passing rates, Haney observed that merely because the ratio of grade nine enrollment to grade twelve enrollment (three years later) increased, many students, after repeating grade nine, could still take the exit exams as tenth graders, if they did not drop out. So, Haney focused on the ratio of grade eleven enrollments to grade six enrollments, five years before. This is sound reasoning. However, it led to the following admission.

> What this suggests is that the majority of the apparent 20-point gain in grade 10 TAAS pass rates cannot be attributed to exclusion of the types just reviewed. Specifically, if rates of progress from grades 6 to grade 11 have varied by no more than 5% for cohorts of the classes of the 1990s, this suggests even if we take this as an upper bound the extent to which increased retention and dropping out before fall grade 11, and add 2% for the increased rate of grade 10 special education classification, we still come up with less than half of the apparent 20-point gain in grade 10 TAAS pass rates between 1993 [sic] and 1998.[17]

Table 6-5. *Ratio of Grade Eleven to Grade Six Enrollment, All Students*

Grade six		Grade eleven		Ratio of grade eleven to grade six
Year	Enrollment	Year	Enrollment	
1989	250,740	1994	205,735	0.82
1990	261,995	1995	213,714	0.82
1991	275,909	1996	225,833	0.82
1992	282,089	1997	234,187	0.83
1993	285,414	1998	240,860	0.84

Source: Data from the Texas Education Agency, Office of Communications, August 2000.

This seems a brave admission, that "less than half of the apparent 20-point gain" is accounted for by adjusting for special education and dropouts. The question is, just how much "less than half" has been accounted for?

In the quotation, Haney referred to "rates of progress from grades 6 to grade 11" as varying by less than 5 percent for "cohorts of the classes of the 1990s." But, the issue is the impact of potential increased dropouts specifically on TAAS passing rates from 1994 to 1998, the period of alleged fraud. What happened to the grade eleven to grade six ratios during this period? If they decreased, this would support Haney's argument. If the ratios increased, they would refute his argument.

Fall enrollments for grade six from 1989 through 1993, and grade eleven from 1994 through 1998, are shown in table 6-5. Students who were recorded as taking the grade ten TAAS exams in the spring of 1994 would show up as eleventh graders in the fall 1994 enrollment figure. Such students would still be in school and (in most instances) would have taken the exit exam the previous spring. Not only did grade eleven enrollments increase each year during this time interval, but the ratio of eleventh graders to sixth graders increased also, by over 2 points (see last column of table 6-5). Using Haney's logic, instead of a downward adjustment to the grade ten TAAS passing rates between 1994 and 1998, there should be an upward adjustment. In fact, the 2.3-point increase in the ratio of eleventh graders to sixth graders almost offsets the 2.4-point increase in the percentage of grade ten special education students. The net result is therefore a wash. In other words, none of the 20-point increase in grade ten TAAS passing rates has been accounted for by the net effects of changes in special education and dropout behavior. So the "Texas miracle in education" is not a myth, nor has fraud been perpetrated by the State of Texas. This analysis flatly contradicts Haney's assertion that Texas's accountability system directly causes an increase in dropouts, which "in turn boosts test scores."[18]

Haney also takes issue with how the State of Texas calculates dropout rates, which figure into the state's accountability formula. Including them was designed to prevent schools from passively allowing low-performing students to drop out, thereby raising TAAS scores. But having made the dropout rate a critical measure of school performance, TEA had to define as precisely as possible the criteria for determining the nonreturning students who are dropouts and those falling into other categories. Students who leave school before normal graduation can be classified into thirty-seven different categories. TEA has been insistent that school districts account for all students who are no longer enrolled. In the most recent report, only 1.1 percent of the students in grades seven to twelve in 1998–99 could not be accounted for the following year.[19] Just 1.5 percent were classified as dropouts. Some critics might prefer that the 0.55 percent who were enrolled in general equivalency diploma (GED) programs be in the dropout category, and perhaps the 0.27 percent who were incarcerated. But then what of the 0.04 percent who died, or the 0.03 percent who enrolled in college, or the 0.53 percent who returned to their country of origin? The point is that the State of Texas has a vastly improved system of accounting for students who fail to graduate. Particular modifications may be warranted in the future, but the system itself appears sound.

Haney cites National Center for Education Statistics (NCES) data to claim that Texas schools have "some of the nation's highest dropout rates."[20] In "The Myth of the Texas Miracle in Education," he presents high school completion rates for all states and the District of Columbia with the following comment: "As can be seen for all three time periods, these data show Texas to have among the lowest rates of high school completion among the fifty states."[21] Low completion rates translate into high dropout rates (or other reasons for leaving school before graduation). For the 1996–98 period, Texas's completion rate of 80.2 percent ranked forty-sixth among the fifty states. Only Arizona, Nevada, New Mexico, and Oregon were worse. Apart from Oregon, the other three states and Texas all share substantial proportions of Hispanic and low-income students.

We conducted a simple regression analysis of these data. It showed that roughly two-thirds of the variation in the NCES retention rates is explained by three factors—the percentage of Hispanic students, the percentage of African American students, and state per capita personal income (not shown here, the analysis used 1997 data). When the states were ranked after controlling for these factors, California's ranking improved from forty-fifth to twenty-fifth, New Mexico's went from forty-seventh to fifth, and Texas's improved from forty-sixth to seventeenth. So while the NCES data do show that Texas has a higher than average dropout rate, the state fares very well when demographic factors are taken into consideration.

TAAS VALIDITY. The Texas Assessment of Academic Skills test is often criticized as inappropriate for measuring academic performance. Individuals skeptical of all standardized testing contend that the TAAS is narrow and does not adequately reflect what students learn during a school year. Others argue that the TAAS is a highly questionable test because its correspondence to national norms is unknown.

Research addressing these concerns has upheld the validity of the TAAS.[22] Test-retest correlations—based on TAAS scores from 1994 to 1998 and conducted with students in the metropolitan Houston area—range from .69 to .81. These are comparable to figures for nationally normed tests. The lowest values occurred during 1994 and 1995 when the current form of the TAAS was implemented. Further, the annual test-retest TAAS correlations were similar in both the reading and mathematics sections of the TAAS across all groups of students classified on the basis of ethnicity or race, gender, economics, LEP, and special education status. Student performance on the reading and mathematics sections of the TAAS were also substantially correlated with student achievement scores on the Iowa Test of Basic Skills, the Metropolitan Achievement Test 7, and the Stanford Achievement Test, Ninth Edition (Stanford 9). Comparing 1999 TAAS scores with 1999 Stanford 9 results, for example, revealed correlations ranging from .82 for third graders to .63 for tenth graders.

Another way to assess the validity of the TAAS is to compare state achievement performance on the National Assessment of Educational Progress (NAEP). A total of forty-three states and five jurisdictions participated in the 1998 round of NAEP tests.[23] Texas non-Hispanic white fourth graders placed second in the nation in mathematics and third in reading. Texas African American fourth graders ranked first in the nation in mathematics and well above average in reading. Texas Hispanic students placed fourth in mathematics and seventh in reading. In writing, Texas non-Hispanic white students tied with New York non-Hispanic white students for second place, Hispanics ranked second only to Virginia Hispanics, and African Americans ranked best in the nation.[24]

In a 2000 study, a RAND research team led by David Grissmer estimated state NAEP score differences for students with similar family backgrounds.[25] Based on seven state reading and math tests administered between 1990 and 1996, Texas ranked first among the forty-four states included in the study. The authors concluded that "aligned standards, assessments, and accountability was the most plausible cause of the gains."[26] Texas's success was also attributed to lower pupil-teacher ratios, a large proportion of children in public prekindergarten programs, and the relative satisfaction of teachers with the level of necessary resources provided them.[27] The report concluded that, although the reforms in Texas were begun in the early 1980s, their full impact has yet to be realized.[28]

IMPACT ON SAT AND ACT RESULTS. Opponents of the accountability system point to the lack of improvement of Texas students on the SAT and American College Test (ACT) as evidence that the accountability system is ineffective.[29] Such judgments seem premature, for the following reasons.

—The charge is based on the SAT and ACT scores of students who were already in middle school in 1993–94, when the accountability system began, and thus were unable to benefit from the improvements in curriculum that were implemented in the critical early grades of schooling.

—The largest gains measured by the TAAS and the NAEP have been in the early grades. The students who registered for them have not yet taken the SAT or ACT.

—So far the accountability system seems to have larger positive effects among minority and low-income students, groups traditionally less likely to take the SAT examinations.

In short, while improvement by Texas students on the SAT and the ACT would be encouraging, realistically it is too soon to draw any conclusions from these tests.

The Impact of the Accountability System on Instructional Practices

A number of additional criticisms center on the extent to which a high-stakes accountability system impairs true learning. Among these are claims that focusing on the TAAS narrows the curriculum, that higher-order thinking skills are ignored or not developed, and that preparing for and administering the TAAS wastes valuable time that could be used to better advantage. Not all interested educational stakeholders in Texas agree with these criticisms, however. For nearly twenty years, the legislature and other state leaders have been attempting to define a curriculum that will prepare Texas students for the rapidly unfolding, high-tech, global economy in which they will be working. Texas has also endeavored to develop a set of tests that will measure whether students are achieving the goals set out in that curriculum, regardless of ethnicity or economic status. The most recent version of these academic requirements, the Texas Essential Knowledge and Skills, neither is narrow nor neglects higher-order thinking skills as normally defined. In fact, some fear that these standards may be too rigorous. For example, the TEKS for mathematics takes seventy-three pages to describe what is expected in this subject alone.[30] For the middle school grades on through high school, the content is by no means trivial. Tests aligned with the TEKS curriculum will be demanding for even the very best students.

Not all of the criticism of TAAS and the accountability system is groundless; difficulties remain that need correction. Teaching to the test under the aegis of the TEKS is likely to result in a comprehensive education. However, teaching to the more narrow essential elements has resulted in the elimination of topics from the curriculum in some schools. During interviews at some inner-city campuses, we were told by principals that the elementary schools had to drop art, music, and other topics that were seen as "detracting" from TAAS preparation.[31]

Many middle-class parents complain that too much attention is paid to TAAS drills at the expense of other, more rigorous topics. Some principals of schools where TAAS passage is almost certain insist nevertheless on endless (and often mindless) exercises to ensure that the students meet minimum expectations. A deputy superintendent in a suburban district recounted that when, at parents' request, some high-scoring students were included in the TAAS drills, their test scores dropped. The administrator attributed the decline to student boredom with the drills and even to the students' retaliation.

Also drawing fire is the practice by the Texas Education Agency of awarding financial incentives to the administrators of schools with high TAAS passage rates. Two of us attended a suburban school district meeting of principals in which checks for $500 to $5,000 were awarded for academic enhancements on school campuses. In times of tight school budgets, financial incentives for high TAAS passage rates can exacerbate the pressure to cheat and may have been an element in recent state testing scandals.[32]

Linda M. McNeil has championed rigorous and culturally relevant instruction in the public schools for many years, criticizing efforts to dumb down the curricula. She noted in 2000 that the Texas accountability system has fostered a narrowing of instruction to the essential elements of the TAAS, which has in turn led teachers and schools to ignore any instruction that will not be tested. In her opinion, excessive amounts of time have been devoted to TAAS drills, expensive TAAS prep materials, student rallies to foster enthusiasm for TAAS, and an endless list of maxims and formulae for finding correct answers on the TAAS.[33] Our own work has corroborated some of McNeil's concerns.[34] Several low-performing, high-poverty campuses have cut back the curricula to include only what the TAAS (under the old essential elements) would test. Despite the rallies and test preparations, these schools' test scores remain low. However, not all schools have responded in this fashion. High-performing, high-poverty schools share much in common with the more affluent high-performing schools: They teach solid content, have high expectations, and exhibit high levels of trust for students and teachers. Some of these schools may engage in TAAS drills, but they are intended to augment a rich curriculum, not to supplant it.

The Impact of the Accountability System on HISD

Progress on TAAS performance in the Houston Independent School District generally mirrors that of the state as a whole. Like most major urban school districts, HISD has more than its share of economically disadvantaged students, many recent immigrants whose native language is not English, and large numbers of students whose parents never attended college. All of these factors make their job more difficult. But in spite of these factors, the percentage of students who passed all tests in all grades tested increased from 43.7 in 1994 to 69.5 in 1998.[35] In 1999 the passing rate for all students in all subjects dropped to 64.3 percent. How this 5-point decline was addressed tells a great deal about the determination of the HISD administration to deal forthrightly and decisively with problems as they arise.

In February 1998 the *Houston Chronicle* published the results of a report commissioned by the Governor's Business Council, a business group. The report noted the percentage of eligible students not included in the accountability system.[36] A large number of campuses tested fewer than half of their enrolled students. At that time, all special education students were excluded from the accountability system, whether the TAAS tests were administered to them or not. In addition, 53 percent of HISD's students were of Hispanic origin, and those of limited English proficiency were exempt from taking the English TAAS for up to three years. At about this time the state began moving to tighten the exemption process, but HISD took the state's initiatives even further. As a result, the percentage of eligible students who were tested went from 67 percent in 1998 to 84 percent in 1999. Instead of 14.3 percent being excluded for being in the special education category in 1998, only 7.3 percent were excluded in 1999. Further, the 5.6 percent exempted in 1998 due to limited English proficiency fell to just 1.6 percent in 1999.[37]

Another action taken by the TEA was to release an analysis of erasures on TAAS answer sheets. The analysis entailed detecting, tabulating, and establishing threshold measures for the percentage of answers that were changed from incorrect to correct choices. Campuses with classrooms that exceeded the limits were on the exception report, including some in HISD. The HISD administration immediately undertook an internal investigation, and ultimately four teachers and one principal were fired.[38] In addition, HISD increased the security surrounding the TAAS test administration in 1999, including inviting volunteers from business and civic groups to assist in school and classroom monitoring.

The substantial increase in the percentage and numbers of students tested, as well as the tightened oversight of the administration of the TAAS in 1999, probably contributed to the 5-point decline in the passing rate that year. The major lesson from these experiences is not that some school personnel attempted to take advantage of loopholes or opportunities to cheat. Instead, the swift and decisive manner in which HISD responded to these situations preserved the integrity of the accountability system and maintained the public's confidence in its school district. A recent Houston area survey reported that 45 percent of its respondents rated the area schools as excellent or good, whereas in 1992 only 27 percent of the respondents felt that way.[39] The author of the survey credited public approval to the accountability system as well as to greater openness on the part of area school districts, of which HISD is by far the largest.

The HISD took an additional step that contributed to public confidence. On its own initiative, the HISD administration adopted the Stanford 9 as another means of checking the district's educational progress. Unlike the TAAS, results on the Stanford 9 allow the district to compare its students' performances with national norms. The most recent results from the Stanford 9 test, given in the spring of 2000, showed HISD students in most grades (except for grades seven and eight) to be performing at the national average.[40] For an urban district with 75 percent of its students in the federally subsidized lunch program, the results are respectable.

Summary and Conclusions

The Texas educational accountability system is forcing everyone (administrators, teachers, parents, and students) to take responsibility for learning. Teachers must teach all students how to read and to do mathematics well. Students must demonstrate that they are proficient in academic subjects. The curriculum is improving; teachers are delivering better instruction; students are achieving higher test scores.

Texas is holding schools accountable for the academic performance of all demographic groups because the future requires it. Hispanic and African American students already compose a majority of elementary and secondary students in Texas, and within a decade Hispanic students alone are expected to outnumber non-Hispanic white students.[41] Without the academic success of the traditionally underserved minority and low-income students, and those whose home language is not English, Texas will fail to sustain its economic, political, and social growth.

Administrators and teachers may never be able to completely abandon subjecting their students to drill and practice. Mastery of the basics often begins with drill and practice. If students do not master basic concepts in math and reading, they face a limited economic future. Granted, students who have demonstrated educational competency should not be subjected to "drill and kill," and schools need to engage in strategies that expand, not limit, the educational horizons of their students. Once students demonstrate that they have mastered the basics, then educational goals should be placed higher.

Maintaining public support for a high-stakes testing system depends upon educators' and policymakers' abilities to competently and fairly manage accountability. Detractors of the Texas educational accountability system cannot simply point to differences in TAAS performance among different economic and ethnic groups to argue that the system is somehow inferior and should therefore be abandoned. State test scores are improving, and performance gaps are narrowing. The accountability system, however, cannot afford to become arbitrary or driven by incentives that overlook the special needs of economically and ethnically diverse students. To provide anything less than adequate resources and competent teachers to help all children reach their potential would give educational critics the moral and ethical justification to reject such a system. Texas and the nation must remain cognizant of the need to maintain an accountability system that does not ignore the educational needs of any student. To do anything less would only perpetuate the inequalities that continue to place the nation at risk.

Notes

1. Craig D. Jerald, "How We Grade the States" (www.edweek.org/sreports/qc00/temp [July 24, 2000]).

2. S. M. Elam, L. C. Rose, and A. M. Gallup, "The 25th Annual Phi Delta Kappa/Gallup Poll of the Public's Attitudes toward the Public Schools," *Phi Delta Kappan*, vol. 75 (October 1993), pp. 137–57.

3. Students have up to eight opportunities to pass each section of the exit exam before their normal graduation date. The Texas Assessment of Academic Skills (TAAS) examinations are not timed tests.

4. Additional recognition is given to districts for student performance in areas beyond the three basic subject areas of reading, mathematics, and writing. For exam-

ple, additional recognition is given if 70 percent or more of the graduates take the SAT or American College Test (ACT) and more than 50 percent of them score 1110 on the SAT or 24 on the ACT composite. A monetary reward system compensates schools making significant gains in performance, and exceptionally outstanding performance can result in exemption from certain state regulations. For low-performing schools and districts that do not meet specified improvement goals, sanctions can be imposed and extra site visits carried out. Parents of children at designated low-performing schools can choose to enroll their children at some other public school, even one located in another school district.

5. Texas Education Agency, *2000 Accountability Manual* (www.tea.state.tx.us/perfreport/account/2000/manual/sec01.html [July 3, 2000]).

6. The Texas Supreme Court finally upheld the Texas school finance system in *Edgewood* v. *Meno et al.* and *Bexar County Education District et al.* (1995).

7. Texas Education Agency, *1999 State AEIS History Report* (www.tea.state.tx.us/perfreport/aeis/hist/state.html [July 25, 2000]).

8. Texas Education Agency, *1999 State AEIS History Report*.

9. To further investigate whether the learning gap decreased among various ethnic or racial groups in the Houston Independent School District (HISD), we attempted to utilize standardized tests based on national norms. Unfortunately, the district has not consistently administered the same nationally standardized test during the period studied. Before the implementation of the Stanford Achievement Test, Ninth Edition (Stanford 9) in 1997, the most recent nationally standardized test given in HISD was the Metropolitan Achievement Test 6 (MAT-6) in 1991. Comparing the average ethnic or racial differences on the 1991 MAT-6 from a sample of more than five thousand HISD students with 1999 mean Stanford 9 scores based on all students in grades three through eight in the district suggests that the test performance gap has not decreased between non-Hispanic white and African American or Hispanic students. However, comparing national scores based on different standardized tests many years apart is not recommended. K. D. Hopkins, J. C. Stanley, and B. R. Hopkins, *Educational and Psychological Measurement and Evaluation*, 7th ed. (Englewood Cliffs, N.J.: Prentice-Hall, 1990), pp. 393–94, point out that a school district's scores depend on which specific standardized test is administered because of differences in the reference groups various standardized tests use to develop national norms. Further, such norms can change considerably over an eight-year period.

10. The phenomenon of a greater proportion of enrollment occurring in the ninth grade is very widely observed. Students who were marginally promoted in elementary and middle school, who were socially promoted, often fail to earn sufficient credits during their first year in secondary school to achieve sophomore or tenth-grade status. The term *retention* is frequently applied to this failure, but it is different in kind from the retention in earlier grades, which results from an explicit decision of teachers, administrators, and often parents to have a child repeat a grade.

11. Walter Haney, as quoted in John Mintz, "An Education Miracle, or Mirage?" *Washington Post*, April 21, 2000, p. A–1.

12. Walter Haney, "The Myth of the Texas Miracle in Education," Center for the Study of Testing, Evaluation, and Education Policy, June 2000, table 3.1 on p. 12 and p. 87. This Haney paper has since been published electronically, at *Education Policy Analysis Archives*, vol. 8, no. 41 (August 19, 2000) (epaa.asu.edu/epaa/v8n41/ [August 19, 2000]). As the electronic version has no page numbers, the page references in this and in subsequent footnotes are to the original unpublished version.

13. Haney, "The Myth of the Texas Miracle in Education," p. 90.

14. Haney, "The Myth of the Texas Miracle in Education," p. 87.

15. Haney, "The Myth of the Texas Miracle in Education," figure 5.3 on p. 72.

16. Haney, as quoted by Mintz, "An Education Miracle."

17. Haney, "The Myth of the Texas Miracle in Education," p. 92.

18. Haney, as quoted by Mintz, "An Education Miracle."

19. Texas Education Agency, *1997–98 and 1998–99 Returning and Non-Returning Students in Grades 7–12* (www.tea.state.tx.us/research/leavers02 [August 10, 2000]).

20. Haney, as quoted by Mintz, "An Education Miracle."

21. Haney, "The Myth of the Texas Miracle in Education," table 7.2 on p. 122 and p. 123.

22. A. G. Dworkin and others, "Comparisons between the TAAS and Norm-Referenced Tests: Issues of Criterion-Related Validity," unpublished technical report to the Texas Education Agency, 1999.

23. "What Is NAEP?" *The Nation's Report Card* (www.nces.ed.gov/nationsreport-card/site/whatis.asp [July 25, 2000]).

24. Darvin M. Winick, "The TAAS and Texas School Reform," presentation to the Texas State Board of Education, November 3, 1999, p. 2.

25. David Grissmer and others, *Improving Student Achievement: What NAEP State Test Scores Tell Us* (Santa Monica, Calif.: RAND, 2000).

26. Grissmer and others, *Improving Student Achievement,* p. 100.

27. Grissmer and others, *Improving Student Achievement,* p. 100.

28. Grissmer and others, *Improving Student Achievement,* p. xxxvi.

29. Haney, "The Myth of the Texas Miracle in Education," p. 143.

30. From Texas Education Code, Section 8.002, Chapter 111. Texas Essential Knowledge and Skills for Mathematics (www.tea.state.tx.us/rules/tac/ch111.html [July 11, 2000]).

31. In response to these criticisms, the Texas Education Agency has broadened the subject matter to be covered on future TAAS exams. The revised required state examinations will include new content pertaining to science and social studies, in addition to reading and mathematics. State education officials are attempting to revise the TAAS to prevent a narrowing of the curriculum.

32. Analyses of TAAS scores suggested that some educational administrators and teachers had attempted to raise campus test scores through illegitimate practices. For example, auditors found that administrators in several Austin public schools changed TAAS answer sheet identification numbers to purposely exclude students who failed the TAAS from overall school results (Associated Press, "Austin ISD Manipulated

TAAS Results, Probe Reveals," *Houston Chronicle*, September 16, 1998, p. 29A). Other indications of cheating on the TAAS tests arose when an unreasonably excessive number of incorrect answers were found to have been changed to correct answers in schools throughout the state (Melanie Markley, "State Suspects Tampering on Tests at 22 Area Schools," *Houston Chronicle*, February 29, 1999, pp. 1A, 8A).

33. Linda M. McNeil, "Creating New Inequalities: Contradictions of Reform," *Phi Delta Kappan*, vol. 81 (June 2000), pp. 728-735; and Linda M. McNeil, *Contradictions of School Reform: Educational Costs of Standardized Testing* (New York: Routledge, 2000).

34. A. Gary Dworkin and others, *Evaluation of Academic Performance in the Houston Independent School District: A Final Report to the Center for Houston's Future* (Houston, Texas: Center for Houston's Future, 1998), appendix 4–A, pp. 18–23.

35. Data obtained from the Texas Education Agency website (www.tea.state.tx.us/perfreport/aeis/99/district.srch.html [June 23, 2000]).

36. Staff, "Accountability Exemptions for Area Schools," *Houston Chronicle*, February 22, 1998, pp. 38A–39A.

37. Data obtained from the Texas Education Agency website (www.tea.state.tx.us/perfreport/aeis/99/district.srch.html [June 23, 2000]).

38. Eric Hanson and Salatheia Bryant, "Houston, Fort Bend Districts Take Action against Six in TAAS Probe," *Houston Chronicle*, April 2, 1999, p. 1A.

39. Mike Snyder, "Hispanic Immigrants Lagging Far Behind," *Houston Chronicle*, June 25, 2000, Section A, pp. 31–32.

40. Melanie Markley, "Low Scores Force HISD to Target Middle Schools," *Houston Chronicle*, July 18, 2000, p. A1.

41. S. Murdock and others, *The Texas Challenge: Population Change and the Future of Texas* (Texas A & M Press, 1997), pp. 142, 150; and Texas Education Agency, Division of Performance Reporting, *Pocket Edition: Texas Public School Statistics,* various editions (Austin, Texas, 1993–2000) (www.tea.state.tx/perfreport/ pocked/ [August 1, 2000]). Data also obtained from HISD reports from the Pupil Accounting Office (1976 and 1980) and from Houston Independent School District, *District and School Profiles* (Houston, Texas, 2000).

7

Schools That Work

ABIGAIL THERNSTROM AND
STEPHAN THERNSTROM

R acial equality is still a dream—and will remain a dream as long as
blacks learn less in school than whites and Asians. It is a simple point,
to which remarkably little attention had been paid until recently. For a long
time, the fact of black underachievement was treated by the media, by civil
rights spokespersons, and even by scholars as a dirty secret—something to
whisper about behind closed doors. As if it were racist to say, there is a problem: black kids, on average, are not doing well in school.

To ignore the racial gap in academic achievement is to neglect black
youth, which is criminal negligence. Education has become the key to racial
equality. Equal earnings depend on equal skills. And thus, if the current drive
for educational reform does not raise black test scores, it will have failed. If
black youngsters remain second-class students, they will be second-class citi-
zens—a racially identifiable and enduring group of have-nots.

In the literature on minority underachievement, the focus has been almost
entirely on the black-white test score gap. But, for the most part, Hispanic
children are doing no better academically than African Americans, and
already they outnumber blacks among the school-age population. Thus,
while we begin with a reexamination of the familiar data on the black-white
test score gap, in the case studies that follow we turn to examples of excellent
education for inner-city children—black, Hispanic, and Asian. We ignore

disadvantaged whites only because no white children were in the schools and classroom we looked at closely.

More Bad News

The Black-White Test Score Gap, the collection of papers assembled by Christopher Jencks and Meredith Phillips in 1998, is the essential starting point for any discussion of racial disparities in academic performance in the K–12 years.[1] But the National Assessment of Educational Progress (NAEP) results that have become available since its publication make the problem seem even more intractable than that volume suggests.

In their introduction, Jencks and Phillips stress that the black-white test score gap, though still very large, had "narrowed since 1970."[2] They offer a supporting figure comparing the NAEP reading and math scores of black and white seventeen-year-olds from 1971 to 1996. Larry V. Hedges and Amy Nowell, in their chapter in *The Black-White Test Score Gap*, draw on a number of sources other than NAEP in reaching their conclusion about "black-white test score convergence."[3] This additional evidence points to some convergence since James Coleman's 1965 Equality of Economic Opportunity survey. But only NAEP provides a consistent instrument administered at frequent enough intervals to draw a clear picture of trends since the 1970s.

Hedges and Nowell's analysis of the NAEP material covers the years through 1994 and seems overly rosy in light of what is now known. They estimate that, at the rate of change visible in reading scores for 1971–94, the gap "would completely disappear in approximately twenty-five years, and that the gap in science would be gone in seventy years."[4]

This optimistic projection is no longer plausible, if it ever was.[5] At the rate of change apparent in reading scores for seventeen-year-olds from 1988 to 1999 (the date of the last NAEP trend assessment), the racial gap will be far larger a quarter century hence. Scores in science do not reveal the same pattern of sharp regression that is so clear in reading, but recent experience gives no grounds for believing that the racial gap in that subject will be closed in the near future. In fact, the racial gap in science was constant and very large from 1982 to 1999, the last date for which we have data.

Hedges and Nowell concede that "neither the gap in math nor that in writing shows a significant narrowing over the years," but this important qualification is not given the emphasis that it deserves.[6] Nor do Hedges and Nowell examine trends in the performance of students at younger ages.

David Grissmer, Ann Flanagan, and Stephanie Williamson's chapter in *The Black-White Test Score Gap* looks at nine- and thirteen- as well as seventeen-year-olds, and it includes evidence through 1996. But the authors examine only reading and math scores, ignoring science and writing. Only briefly do they note that the pattern of progress for black thirteen- and seventeen-year-olds reversed in the 1990s, with the gap in both reading and math widening again. Instead, their emphasis is on the progress achieved in the 1970s and 1980s. In reading and math "at all ages," they conclude, "black students improved a great deal while white students improved only a little."[7]

Reviewing the latest (1999) NAEP trend data for all age groups and subjects, we draw gloomier conclusions. The data in figure 7-1 reveal how well black students have been performing compared with their white classmates by indicating where their mean scores fall in the white percentile distribution. If there were no racial gap at all, black mean scores would consistently be at the 50th percentile. However, black students are nowhere near the 50th percentile in any subject, and none of the trend lines looks encouraging.

The racial gap has fluctuated more in reading than in any other subject. In 1971 black students at ages nine, thirteen, and seventeen were appallingly far behind whites, ranking in the 14th, 13th, and 11th percentiles, respectively. Scores edged upward thereafter, beginning with the youngest students, and by 1988 black nine-year-olds ranked in the 23rd percentile, thirteen-year-olds in the 30th percentile, and seventeen-year-olds in the 29th percentile. At this heartening rate of gain, it was possible to foresee the complete closing of the gap within a generation or so.

The high-water mark, however, was 1988. Over the next eleven years, the rank of black students declined fairly consistently, a drop large enough to be statistically significant for both thirteen- and seventeen-year-olds and close to it for nine-year-olds. In 1999 the two older groups scored about the same as they had fifteen years before, and nine-year-olds were performing at the low level they had achieved twenty-four years earlier. The results of the 2000 reading assessment for fourth graders were released in 2001, and they fit this pattern as well. For a dismayingly long time, the racial gap in reading has not been narrowing at all.

Reading is perhaps the single most significant skill that can be tested, but reading scores have nonetheless attracted what seems to be disproportionate attention. A command of mathematics is also manifestly of great importance in American society, and that picture is distinctly bleaker. Black nine-year-olds made no statistically significant progress in math between 1978 and 1999.[8] Although their peers four and eight years older made substantial gains over the course of the 1980s, significant regression followed, mirroring the pattern of decline in reading. In 1999 the two groups ranked in the 15th and 14th percentiles, respectively—a dismal showing.

Figure 7-1. *Percentile Ranking of Black Students on National Assessment of Educational Progress*

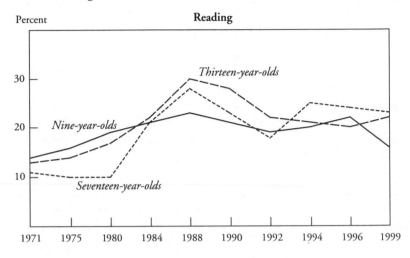

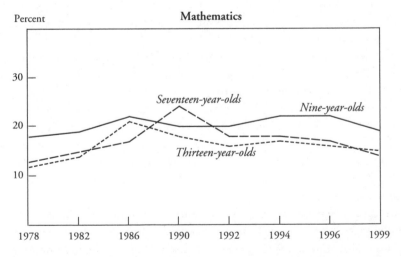

continued on next page

Figure 7 1. *Percentile Ranking of Black Students on National Assessment of Educational Progress (continued)*

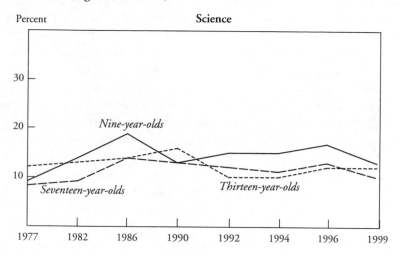

Percent   **Science**

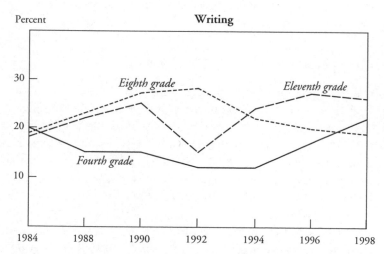

Percent   **Writing**

Source: Calculated from trend data on the National Assessment of Educational Progress website (nces.ed.gov/nationsreportcard).

Note: The black mean score was subtracted from the white mean score for each test to determine the racial gap, the point gap was divided by the white standard deviation, and the resulting z-score was translated into a percentile rank.

The science scores revealed less both in the way of initial progress and of subsequent regression. Between 1977 and 1982, black nine- and thirteen-year-olds made statistically significant gains, but no further progress was achieved over the seventeen years that followed. Most important, seventeen-year-olds made no statistically significant progress over the entire twenty-two-year period. In 1999 as in 1977, more than half of all black students were as ignorant of science as whites in the bottom tenth of the distribution.

Nor was there any narrowing of the racial gap in writing skills over the fourteen-year period in which that subject has been tested. The earliest writing scores for black students look a little better than in other subjects, probably because the earliest writing test was in 1984. Had writing been tested in the 1970s, the gap likely would have been wider, as was the case in reading and math. Nevertheless, it is depressing that black students were as far behind whites in writing skills at the time of the most recent test, 1998, as they were when the first was administered fourteen years earlier.

In sum, some progress has been made in narrowing the racial gap in reading. But in the five reading tests since 1988 the trend has been backward, not forward. And in the other three subjects for which NAEP trend data are available, the gap has been largely constant for an even longer period. Thus, whatever is being done to close the gap is not working sufficiently to register in tests administered to representative national samples of students.[9]

Common Explanations That Do Not Work

This dismal picture is somewhat surprising. A number of the factors assumed to explain black academic progress in the past have continued to operate. David J. Armor's 1992 *Public Interest* piece, "Why Is Black Educational Achievement Rising?" was one of the earliest discussions of racial trends in achievement in the 1970s and 1980s.[10] NAEP gains by black students that seemed so impressive a decade ago were largely the result of the rising socioeconomic status of black parents, Armor argued. But what explains, then, the pattern of regression—or (at best) stagnation—in NAEP over the past dozen years? The size of the black middle class has neither shrunk nor stagnated. Armor relied on data on parental education from 1971 to 1990 in describing the rising socioeconomic status of black parents. Figure 7-2 carries the story forward to 1999, and it plainly reveals no slackening of progress in the 1990s and certainly no widening of the racial gap in parental educational levels. The racial gap—if Armor's theory were right—should have continued to narrow, and yet it did not.

Figure 7-2. *Education of Mothers of Children Age Six to Eighteen, by Race, 1974–99*

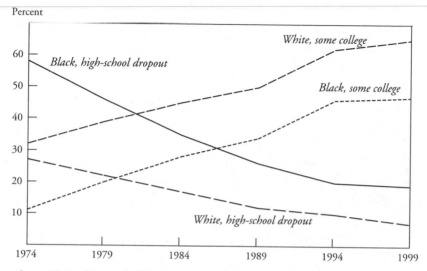

Percent

Source: National Center for Education Statistics, *The Condition of Education, 2000* (U.S. Department of Education, 2000), p. 124.

The analysis of data from the state NAEP tests for 1990–96 by David W. Grissmer and his colleagues advances other arguments that do not seem to fit well with the national NAEP patterns.[11] Grissmer's book contends that increasing the proportion of children in public prekindergarten programs and cutting pupil-teacher ratios improve overall educational performance and narrow the racial gap. But the point about the availability of pre–K instruction is difficult to square with the evidence in figure 7-3.

If exposure to pre–K programs is as beneficial as Grissmer's book suggests, the NAEP scores of black and white students alike should have been rising impressively over the past three decades. Enrollment in nursery school or prekindergarten programs has grown strongly and steadily, from just one out of ten in 1964 to approximately half by the mid-1990s. But overall scores have improved little. And it is hard to see from the slight racial differences in enrollment rates over these three decades any explanation for the changing pattern of the racial gap on NAEP performance (see figure 7-3).

Figure 7-4 tests another proposition put forth by Grissmer and his colleagues—that reductions in class size result in a narrowing of the racial gap—against the national data. This argument, too, does not square well with the

Figure 7-3. *Percent of Black and White Three- and Four-Year-Olds Enrolled in School, 1964–96 (Three-Year Moving Averages)*

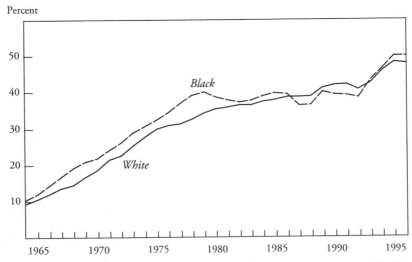

Source: Data as given in Mark S. Littman and Deirdre A. Gaquin, *Education Statistics of the United States* (Washington: Bernan Press, 1999), table A-21, transformed into three-year moving averages.

pattern in the admittedly crude national-level data. Between 1965 and 1998, the pupil to teacher ratio in American elementary schools (the level at which class size seems to matter most) fell by more than a third, from 28.4 to 18.3. The corresponding figure for students in secondary schools dropped from 20.6 to 14.0, also a decline of about a third.[12] And yet NAEP scores in general have not risen correspondingly. Furthermore, the shape of the trend lines do not provide any clues that shed light on the narrowing and subsequent widening of the racial gap. The issue is far from settled. The evidence from the Tennessee Project STAR experiment does show some class-size effects in the early elementary years, but there are reasons for caution about making too much of them.[13] It is hard to believe, at present, that reforms focused on class size alone will dramatically narrow the racial gap in school achievement.

Great Teaching, Great Results

The data on black student performance are depressing. Two states, North Carolina and Texas, have made some progress in raising NAEP scores overall, but the black-white gap even in those states is unchanged, while the Hispanic disparity has narrowed only modestly. If all students are learning more, then

Figure 7-4. *Pupil-Teacher Ratios in American Elementary and Secondary Schools, 1965–98*

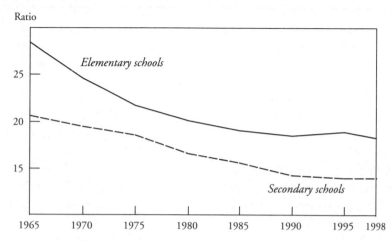

Source: National Center for Education Statistics, *Digest of Educational Statistics: 1999* (U.S. Department of Education, 1999), p. 75.

education is improving. No one should uncork the champagne, however, until the racial and ethnic disparities lessen significantly.

The picture seems bleak, and yet scattered across the educational land-scape are pockets of superb education. They are few in number and all are atypical within their own districts. Nevertheless, their record of success suggests that truly radical reform can change the lives of inner-city students, whatever their race or ethnicity.[14] The goal is thus clear. But how to get there? The road is littered with obstacles. They may be insurmountable.

We focus on one classroom and two schools—all three closely connected. We chose these particular examples of fabulous education only because we happen to know them best. The classroom is that of Rafe Esquith, who has been teaching fifth grade at the Hobart Elementary School in Central Los Angeles since 1985. The two schools are the KIPP Academies in New York and Houston, whose founders learned much from Esquith and had the courage to take a number of his core ideas and build two schools in part upon them. Esquith is the KIPP Academies' greatest fan, and David Levin, principal at KIPP in New York (until the fall of 2001), has described Rafe Esquith as "awesome." We are most familiar with New York's KIPP and Esquith's class. One of us made only a single two-day visit to the original KIPP Academy, located in Houston. But while the two KIPPs are somewhat different, it is evident that both are superb—for similar reasons.[15]

The Hobart Elementary School is an inner-city educational factory, serving twenty-four hundred students in grades K–5. Its drab stucco buildings are scattered across an expanse of concrete surrounded by a high, protective chain link fence—essential in a neighborhood of gangs, drugs, and violence. There is nothing educationally noteworthy about Hobart, but Rafe Esquith is, in effect, running a one-room schoolhouse for one grade, with little connection to the rest of the school, which contains a dozen other fifth-grade classrooms. His class is split roughly down the middle, with half the children Hispanic, and half Korean. But a high percentage from both groups comes from single-parent, impoverished households with a multitude of too-familiar problems.

Why discuss a classroom made up of Hispanic and Korean American students in an essay focused on the black-white test score gap? The principles Esquith has developed and applied so successfully are relevant to all pupils from disadvantaged minority backgrounds. The proof that they work specifically with African American students can be found in the record of New York City's KIPP Academy, whose founder acknowledges his debt to Esquith. Approximately half of the students at KIPP in New York are black; half are Hispanic.

KIPP is an acronym for Knowledge Is Power Program, and both academies are small middle schools. New York's KIPP serves grades five to eight; the Houston school has added a ninth grade for those who need an extra year before entering a competitive high school. New York's KIPP is in the South Bronx—high on the list of the city's worst neighborhoods. It has roughly 250 students and shares a building with three other schools, with which it has nothing in common. Most of its students live in low-income housing projects. In Houston, KIPP is located on the southwest side of the city, and almost all of its students are second-generation Latino, the overwhelming majority of whom qualify for free lunch. Both are now charter schools, but New York's KIPP was a regular public school for its first five years—until the fall of 2000.

In theory, Rafe Esquith's kids are part of a gifted program, although the school's definition of *gifted* means he has a mixture of academically talented and struggling youngsters. KIPP's students are admitted on a first-come, first-served basis, although parents do need to apply, and both they and their children must sign a contract that, at least on paper, commits them to the program.

Students must agree, for instance, to "always work, think, and behave in the best way [they] know how and . . . do whatever it takes for [them] and [their] fellow students to learn." They must promise to attend school faithfully, do their homework, and "behave so as to protect the safety, interests, and rights of all individuals in the classroom." And they must understand that they are "responsible for [their] own behavior." The contract parents sign is similar, but it includes provisions on helping their "child in the best way we know how" and making themselves available to their children and the school. They, too, must agree that the ultimate responsibility for the "behavior and actions" of their child lies with the family.

These contracts, however, do little more than set expectations. With almost no exceptions in New York, and very few in Houston, children and parents who violate the terms are not asked to find another school.

The most obvious measure of excellent education is how much kids know—that is, how well they do on standardized tests. The quality of these tests is uneven, but most do assess the minimum skills that all students need to succeed in school and in the workplace. By that standard, Rafe Esquith's students are doing spectacularly. The average fifth-grade score in reading on the Stanford Achievement Test, Ninth Edition (Stanford 9) at Hobart Elementary School is at the 32nd percentile nationally; in math, the students are at the 52nd percentile. Those scores include Esquith's class, which raises the school-wide fifth-grade average significantly. The average reading score for Esquith's class is at the 82nd percentile, with math at the 95th percentile.[16] Esquith is rightly pleased with this record, but even more proud of the fact that his kids' scores reflect dramatic improvement over their fourth-grade performance.

At KIPP, too, for the most part the students are doing splendidly. The latest figures show that when the Bronx students entered the fifth grade in the fall of 2000, a minority were at grade level in math. By the end of the year, 82 percent were at or above grade level on the CTB/McGraw Hill tests used in New York (and elsewhere). In the 2000–01 school year, KIPP's eighth graders ranked seventh in math and twenty-fifth in reading in all of New York City. For the fifth straight year the academy was the highest performing public middle school in the Bronx. Its daily attendance averages 96 percent, among the highest in the state. This is a stunning achievement. And it accounts for the fact that many of KIPP's former students—including those who have earned scholarships to competitive private schools—are among the best in their high schools in math.

Esquith has a class with some truly academically talented kids, and a number of his students have ended up at Ivy League colleges, although he started them down that road of success and nurtured them along with way. Most would not have made it without him. David Levin has some students who go on to highly selective schools, but his main goal, as he puts it, is a "shift in the bell curve of achievement to the right" for those students whose academic gifts put them in the middle 80 percent. His success in doing so for such a highly disadvantaged population makes his school remarkable.

The KIPP Academies and Esquith's class raise extra funds. In Esquith's case, some of the money comes from outside contributors, some from awards. KIPP receives approximately $7,000 per child in public funds, to which it adds roughly $3,000 from donors, which still brings the total under the amount that regular New York City public schools receive on a per pupil basis.

Hard Work, High Standards

The walls of both KIPPs are plastered with messages, some of which originated many years ago in Rafe Esquith's class: "There Are No Shortcuts." "Be Nice!!! Work Hard!!!" "No Excuses." In Houston KIPP's new gym, the students read these mottos—painted on the floor—as they play sports. Civility, hard work, high standards, and superb teaching are the not-so-secret formula that gets the results reflected in the test scores of Esquith's students and of KIPPsters (as they are called).

"We don't do anything that doesn't improve reading, writing, and math skills," David Levin notes. The school has only one major extracurricular activity: music. Every child plays an instrument, and there is a superb school orchestra. Otherwise, however, almost the entire day is devoted to learning core subjects.

That day is long. Both KIPPs have 67 percent more instructional time than the normal public school. Students arrive at 7:25 a.m. (or 7:00 a.m. if they want breakfast) and leave at 5:00 p.m. They go home with hefty homework assignments. During the regular academic year, classes are held on Saturday (9:00 a.m. to 1:00 p.m.) as well. School is in session for three weeks in the summer. All fifth-grade students get double reading and double math classes. Those who do not get their work done stay "Wall Street hours," as KIPP calls them. In other words, they remain in school, working late, like attorneys on Wall Street. The school also contacts the parents, making sure they understand they have a role to play.

"Kids have too much free time in our country and we're paying for that," Rafe Esquith is convinced. His students are one class in a conventional public school, which runs from 8:00 a.m. to 2:48 p.m. But he is there at 6:30 a.m. teaching an early math class and stays until 5:00 p.m. With few exceptions, his kids voluntarily put in the same long hours. Thus the school day for his students is 60 percent longer than for their peers in other classes.

Moreover, Esquith runs his class fifty weeks a year, cutting down radically on the seventeen weeks of vacation the system provides. Over the course of a year, his students spend over twice as much time in class—or on trips that are, in effect, a class—as other fifth graders in Los Angeles public schools.

Esquith also holds Saturday sessions for his former students who want to continue to build their skills and prepare for the SAT under his guidance, and impressive numbers show up regularly. "I have a definite point of view," he says. "Kids need to work much harder than they've been working, much longer than they've been working, and with much more discipline than they've been working." He is certainly their role model. For years he even walked the five miles to school and back every day, despite the long hours he put in, because his wife needed their only car. The extra hours he works are not compensated. He gets the standard, very low salary to which a teacher without a master's degree or points collected by attending professional development courses is entitled.

The long hours that Esquith and his kids put in are in part devoted to reading and then producing a Shakespeare play, the after-school activity for which he is most famous. His "Hobart Shakespeareans" (as the kids are called) have performed with Britain's Royal Shakespeare Company and have, in effect, been adopted by British actor Sir Ian McKellen, who comes to see them perform. Why Shakespeare? Esquith loves the plays himself, and he decided there was no better way to teach English to children whose first language is either Spanish or Korean. Furthermore, as Esquith says, the Bard "tackles the big issues—love, violence, jealousy, comedy, and humorous situations . . . in a language that nobody has ever duplicated."

To watch his class read and analyze a Shakespeare play is an amazing experience. "We go over everything word by word, explaining every conflict, every bit of symbolism," he says, and they do. *King Lear* is the play he has chosen for his nine- and ten-year-olds to perform in the spring of 2001. "Who's the smartest in the play?" Esquith asks his class. "The fool," one student answers. "But Kent is smart too," Esquith responds. And what about "bedlam beggars"? What does that mean? There are fifty-five students in the room, some from other classes who come only for Shakespeare. Almost everyone is following along totally enraptured. "Should you stop at the end of all the lines?" The students agree that you should not. "Why does Shakespeare talk of 'roaring voices'?" Hands go up with each question. In the spring, his young Shakespeareans, wearing regular clothes except for "Will Power" tee shirts, put on eight performances just in the classroom, an event that McKellen regularly flies in for—all the way from New Zealand in April 2001. One of us saw the final production of *King Lear*—an unforgettable experience. Why the classroom setting? "A real stage and costumes are show biz," Esquith explains. "This is about education." And because he adds music, played and sung by the students, every member of the class has a chance to participate.

High expectations are current educational buzzwords, with much hand-wringing about just how high those expectations can be for black and Hispanic children in poverty. There is no hand-wringing at KIPP or by Esquith. All of KIPP's eighth graders have completed a two-year high school level algebra I class by the time they graduate. Part of the secret is a lack of ambivalence about the need to memorize basic mathematical strategies for solving problems. Levin himself teaches math, and he turns, for instance, the speed with which kids can accurately run through the times tables into a competition, the object of which is to beat his own time. To watch him explain to new fifth graders (with minimum preparation for the academic demands of KIPP) how to tell which of two numbers is the larger is to see a level of sophistication in illuminating the structure of math that is rare.

KIPP's sixth graders are expected to spell such words as *audible, audience, confidential, hyperbole, hypertension,* and *pianist.* Rich vocabularies open literary doors. In Houston, on a day we visited, an eighth-grade English class was engaged in a close textual analysis of *The Lord of the Flies.* Later that day in a thinking skills class, Michael Feinberg, the principal, led a sophisticated discussion of the federal highway program, the power of Congress over interstate transportation, and the political pressures behind appropriation decisions.

Esquith's fifth graders play mental mathematical games—no pencil and paper allowed. Take the total intelligence quotient (IQ) of everyone on the board of education ("Zero!" he says with a twinkle), add 8, multiply by 7, subtract 5, and divide by 17. In a flash the students hold up tiles with the number 3 on it. Take the number of holes on a golf course, add the number of years in a decade, add the number of weeks in a fortnight, add 19, and take the square root. Up come the number 7 tiles with amazing speed. These are inner-city kids, but Esquith does not ask inner-city questions. He wants them to know, for example, what a golf course looks like.

Esquith pushes the kids hard and believes "facts are good." But there is nothing grim about his class. (We saw kids at lunchtime shouting, "Let's skip lunch," so they could keep working.) He plays games with history, geography, and literature as well. Who campaigned in support of the ratification of the Constitution? Who was the ruler of England during the Revolutionary War? Who was the British prime minister during the French and Indian War? Name the country directly east of Libya. Name the country north of the Sudan. Name the country south of Libya with four letters. How many states border the Pacific Ocean? (This is a trick question because they might forget Hawaii and Alaska.) Five states border the Gulf of Mexico—what are they? Let's see how many Shakespeare plays we can name. He goes around the room, and almost all hands are raised.

This is great preparation for any standardized assessment. Both KIPPs and Esquith's class spend considerable time taking tests, practicing for state exams, and learning to become test-savvy. "I love tests," Levin says. Esquith gives a math test every two weeks, a geography test every month, and a spelling test every Friday. Writing assignments do not get graded, but essays must be rewritten until they are right. His students practice the Stanford 9 for about thirty minutes twice a week. He even has his students figuring out what wrong answers might be offered as options on a multiple-choice exam—that is, what sorts of traps those who design the Stanford 9 might logically set.

Not by Math Alone

In 1997 the College Board organized a National Task Force on Minority High Achievement. The group contained no dissenting voices from civil rights orthodoxy, and the College Board, itself, tends to stick to safe ground. And yet *Reaching the Top*, the task force report released in October 1999, courageously placed considerable stress on the culture of the home, drawing a contrast between East Asians and non-Asian minorities.[17]

The report described the problem of underachievement as emerging "very early," and it referred to the "cultural attributes of home, community, and school," talking at length about the views toward school and hard work that Asian parents transmit to their children. "East Asian American high school and college students . . . spend much more time on their studies outside of school and are more likely to be part of academically oriented peer groups." In addition, "East Asian parents are more likely than Whites to train their children to believe success is based on effort rather than innate ability," and thus they instill in their children the values of hard work, "diligence, thoroughness, and self-discipline."[18] It was a point that Laurence Steinberg, in *Beyond the Classroom*, had made three years earlier. "In terms of school achievement . . . ," he wrote, "it is more advantageous to be Asian than to be wealthy, to have nondivorced parents, or to have a mother who is able to stay at home full-time."[19]

"Culture," George Farkas has written, "is best seen not as a matter of "values" but as "a tool kit of *skills*, the means by which strategies of action are constructed." Low-income parents do value education, stable marriages, steady jobs, and other "middle class" objectives, his argument runs. But they differ in the "culturally-shaped skills, habits, and styles" that facilitate the realization of those aspirations.[20] Were there strategies that the College Board could identify that successfully addressed the problem of counterproductive "culturally-shaped skills, habits and styles"? Except for its advocacy of after-school and other supplementary educational programs, the report skirted the question.

Neither Rafe Esquith nor the KIPP Academies skirt the issue, however. They confront it head on. The values of "diligence, thoroughness, and self-discipline" are precisely those they try to instill, a task particularly daunting for David Levin. His South Bronx black and Hispanic students all reside in a neighborhood in which, as the school's literature puts it, "illiteracy, drug abuse, broken homes, gangs, and juvenile crime" are rampant.

"We are fighting a battle involving skills and values," Levin notes. "We are not afraid to set social norms." In effect, he has adopted James Q. Wilson's "broken windows" theory and applied it to schools. To ignore one piece of trash on the floor ("I hate trash," Levin remarks on our first visit to the school), one inappropriately dressed teacher or student, one fight between kids, one hint of verbal abuse in a classroom would send a disastrous no-one-cares message. And thus, at KIPP, the staff responds to every sign of disorder—however slight. The result is that, even in the lunchroom, the students talk quietly and need little supervision. The disciplined atmosphere also allows large classes, reducing the number of teachers on the payroll, with the result that discretionary funds are used for other purposes. "Class size is not an issue if teachers know how to manage kids," Levin notes.

A 1992 survey of a representative sample of the metropolitan Detroit, Michigan, population found that young unemployed blacks failed to grasp the importance of dress and appearance to potential employers.[21] Those are not skills overlooked at KIPP. Its education in "self-discipline" includes learning how to dress for success and how to sit in a classroom chair (no heads on desks), the importance of looking directly at the person to whom you are talking, and the point of standing when greeting someone.

The school has a dress code, although there are no uniforms. The rules consist of such items as closed shoes, shirts with sleeves, skirts to the knees, no big earrings or other jewelry, and belts (when needed) to hold pants up. KIPP students spend hours at the beginning of the fifth grade learning the school's code of behavior. And every moment in class the teachers themselves are role models. They, too, dress professionally and are invariably courteous. Levin knows the name of every student and never walks by a kid without saying hello. Civility and decorum permeate the school. He has been asked,

"Who are you to set behavioral standards?" The answer: "I'm the boss." Understanding who is in charge (in any school and most jobs) is also integral to a good education.

Esquith, too, sets behavioral standards, although as the lone teacher in a contained classroom, he does not need a dress code or the same drill in moving expeditiously between classes. A student from another teacher's class comes to his early morning math lessons. "Everything is noisy and rude in my classroom," he says. Esquith takes his kids to concerts, ballgames, and restaurants, but he expects perfect behavior. They learn to sit quietly at a concert and to clap at the right time. Their presence at a restaurant never disturbs the other patrons. "Teachers can't say at the last minute [as the class leaves for a field trip], I want you to be on your best behavior," Esquith notes. "By then, it's too late." "Best behavior" takes practice.

The 1992 Detroit survey did not ask respondents to rate the importance of the "diligence" and "thoroughness" to which the College Board referred. But the KIPP Academies and Rafe Esquith both stress the importance of disciplined work habits. "Oh, Steven, you weren't listening? Sorry to bother you," Esquith says to a student who cannot answer a question because his attention has wandered. Total attention, diligence, and thoroughness are also expected when the students participate in a sports program Esquith has added to the normal school day. On one of our visits, he is teaching volleyball. For two months, he has the kids practicing handling the ball and moving properly, but without any net in place. They play the actual game when they are ready to do so well. Good athletes, these students learn, pay meticulous attention to their craft. Excellence in every endeavor requires discipline.

At KIPP students chant rules in unison:

We 'slant' at all times.
We listen carefully at all times.
We follow the teachers' instructions.
We answer when given the signal.
We stay focused to save time.
We will always be nice and work hard.

"Slant" is an acronym for: Sit up. Listen. Ask and answer questions. Nod your head so people know you are listening and understanding. Track your speaker by keeping your eyes on whoever is talking.

KIPPsters learn to avoid wasting time by walking down halls rapidly in orderly lines and sitting in their classroom seats immediately. They are taught small habits that make a big difference—like using a finger on their left hand to keep track of their place in a book while the right hand is raised to ask a question. They learn to organize their pencils, notebooks, and assignment sheets. Six rules for notebook organization are spelled out on a handout. "God wants you to be organized, whatever God you believe in," Levin tells a class. At Houston's KIPP the students pick up worksheets as they walk into school and do the problems in their spare moments.

Ronald F. Ferguson, who has been studying middle-class black students in Shaker Heights, Ohio, and elsewhere, has found that 21 percent of black males in the lower track in school say, "I didn't try as hard as I could in school because I worried about what my friends might think." He also notes the "misguided love" of many teachers who "are a little too sympathetic[,] . . . [letting] the black kids in elementary school get away with more, just relax, doze off in class, or not pay much attention."[22] KIPP and Esquith both want their students to think it is cool to work hard to get good grades. And Levin has zero tolerance for teachers whose definition of love is letting kids doze off.[23]

In the Detroit survey, young blacks (both employed and unemployed) underestimated the degree to which employers expected those whom they hired to be a "team player."[24] Esquith has created a supportive and nurturing community within the school. "Who has a compliment to give someone today?" he frequently asks. "We're a team," a KIPP teacher says. "Everyone ready? We wait until they are." To an incoming group of fifth graders, Levin explains: A team is a family. We do not make fun of teammates. If you make other students feel bad, they will not concentrate in class. They will be think-ing about how to get back at you. And that will make you feel terrible, and around and around it will go. At the end of the year, that is what you will have spent your time on. But there will be no questions on the state test about being mean. "You are all KIPPsters," he concludes. "We're only wor-ried about everyone moving ahead together." The stress on teamwork affects work as well as behavioral habits. The student who cannot spell a word, for example, is letting the family down.

Levin is "trying to break a complicated cycle" (as he puts it) in which the kids who start behind stay behind. And as part of that effort he makes the connection between hard work, good behavior, and rewards in life very clear. The school, in effect, is the employer they will later encounter. There are weekly paychecks, which reflect (in KIPP dollars) such qualities as atten-dance, promptness, organization and neatness, hard work, and the respect given other teammates. Checks are given out on Mondays and must be signed by parents. Those who meet the school's standards are eligible for trips to places such as Utah, California, and Washington, D.C.

Grades do not figure into the KIPP paychecks, but plenty of rewards are offered for academic accomplishment: a Wall of Honor in the hallway, award assemblies, "students of the week" listed on the classroom walls, along with "Homework Champs" and "Reading Champs" and samples of excellent writ ten work.

Esquith, too, has a complicated system of paychecks, points, and awards. In class, students lose more points by giving a wrong answer than they gain by a correct one. He wants them to think before speaking. Trips to Washington, D.C.; Muir Woods in California; Philadelphia, Pennsylvania; the Oregon Shakespeare Festival; and elsewhere have long been integral to the education he offers. They reward mature behavior. A role in a Shakespearean production is also earned, in part by a willingness to spend countless hours working on the play, putting the classroom in order after hours, and so forth. But paychecks in Esquith's class reflect grades as well as behavior. Everyone has a checking account, and once a month an auction is held in which the students bid on such items as pens, calculators, and chess sets. Designated bankers have ledgers in which they keep track of how much money each student has.

Property, as well, is bought and sold at the auctions. Classroom seats are real estate—with some locations worth more than others. The students pay rent, but if they have earned and saved enough, they can buy their seat as a condo. They also can buy other students' seats, at which point rent is paid to them. (The kids know that if they are profligate and cannot pay rent, they could be "homeless" and find themselves sitting on the floor, although we saw everyone safely in their chairs.) All students pay income taxes, and seat-owners pay property tax as well. "This is like Monopoly," one youngster notes. To which Esquith answered, "Buddy, this is real life." His kids are learning the rules of the American game—which they can choose to join or reject.

Intertwined Messages

A variety of messages are intertwined in the training the children receive.

In a KIPP phonics class, the teacher asks, "What room is this?" The students chant the answer: "This is the room that has the kids who want to learn to read more books to make a better tomorrow." "We are giving the kids the skills and confidence to take them to someplace better," David Levin says.

"Someplace better" is the world of opportunity that awaits them if they are ready to take advantage of it. Getting ready is the point of working so hard. "Good things happen," Levin says, letting the students finish the sentence: "when you do the right thing." He goes on: "You never know when good things are going to happen. You want to be in a situation in which nothing is ever denied you."

On one of our visits, Levin has extra tickets to a Yankees game. They go to the students with the highest paycheck averages—the students who have met the behavioral demands of KIPP. And while grades are not part of the mix, hard work (essential to learning) is. In a thinking skills class, Levin rhetorically asks: "Why do you have to finish work at home that you didn't finish here?" The answer: "You want knowledge." KIPP, it is important to recall, stands for Knowledge Is Power Program. Knowledge provides the power to get you to that better place.

Both KIPP and Esquith, in a multitude of ways, remind the students of what they are striving for. KIPP names classrooms after various colleges. Esquith has long had college banners from elite schools decorating his walls, with the names of the students admitted to them underneath. When he takes his kids on trips, they stay at good hotels and eat at good restaurants. "I want to show them what they're working for," he says. "In our neighborhood, you look outside your window and you see burned buildings," one of his students, quoted in the *Los Angeles Times* some years back, noted. But, she went on, he "teaches us that there is more to life than just [what is] outside the window."[25]

Levin and Esquith are helping their students get ready for a life beyond the burned buildings, but they cannot do the job for them. They must take responsibility for their own lives. "You've got to be ready in life," Levin tells his KIPPsters. "We deliver an explicit message to the kids: that's the outside world, and we cannot change certain things. This is the only place we can control. We'll do everything we can for you . . . but at a certain point you have to do it on your own. Ultimately it's up to you to choose your future." Esquith says much the same thing. "My job is to open a lot of doors for those kids. Their job is to choose which ones to walk through." They make choices, and choices have consequences. "It's not my job to save your souls," he tells his class. "It's my job to give you an opportunity to save your own soul."

It is an optimistic message about America and about the rules that govern social mobility—the climb out of poverty to greater affluence. "There Are No Shortcuts" on the road to success, although doors are open for those determined to walk through them. Neither KIPP nor Rafe Esquith promises a rose garden—a future in which race and ethnicity will not matter. But the opportunities outweigh the barriers, they suggest. Skills and persistence will pay off.[26]

In any case, barriers too easily become an excuse for failure. In May 2001, the *New York Times* quoted a Massachusetts teacher, James Bougas, on the subject of the statewide testing to which he objected. "Low scores," he said, "can reflect family hardship, not lack of effort or teaching."[27] Such rhetoric reflects a very different philosophy from that which informs KIPP. "You live in a world in which things are often not fair," Levin tells a sixth-grade class. But the road to success is not paved with excuses. Or second chances. At both KIPP and in Esquith's class, if you goof off or violate the rules of behavior, predictable and immediate consequences follow. No sob stories could persuade Levin to let a student go to the Yankee game unless he or she had earned a ticket. "You can't argue your way into privilege," Levin tells the sixth graders. "You've got to earn it step-by-step." A disruptive student asks Esquith, "Can we talk about it?" "No," he replies without hesitation. A young girl is not listening to a classmate reading *King Lear*. "Tomorrow if you're not listening, what's going to happen?" he asks. "I'll have to leave," she whispers. "Yes, and how long will you be outside? The rest of the year, yes." They know he means it.

Plenty of middle-class kids need to hear the same message, but, as with inadequate instruction in math and other core subjects, when schools fall down on their job, those who suffer most are the students who come to class with the least. Much is made of the fact that more affluent children have parents who read to them and that they arrive in school with larger vocabularies and a knowledge of numbers, letters, and colors. Low-income children certainly need help in beginning to acquire academic skills at an early age. But arguably the more difficult job is to teach "desire, discipline, and dedication," the watchwords painted in red and blue letters on sidewalks throughout Houston's KIPP. "We want students who, when we say, run through that wall, will run because they believe something is good on the other side," Levin tells a group of goofing-off students. "Fire, trust, the will to succeed is what we want to see. If you have that fire, it should show every day." It is hard to find that fire in any school—whatever its demographic profile. Analyzing a survey of twenty thousand teenagers in nine high schools in the decade 1985–95, Laurence Steinberg found widespread disengagement from academic work.[28] But, again, the consequences are particularly severe for those students who do not come to school with the "tool kit" of "culturally-shaped skills, habits, and styles" they need to succeed.

The effort to put disadvantaged youngsters on the traditional ladder of social mobility has another component, never explicitly articulated. Esquith and KIPP introduce their students (black, Hispanic, and Korean) to great writing, great music, and great documents. The Declaration of Independence, the words to "America (My Country 'tis of Thee)," and quotations from Henry David Thoreau and Oliver Wendell Holmes—as well as Michael Jordan and others—decorate the walls in the KIPP Academies in Houston and New York. On one of our visits to Hobart Elementary, Esquith and his kids were reading *The Adventures of Huckleberry Finn* out loud, and on another, *Animal Farm*. Esquith and KIPP are guiding their students down the road that Ralph Ellison walked almost seven decades ago. "In Macon County, Alabama," Ellison wrote in 1963, "I read Marx, Freud, T. S. Eliot, Pound, Gertrude Stein and Hemingway. Books which seldom, if ever, mentioned Negroes were to release me from whatever 'segregated' idea I might have had of my human possibilities. I was freed not by propagandists . . . but by composers, novelists, and poets who spoke to me of more interesting and freer ways of life."[29]

Even in the Jim Crow South, Ellison thought of himself as a writer and an American. ("The values of my own people are neither 'white' nor 'black'; they are American," he wrote.)[30] Today, however, in too many schools minority children are offered a "'segregated' idea" of their potential. And yet, as Ellison argued, that notion of race-as-destiny stifles the development of individuality and nurtures "that feverish industry dedicated to telling Negroes who and what they are"—an industry that "can usually be counted upon to deprive both humanity and culture of their complexity."[31] The industry to which he referred was populated by both blacks and whites. "If white society has tried to do anything to us," he noted in the 1970s, "it has tried to keep us from being individuals"—to deprive blacks of the understanding that "individuality is still operative beyond the racial structuring of American society."[32]

Both Esquith and KIPP are trying, in effect, to teach children the lessons Ellison had to figure out in terrible racial circumstances. The extraordinary amount of time their students spend in school, the serious academic demands made upon them, and what they read are all aimed, in part, at helping students define themselves as individuals and Americans in a society rich with opportunity. If these students come to think of themselves as unique, free to choose their identity, to emphasize their racial and ethnic group ties as much or little as they wish, they will have an excellent chance, with solid skills, of going far. This is not a truth confined to racial and ethnic minorities. The traditional ticket to social mobility in America has been the ability of individuals to define themselves apart from the group (as defined by social class, geographical location, and a variety of other indicators) into which they were born.

We have offered a picture of settings in which high-level learning is taking place in extremely inauspicious circumstances. These are tiny experiments, and even a more rigorous analysis than we have been able to provide would not yield a foolproof recipe for revamping the many undistinguished inner-city schools in which kids are learning much less than they should. Nevertheless, these small examples of superb education perhaps suggest some principles that have wide applicability. Or that, in any case, is our hope.

Notes

We are indebted to J. Michael Ross of the National Center for Education Statistics at the U.S. Department of Education, Ronald F. Ferguson of the John F. Kennedy School of Government at Harvard University, David Levin of the KIPP Academy, New York, and Rafe Esquith of the Hobart Elementary School, Los Angeles, for their criticisms of an earlier draft of this essay.

1. Christopher Jencks and Meredith Phillips, eds., *The Black-White Test Score Gap* (Brookings, 1998), p. 1.

2. Jencks and Phillips, *The Black-White Test Score Gap*, p. 1.

3. Larry V. Hedges and Amy Nowell, "Black-White Test Score Convergence since 1965," in Christopher Jencks and Meredith Phillips, ed., *The Black-White Test Score Gap* (Brookings, 1998), pp. 149–81.

4. Hedges and Nowell, "Black-White Test Score Convergence since 1965," p. 155. Since the standard deviation for math scores before 1978 has not been published, it is not clear how the authors calibrated the pre-1978 math scores given here.

5. It seems to have been an unduly optimistic judgment even at the time it was written. Our own discussion of trends in the National Assessment of Educational Progress (NAEP) data through 1994, published in 1997, noted the same positive trends but went on to stress that toward the end of the 1980s they were reversed and the gap began to widen again. See Stephan Thernstrom and Abigail Thernstrom, *America in Black and White: One Nation, Indivisible* (Simon and Schuster, 1997), pp. 352–58. The 1996, 1998, and 1999 NAEP results, which became available since our book went to press, strongly confirm our more pessimistic assessment. In *America in Black and White* we employed John Bishop's method for translating racial gaps in NAEP scores into estimates of the number of school years black students lagged behind their white peers. The critique of this method set forth in Jencks and Phillips, *The Black-White Test Score Gap* (pp. 26–27, 230–32) has persuaded us to abandon it in our current work. The most recent overly optimistic assessment of recent trends to appear is Marshall S. Smith, "Assessment Trends in a Contemporary Policy Context," in David W. Grissmer and J. Michael Ross, eds., *Analytic Essays in the Assessment of Student Achievement,* NCES 2000–050 (U.S. Department of Education, National Center for Education Statistics, 2000), pp. 264–72. Because the NAEP trend data have been based on relatively small samples since the mid-1980s and because their fixed format is not responsive to curricular changes, Smith focuses on the "main" NAEP assessments of the 1990s and concludes that "the scores are now moving in the right direction." But the overall gains he emphasizes seem very small to us, and he

does not indicate which—if any—of them are statistically significant. He mentions the point that interests us most in his table 4 (on reading trends for 1992–98) in just one sentence: "Note, however, that there is no evidence of the black-white gap's closing." And his discussion of table 5, on trends in mathematics for 1990–96, is similarly succinct on this matter: "Again, there is no sign of a reduction in the gap." Given that much of Smith's essay focuses on the racial gap in academic achievement, consigning the bad news to two brief sentences seems curious.

6. Hedges and Nowell, "Black-White Test Score Convergence since 1965," p. 155.

7. David Grissmer, Ann Flanagan, and Stephanie Williamson, "Why Did the Black-White Test Score Gap Converge in the 1970s and 1980s?" in Christopher Jencks and Meredith Phillips, ed., *The Black-White Test Score Gap* (Brookings, 1998), quote on p. 186.

8. The results of an earlier mathematics assessment, in 1973, cannot be used here; likewise with the science assessments of 1968–70 and 1973. The only results for these years that are available for gauging trends by race are extrapolated, and no standard deviations are available for them.

9. Some educational researchers believe that the NAEP trend data we rely upon here are so problematic that no one can be sure what has happened since the late 1980s, except that progress in narrowing the gap unquestionably came to a halt. But the widening in the gap that we see is, in most cases, large enough to be statistically significant. If the NAEP trend data are as deficient as some suggest, there would be little point in any elaborate statistical analyses of what they might reveal about the issue. But in the absence of alternative evidence, NAEP is what we have to work with, and we think that the patterns we describe do exist, though it certainly would be better to have more solid evidence.

10. David J. Armor, "Why Is Black Educational Achievement Rising?" *Public Interest*, no. 108 (Summer 1992), pp. 65–80.

11. David W. Grissmer and others, *Improving Student Achievement: What State NAEP Test Scores Tell Us*, MR–924–EDU (Santa Monica, Calif.: RAND Corporation, 2000).

12. Kirk A. Johnson's recent analysis of reading scores from the 1998 NAEP also calls into question the Grissmer hypothesis. Johnson finds no statistically significant benefit from small class size. See Kirk A. Johnson, *Do Small Classes Influence Academic Achievement? What the National Assessment of Educational Progress Shows* (Washington: Heritage Foundation, June 2000.)

13. For the latest word from a leading skeptic, see Eric A. Hanushek, "Evidence, Politics, and the Class Size Debate," Stanford University, Department of Economics, March 2001.

14. We focus here on schools in the inner city, where the problem is most severe. But black students are underachieving in suburban settings as well. For an analysis of the issue in Shaker Heights, Ohio, see Ronald F. Ferguson, "A Diagnostic Analysis of

Black-White GPA Disparities in Shaker Heights, Ohio," *Brookings Papers on Education Policy, 2001* (Brookings, 2001), pp. 347–96.

15. Quotations by Rafe Esquith, fifth-grade teacher, Hobart Elementary School, Central Los Angeles, and David Levin, principal, KIPP Academy Charter School, New York, made in personal communications with the authors or made to their students.

16. Data from the website of the Los Angeles Unified School District and from Rafe Esquith (www.lausd.k12.ca.us/[January 2001]).

17. The College Board, *Reaching the Top: A Report of the National Task Force on Minority High Achievement* (New York: College Board Publications, October 1999).

18. The College Board, *Reaching the Top*, pp. 7, 14, 17, 18.

19. Laurence Steinberg, *Beyond the Classroom: Why School Reform Has Failed and What Parents Need to Do* (Simon and Schuster, 1996), p. 86.

20. On this perspective, see the views of Anne Swidler, which are ably summarized and applied to schooling issues in George Farkas, *Human Capital or Cultural Capital? Ethnicity and Poverty Groups in an Urban School District* (New York: Aldine de Gruyter, 1996), pp. 11–13.

21. Reynolds Farley, Sheldon Danziger, and Harry J. Holzer, *Detroit Divided* (New York: Russell Sage Foundation, 2000), table 5.7, p. 142.

22. "Brookings Papers on Education Policy Conference on National Standards," unpublished transcript, Brookings Institution, Brown Center on Education Policy, May 15-16, 2000.

23. In strenuously combating the notion that academic work has a "whites only" sign on it, Rafe Esquith and KIPP are creating an alternative high-achieving peer group for their students, which, they hope, will have the additional benefit of keeping them from the clutches of a gang. For a good recent description of the hazards of gang life for young black males, see Orlando Patterson, *Rituals of Blood: Consequences of Slavery in Two American Centuries* (New York: Basic Civitas, 1998), pp. 137–45.

24. Farley, Danziger, and Holzer, *Detroit Divided*.

25. Sandy Banks, "Disney Awards Teacher with a Touch of Class," *Los Angeles Times*, December 6, 1992, p. B1.

26. In a 1990 study, Roslyn Mickelson found that black students believe that "achievement and effort in school lead to job success later on." But they were more doubtful when asked about the likelihood of fair treatment in the workplace. Cited in Ronald F. Ferguson, "Teachers' Perceptions and Expectations and the Black-White Test Score Gap," in Christopher Jencks and Meredith Phillips, eds., *The Black-White Test Score Gap* (Brookings, 1998), pp. 292–93.

27. Quoted in Richard Rothstein, "The Growing Revolt against the Testers," *New York Times*, May 30, 2001, p. A19.

28. Steinberg, *Beyond the Classroom*, passim.

29. Ralph Ellison, "The World and the Jug," in John F. Callahan, ed., *The Collected Essays of Ralph Ellison* (New York: Modern Library, 1995), p. 164.

30. Ralph Ellison, "The Shadow and the Act," in John F. Callahan, ed., *The Collected Essays* (New York: Modern Library, 1995), p. 299.

31. Ellison, "The Shadow and the Act," p. 57.

32. Ralph Ellison, "Indivisible Man," in John F. Callahan, ed., *The Collected Essays* (New York: Modern Library, 1995), p. 394; and " 'A Completion of Personality': A Talk with Ralph Ellison," in John F. Callahan, ed., *The Collected Essays* (New York: Modern Library, 1995), p. 799.

8

High Achievement in Mathematics: Lessons from Three Los Angeles Elementary Schools

DAVID KLEIN

W hat can elementary schools do to promote high achievement in mathematics for their students? While much knowledge has been gained in recent years about the teaching of reading, relatively little is known about what constitutes effective mathematics programs.

This paper describes characteristics and policies of three low-income schools with unusually successful mathematics programs in the Los Angeles area. It should be conceded from the outset that this is not a scientific study, and any conclusions and recommendations for the establishment of successful mathematics programs in this report are necessarily speculative. The descriptions of the mathematics programs that follow are based on my conversations with the principals and some teachers at these schools and on site visits.

This report also identifies and discusses barriers to student achievement in mathematics, which exist for a great number of schools in the Los Angeles area. The observations in this regard stem from my work with the Los Angeles County Office of Education (LACOE) between July 1, 1999, and June 30, 2000. During that year, I took a leave of absence from my normal duties as a professor of mathematics at California State University–Northridge to serve as a mathematics consultant for LACOE. My responsibilities during that time included directing eight math specialists toward increasing student achievement in mathematics in Los Angeles County schools and making teachers and administrators aware of the California state mathematics standards and a variety of educational resources to support them.

Three High-Achieving Elementary Schools

Robert Hill Lane Elementary School is located in Monterey Park and is part of the Los Angeles Unified School District (LAUSD). Bennett-Kew Elementary School and William H. Kelso Elementary School are part of the Inglewood Unified School District, located near the Los Angeles International Airport. These schools are exceptional. Among elementary schools with 95 percent or more of the students tested on California's Standardized Testing and Reporting (STAR) exam, 25 percent or more of the student body categorized as Limited English Proficient (LEP), and at least 70 percent of the students on free or reduced-price lunch, Kelso ranked highest in the state in terms of the Academic Proficiency Index (API) score, Bennett-Kew was the second highest, and Robert Hill Lane Elementary was the fourth highest in California in 1999.[1] Spring 2000 Stanford Achievement Test, Ninth Edition (SAT-9) average percentile scores by grade level are summarized in table 8-1.

At Robert Hill Lane, 90 percent of the student body is Latino, 36 percent of students are not fluent in English, and 85 percent qualify for free or reduced-price lunch. Yet the school's performance in mathematics is typical of relatively affluent schools.

The entire Inglewood Unified School District has received national attention because of the high academic achievement of its elementary schools and the modest resources of the student population.[2] Almost 75 percent of Inglewood's elementary students qualify for subsidized lunches, a standard measure of poverty among schoolchildren, and 45 percent of the teachers hold emergency credentials. More than one-third of the students are not fluent in English, and 98 percent of the student population is Latino or African American. At Bennett-Kew, 51 percent of the student body is African American, and 48 percent is Latino. Seventy-seven percent of all students qualify for free or reduced-priced lunch, and 29 percent are not fluent in English. At Kelso, 44 percent of all students are African American and 53 percent are Latino. Eighty-nine percent of all students qualify for free or reduced-priced lunch, and 34 percent are not fluent in English.

Bennett-Kew and Kelso are the two highest achieving schools in Inglewood, and they have led the district in implementing successful reforms. McKinley M. Nash, as superintendent of Inglewood Unified, organized the other elementary schools to emulate Bennett-Kew and Kelso. He pushed the district's adoption of Open Court, the reading program that Bennett-Kew

Table 8-1. *Average SAT-9 Percentile Scores, by Grade Level, Spring 2000*

School(s)	Grade two	Grade three	Grade four	Grade five
Bennett-Kew Elementary School	80	83	65	58
William E. Kelso Elementary School	81	82	69	73
Robert Hill Lane Elementary School	64	72	64	67
Los Angeles Unified School District schools	41	42	35	35
Los Angeles County schools	51	51	44	44

Note: SAT-9 = Stanford Achievement Test, Ninth Edition.

and Kelso had used for many years. He also required all elementary school principals in the district to report student reading scores to him. Those reforms began to take root in the district around 1997 as test scores started to rise in Inglewood.

Bennett-Kew

Nancy Ichinaga, the principal of Bennett-Kew until she retired in June 2000, describes the beginning of her tenure as principal as follows.

> When the scores of the first California Assessment Program at the third grade level were released in October, 1974, I had been principal at Bennett-Kew for just a little over a month. Bennett's third graders ranked at the third percentile in the state. Reacting with shock and dismay, I told the staff that the third percentile meant that: 1) 90% of our kids were retarded or 2) the Open Structure Program, in its fourth year at Bennett, was not working. The teachers admitted that their program had created a school full of illiterate children, and they were ready for a change. They agreed that they needed to teach all children to decode and encode in a structured, systematic beginning reading program. They also agreed that to make children truly literate they needed to expose them to the best of children's literature from all over the world.

To improve mathematics instruction, Ichinaga directed teachers first to study the major standardized tests for mathematics, then categorize and sequence the topics to develop a curriculum for the school. This process took several years, but the result was a program that elevated student test scores up to and beyond the 50th percentile on standardized tests. A key component to the mathematics program was that Ichinaga collected and analyzed results of diagnostic tests from teachers and responded to deficiencies in student performance. Especially significant to student success in mathematics, according to Ichinaga, is a clearly defined curriculum. The school uses direct instruction with an emphasis on basic skills as prerequisites to problem solving. Calculators are rarely, if ever, used. Parents contribute to every aspect of the school, from making curriculum and budget recommendations to painting classrooms and planting flowers.

In the fall of 1998, Bennett-Kew began a pilot program using Saxon Mathematics, a K–6 curriculum that in 1999 became one of several approved by the California State Board of Education. One class at each grade level used the curriculum, and resulting increases in student performance motivated the teachers to adopt the program schoolwide in the autumn of 1999. During the first year with the pilot program in 1998, one third-grade class in a Gifted and Talented Education (GATE) program scored on average at the 89th percentile using the old curriculum. Ichinaga and the teaching staff were surprised, however, when a regular third-grade class using the Saxon program scored at the 95th percentile that same year.

Although more than one in four students at Bennett-Kew does not speak English fluently, the school never practiced bilingual education during the decades of Nancy Ichinaga's tenure as principal. Instead, entering kindergartners are immersed in English, and those who still require help beyond that year enroll in "junior first grade," where language and math skills are also bolstered in preparation for first grade. For entering students in higher grades, there are English language development classes and bilingual aides in classrooms to assist identified students in specific content areas. As a child, Nancy Ichinaga faced similar language barriers as her own non–English speaking students. As Ichinaga explains, "My kids come to school much like I was, with very little English." She was raised in a Japanese-speaking home on a Hawaiian sugar cane plantation but attended schools that taught in English. The immediate effect of this policy on mathematics instruction is that all mathematics classes are conducted in English using the same program.

Nancy Ichinaga selected her teachers carefully, and it shows. During a visit to several classrooms at Bennett-Kew, I observed clear and well-organized instruction. The teachers exhibited warmth toward their students while simultaneously making no secret of their high expectations and demands on performance. The students appeared to understand the lessons and were able to solve problems independently. In several cases, students solved problems at the white boards at the front of the class and briefly provided cogent instruction themselves to the rest of the class. The teachers were not warned in advance of my visit.

An interesting and slightly different perspective was given to me by Juliet Anekwe, a fourth-grade teacher at Bennett-Kew. Anekwe commented that the teachers at Bennett-Kew are really no different from teachers at other schools. When I asked her to identify factors leading to Bennett-Kew's successful mathematics program, she replied, "Perhaps a significant factor in the school's success is the fact that we work together and we are very structured as a team. All teachers use the same textbooks, and this was encouraged and enforced by Mrs. Ichinaga." Other schools allow different programs even within the same grade level, or they impose ineffective or even damaging programs on teachers.

Not all teachers can accept the kind of environment one finds at Bennett-Kew. Newly credentialled teachers from prestigious universities are sometimes turned away after a semester or two. Education college doctrine is often at odds with what works at Bennett-Kew, and Ichinaga has found that in some cases noncredentialled teachers provide better instruction than credentialled ones.

Kelso

Marjorie Thompson was the principal at Kelso Elementary School for more than two decades until she retired in February 2000. She and Nancy Ichinaga have been friends for many years and developed similar policies at their schools. In 1988 Nancy Ichinaga shared the curriculum developed at Bennett-Kew with Marjorie Thompson. Both started using Open Court for reading in the mid-1980s, and both schools have similar policies such as "junior first grade" and close cooperation with parents in educational programs. The capable new principal at Kelso, Jacqueline Moore, was head of the Reading Alliance program sponsored by the Packard Humanities Foundation, and she spent time at Bennett-Kew. As with Bennett-Kew, Kelso has a strong focus on basic skills, and calculators are rarely used. Kelso also rejected bilingual education two decades before California voters ended it through Proposition 227 on June 2, 1998.

While principal, Marjorie Thompson tested all new entering nonkindergarten students to place them in appropriate grade-level classes. Thompson required parents to be present at those placement sessions. During the height of the whole language era, she estimates that roughly 80 percent of the new students were placed at a lower grade level at Kelso than they would have been if they had continued at their previous schools. Principal Jacqueline Moore continues this placement policy with parental agreement.

Kelso has some distinguishing features that undoubtedly contribute to its high test scores. More than an hour each day is devoted to mathematics instruction. Some fourth- and fifth-grade teachers are paid to stay an extra forty-five minutes at the end of each school day to provide additional instruction. Each morning begins with twenty to thirty minutes devoted to reviewing concepts and skills in reading, math, and language. Marjorie Thompson has for years recognized the value of repeated exposure to topics in mathematics. A topic is usually reviewed during at least two of the morning sessions of the week; it is presented and reviewed less frequently thereafter. In this respect, the program at Kelso is similar to the Saxon math program used at Bennett-Kew; repeated exposure and review is an important component of both mathematics programs. Kelso uses a standard curriculum from the publisher Silver-Burdett-Ginn with supplementary material from "Excel Math" of AnsMar Publishers and materials generated within the school.

Instruction at Kelso is data-driven. Kelso conducts regular uniform diagnostic assessments for reading and mathematics as part of its curriculum. Thompson has considered the effect of a strong reading program on mathematics performance. She suggests that language mastery facilitates the mental trial-and-error methods upon which solving math problems depends. Literary abilities and mastery of the language contribute to mathematical proficiency, and therefore a strong reading program aids mathematics instruction in fundamental ways. Principal Moore concurs with this point of view, and both principals firmly believe that high expectations of students are essential to produce high achievement in both language and mathematics.

Kelso has four year-round tracks. Up to two-thirds of students in third through fifth grade attend math classes during the interim sessions, while other children on the same tracks at different schools are on vacation. Some intersession classes are devoted solely to math. Kelso teachers who are off-track work as substitute teachers at Kelso as needed and also supply instruction during the interim sessions. In this way, Kelso teachers contribute to the overall consistency and uniformity of instruction. As with Nancy Ichinaga, Marjorie Thompson was highly selective in hiring teachers for her school and found that noncredentialled teachers sometimes perform better in the classroom than credentialled teachers, even when their degrees come from prestigious universities. In several cases, newly hired credentialled teachers followed their college of education training by opposing direct instruction and not giving sufficient attention to basic skills. Those teachers left the school when it became clear that they were not meeting standards set by Principal Thompson. I asked the vice principal at Kelso, Clark Osborne, what he believed to be the most important factor in the high achievement of Kelso students in mathematics. He identified the high quality of the Kelso teachers as the single most important factor and gave full credit to Marjorie Thompson for Kelso's excellent faculty.

Robert Hill Lane

Robert Hill Lane Elementary School is the recipient of the Los Angeles Educational Excellence Award in 1999. The principal, Sue Wong, explained that for the past two years she held many meetings with teachers to find ways to improve student achievement and develop grade-level pacing plans aligned to the California standards. Every teacher at the school has a copy of the California Mathematics Framework to assist in that effort.

Sue Wong provides a handbook governing student behavior and has a student compact that includes a code of conduct listing expectations and responsibilities. Parents, students, and teachers are expected to sign this document. There is a high degree of parental involvement in the school, with 91 percent of students' parents attending parent-teacher conferences according to Wong.

About one-third of the student body is classified as Limited English Proficient. Of these students, about 80 percent use "Model A," or English immersion for instruction. Instruction is in English, but clarification is given in the primary language of the students. The remaining 20 percent of LEP students receive instruction using "Model B," which includes instruction in English, but also includes occasional previews of lessons in Spanish.

Robert Hill Lane emphasizes systematic, direct instruction and the teaching of basic skills in mathematics. Calculators are rarely used. Like Nancy Ichinaga and Marjorie Thompson, Principal Wong conducts extensive hiring interviews for teachers, and she is very selective. She finds that sometimes noncredentialled teachers are better in the classroom than credentialled teachers. For kindergarten through second grade, the school uses a curriculum by Scott-Foresman. In subsequent grades, teachers use a Silver-Burdett-Ginn curriculum, but Robert Hill Lane plans to buy a California state-approved supplementary math program aligned to the California mathematics standards.

Robert Hill Lane employs a school-based management system and works on a LEARN (Los Angeles Educational Alliance for Restructuring Now) calendar, so it does not operate year-round. The school has an intervention program with after-school tutoring and two hours of Saturday classes with one hour for reading and one hour for math. Students in the intervention program are identified by test scores from an assessment created by the teachers and other forms of teacher evaluation. The tutors come from the Math and

Engineering Club of East Los Angeles College and from Garfield High School during the high school's off-track periods.

Barriers to Mathematics Achievement

There are many barriers to student achievement in mathematics beyond the control of school districts. Poverty is the most debilitating. In the eighty school districts within the boundaries of Los Angeles County, there are tens of thousands of public school children who are homeless. For such children the very concept of homework is problematic, and the heart-wrenching effects of their day-to-day plight cannot be completely compensated by the limited resources of schools. Beyond these extreme cases, there are multitudes of other children who are not homeless, but their sources of support are meager. Many schoolchildren have unschooled single mothers with only limited knowledge of the English language, holding down two or three low-paying jobs in order to support their children. Though not commensurate with the scale of poverty in Los Angeles, the heroic efforts of legions of teachers who dedicate time, energy, and their own limited resources to helping such children should be acknowledged and honored.

Despite these barriers, schools are not powerless. Bennett-Kew, Kelso, and Robert Hill Lane, whose poverty rates range from 77 percent to 89 percent, clearly demonstrate that high levels of academic achievement for children are attainable and should be expected, regardless of their social standing and ethnicity.

There are important barriers to student achievement in mathematics that are self-imposed by school districts and that could easily be eliminated. During my conversations with them, the principals of Bennett-Kew, Kelso, and Robert Hill Lane were adamant in their insistence on holding students to high expectations. They were dismissive of excuses and highly directed toward results. This is a key factor in their academic successes, and it deserves further illumination because declaring one's high expectations for all students by itself is of little value.

No one declares low expectations for girls or minority students. Such a pronouncement would be unthinkable for any responsible school administrator. But administrators do embrace the notion of different learning styles correlated with gender and ethnicity, and the result is much the same: expectations are lowered. Jack Price, a former president of the National Council of Teachers of Mathematics (NCTM), in 1996 expressed the views of many administrators and local math curriculum specialists.

What we have now is nostalgia math. It is the mathematics that we have always had, that is good for the most part for the relatively high socio-economic anglo male, and that we have a great deal of research that has been done showing that women, for example, and minority groups do not learn the same way. They have the capability, certainly, of learning, but they don't. The teaching strategies that you use with them are different from those that we have been able to use in the past when young people—we weren't expected to graduate a lot of people, and most of those who did graduate and go on to college were the anglo males. . . .

All of the research that has been done with gender differences or ethnic differences has been—males for example learn better deductively in a competitive environment, when—the kind of thing that we have done in the past. Where we have found with gender differences, for example, that women have a tendency to learn better in a collaborative effort when they are doing inductive reasoning.[3]

The view that African Americans, Latinos, and girls have learning styles for mathematics different from the learning style of white males (and presumably Asians of both genders) has contributed to the creation and widespread use of low-quality mathematics textbooks and curricula in the United States—and in the Los Angeles area in particular. Many of these curricula radically deemphasize basic skills in arithmetic and algebra, as well as deductive mathematical arguments and proofs. They tend to emphasize inductive reasoning, with a particular focus on extending patterns. Such activities have little or no mathematical significance. Extensive use of calculators is promoted at all grade levels, even at the kindergarten level in some cases, where kindergartners are encouraged to use calculators to learn to count.[4] Such approaches are advertised as math for all students, as opposed to white males, but the word *all* is a code word for minority students or girls and women or both. These curricula attempt to redefine mathematics in a way that is accessible to different learning styles. The federal government has actively funded the creation and distribution of these programs, sometimes referred to as *integrated math*, *reform math*, *new new math*, or *whole math*. The last designation draws an analogy to the whole language approach to teaching reading.

In October 1999, the U.S. Department of Education released a list of ten integrated math programs that it designated as "exemplary" or "promising." The following month, I sent an open letter coauthored with mathematicians

Richard Askey, R. James Milgram, and Hung-Hsi Wu, with more than two hundred other cosigners to U.S. education secretary Richard Riley urging him to withdraw the Department of Education's recommendations.[5] Among the endorsers are many of the nation's most accomplished scientists and mathematicians. Sixteen department heads, including the chairs of the math departments at California Institute of Technology, Stanford University, Harvard University, and Yale University, along with two former presidents of the Mathematical Association of America, added their names in support. Seven Nobel laureates and winners of the Fields Medal, the highest international award in mathematics, and several prominent state and national education leaders also cosigned the open letter. The open letter was well covered in the national press and appeared as a full-page ad in the *Washington Post* on November 18, 1999.

Among the programs criticized in the open letter is an elementary school program called MathLand. This program is based on student discovery and has no student texts for any of the grades kindergarten through grade six. It makes excessive use of calculators and does not develop the foundations of arithmetic. It does not even include instruction on the standard algorithm for multiplication. MathLand has become a target of ridicule among university mathematicians and dissatisfied parents.[6] It is not a state-adopted mathematics program, and it is not aligned to the California mathematics standards on which students are tested. Yet, MathLand has been heavily promoted by LAUSD math education specialists who continue to advise the Los Angeles Board of Education. Several LAUSD math education specialists have opposed the California mathematics content standards, and yet they are called upon to implement those standards.[7]

The Achievement Council is a nonprofit organization in Los Angeles dedicated to improving the achievement of minority students. The Achievement Council advises the Los Angeles school board about mathematics curricula and other matters, and it receives funding from LAUSD as well as from several private foundations. The Achievement Council has taken a public position in support of integrated math programs not aligned to the California mathematics standards on the grounds that they are somehow better for minority students. The organization explicitly defends MathLand, and the LAUSD board president, Genethia Hayes, has publicly aligned herself with the mathematics policies of the Achievement Council.[8] The 1999–2000 interim superintendent, Ramon Cortines, ordered LAUSD schools not to purchase new state-adopted mathematics programs for the school year beginning in fall 2000, even for grades K–3, where the materials are mostly consumable. MathLand elementary schools were required to remain MathLand elementary schools for at least another year. In the spring of 2000, the LAUSD board supported Cortines's mandate even in the face of contradictory advice from Nancy Ichinaga, now a member of the California State Board of Education; Barry Simon, the chair of the mathematics department at Caltech; Jaime Escalante, of *Stand and Deliver* fame; and many others. Principal Sue Wong explained to me during an interview that she was limited by the LAUSD mandate to purchasing only supplemental materials for mathematics for the school year beginning in fall 2000. Thus, a majority of LAUSD students are required to use inferior curricular materials, partly on the supposition that what works for white males is inappropriate for minority students. Sadly, LAUSD is not the only Los Angeles area school district that continues such misguided policies.

In addition to the use of deficient mathematics programs and curricula, there is another important barrier to student achievement in mathematics, again self-imposed by school districts. Many, and perhaps most, mathematics curriculum specialists are mathematically weak. They give bad advice, not only because they support a misguided notion of learning styles for minority students and girls, but also because they simply do not understand mathematics very well themselves. Their level of understanding is generally far below that of classroom mathematics teachers in the schools they serve.[9] The mechanism leading to this paradoxical state of affairs is that the weakest math teachers are usually the first to embrace education fads and are consequently rewarded by principals and other administrators for their willingness to be innovative. Unfortunately, innovation for its own sake has a higher priority than proven effectiveness for most administrators. The result is that the least competent teachers advise senior administrators and gain authority over mathematics programs in the schools. A particularly unfortunate consequence is that the staff development programs and in-services for math teachers are typically of low quality.

The growing pressure on teachers to incorporate computers and the Internet in their daily instruction, whether it does any good or not, also interferes with effective instruction. The California Mathematics Framework warns against the overuse of technology in mathematics instruction.[10] According to an informal estimate published in the *Los Angeles Times*, "Sixty percent of the eighth-graders in L.A. Unified, it is estimated, do not yet know their multiplication tables."[11] Flooding classrooms with expensive, advanced technology when a substantial proportion of middle- and upper-grade students in Los Angeles have not mastered basic arithmetic may create future customers of technology, but it will not address fundamental shortcomings in mathematics education.

The Simplicity of Success

During my discussions with Nancy Ichinaga, Marjorie Thompson, and Sue Wong, I asked them in a variety of different ways why they were so successful. On more than one occasion, they each explained (separately) that they did not think they were doing anything special. All of these outstanding principals wondered why other schools do not do better by simply using common sense.

There are three fundamental ingredients for student achievement in mathematics:

1. A clear set of high-quality grade-by-grade standards.
2. Textbooks and curricula for teachers and students that are aligned to the standards.
3. Sufficiently high teacher knowledge of mathematics to teach to the standards.

The first ingredient is free. The California mathematics standards are clear and specific, and they are held in high regard by university mathematicians and experts on educational standards. The Fordham Foundation ranked them the best mathematics standards in the nation.[12] As for the second ingredient, the California State Board of Education has approved specific textbooks aligned to the standards, and state funds are provided for schools to purchase them. Unfortunately, because of the resistance of senior administrators, making these resources available to children has been problematic. The third ingredient, increased teacher knowledge, is difficult to attain, but under California's Assembly Bill 1331, good programs and funding for professional training are available.[13] Clearly, teachers need to know more mathematics than what they expect students to learn. Here again, senior administrators and their mathematics education advisers have resisted making sound, content-oriented training available to classroom teachers, especially in LAUSD.

At the school level, leadership from the principal is essential for a school to implement an effective mathematics program. During my discussions with Principals Nancy Ichinaga, Marjorie Thompson, Sue Wong, and Jacqueline Moore, I was struck by their own probing inquisitiveness and interest in improving their schools' mathematics performance beyond what they had already achieved. In contrast to the defensiveness one often encounters in principals from low-achieving schools, these principals pursue new ideas, but at the same time they are decisive in their rejections of faddish programs that are not likely to promote high academic achievement.

Los Angeles County's fifth-grade SAT-9 math scores rank it fiftieth among the fifty-eight counties in California. LAUSD, the largest school district in

California, includes slightly less than half of all students in Los Angeles County, and LAUSD math scores are well below the county average. With the spring 2000 appointment of Nancy Ichinaga to the California State Board of Education, a culture of genuinely high expectations could gain a foothold in Los Angeles schools. It is difficult to imagine an education leader more capable of moving schools beyond the mere rhetoric of high achievement and guiding them directly to its substance. However, without the support of local district school boards, little will change. School board members would do well to demand the implementation of math curricula aligned with the California standards and to dismiss administrators who cling to the empty rhetoric and dismal failures of the past decade.

Notes

1. I am indebted to Professor Wayne Bishop of the mathematics department at California State University, Los Angeles for the collection and analysis of these data.

2. Duke Helfand, "Inglewood Writes Book on Success," *Los Angeles Times*, April 30, 2000, p. A1.

3. Radio interview, Jack Price, National Council of Teachers of Mathematics president; John Saxon, independent textbook publisher; and Mike McKeown, cofounder of "Mathematically Correct," KSDO, April 24, 1996. The radio show on mathematics education, hosted by Roger Hedgecock, was held in conjunction with the annual meeting of the National Council of Teachers of Mathematics, in San Diego, California, 1996 (mathematicallycorrect.com/roger.htm [August 1, 2000]). For examples of learning styles correlated with race and gender, see, David Klein, "Big Business, Race, and Gender in Mathematics Reform," in Steven Krantz, ed., *How to Teach Mathematics*, 2d ed. (Providence, R.I.: American Mathematical Society, 1999). A more recent defense of differing learning styles and the math curricula based on them was given by Judith Sunley, interim assistant director of the National Science Foundation, in "Intersections in Mathematics and Education: Learning, Teaching, Creating, Using," *Notices of the American Mathematical Society*, vol. 47, no. 6 (June/July 2000), pp. 658–61.

4. David Klein, "Math Problems: Why the U.S. Department of Education's Recommended Math Programs Don't Add Up," *American School Board Journal*, vol. 187, no. 4 (April 2000) (www.mathematicallycorrect.com/usnoadd.htm [August 1, 2000]).

5. "An Open Letter to United States Secretary of Education, Richard Riley," November 1999 (www.mathematicallycorrect.com/riley.htm [August 1, 2000]).

6. See, for example, Martin Scharlemann, "Open Letter on MathLand," October 11, 1996 (mathematicallycorrect.com/ml1.htm [August 1, 2000]).

7. Michael McKeown and others, "The National Science Foundation Systemic Initiatives: How a Small Amount of Federal Money Promotes Ill-Designed Mathe-

matics and Science Programs in K–12 and Undermines Local Control of Education," in Sandra Stotsky, ed., *What's at Stake in the K–12 Standards Wars: A Primer for Educational Policy Makers* (New York: Peter Lang Publishing, 2000).

8. David R. Baker, "Math-Teaching Issue Debated," *Los Angeles Daily News*, May 3, 2000.

9. For a partial history of the opposition from mathematics specialists and education leaders to the teaching of long division and standard arithmetic procedures in elementary school, see David Klein and R. James Milgram, "The Role of Long Division in the K–12 Curriculum" (ftp://math.stanford.edu/pub/papers/milgram/long-division/longdivsiondone.htm [August 1, 2000])

10. "Chapter 9: The Use of Technology," in Janet Lundin and Sheila Bruton with Catherine Barkett and Mary Sprague, eds., *Mathematics Framework for California Public Schools: Kindergarten through Grade Twelve* (California Department of Education, 1999) (www.cde.ca.gov/cdepress/schoolbag/events.html [August 1, 2000]).

11. Quoted in Richard Colvin, "Debate over How to Teach Math Takes Cultural Turn," *Los Angeles Times*, March 17, 2000, p. A1.

12. Ralph A. Raimi and Lawrence S. Braden, *State Mathematics Standards*, Fordham Foundation report, vol. 2, no. 3 (March 1998) (www.edexcellence.net/standards/math.html [August 1, 2000]).

13. For example, the Winning Equation program for fourth- to seventh-grade teachers was developed by the Curriculum and Instruction Steering Committee of the California County Superintendents Educational Service Association. As a referee, I recommended approval of this program to the California State Board of Education. The program was subsequently approved and has been widely used outside of the Los Angeles Unified School District.

9

Tracking and the Achievement Gap

SAMUEL R. LUCAS AND ADAM GAMORAN

Education policy writers often call for eliminating tracking as part of a strategy of reducing racial inequality in education.[1] Yet, many national and regional studies have shown that blacks are more likely to be assigned to the college track than are whites, once achievement and social background are controlled.[2] Adam Gamoran and Robert D. Mare replicated this common finding, but the implications for achievement were clearer because they used statistical models that accounted for the nonrandom assignment of students to tracks.[3] In this context, their finding that black students were more likely to be enrolled in college preparatory programs than whites of equivalent achievement and family background implied that tracking produces less net black-white inequality than would obtain in the absence of tracking. This particular conclusion has major implications for efforts to reduce racial gaps in test scores.

However, a potentially serious weakness of Gamoran and Mare's study was its reliance on self-reported indicators of students' track locations. Because tracking was measured by asking students what program they were in, one may question whether the assignment pattern favoring blacks reflected differences in the curricula followed by blacks and whites or if it resulted from differences in how blacks and whites perceive their curricular programs. This issue reflects a larger concern with the way tracking has been measured in U.S. survey studies.

In response to this limitation, Samuel R. Lucas and Adam Gamoran used structural measures of track location based on students' course taking to reassess the Gamoran and Mare finding.[4] In addition, they investigated the relationship between the self-report, the structural measure, and race/ethnicity. Lucas and Gamoran found a complex relationship between these factors and, in contrast to Gamoran and Mare, no net effects of race on assignment to the college track. Given that Lucas and Gamoran used the same data set that Gamoran and Mare analyzed, they concluded that findings concerning race and track assignment were sensitive to the measure of track location used.

In this paper, we use data from a cohort of 1990 sophomores to update the Lucas and Gamoran analysis. An updated investigation of these issues is potentially useful because changes in tracking, under way before 1981, have only continued. In the aftermath of *A Nation at Risk,* published in 1983, many state legislatures pushed schools to require more coursework of students. Other waves of reform attempted to increase the academic concentration of students. These policy efforts may have reshaped the landscape students navigate and may have had complex implications for whether and how tracking matters for racial inequality in test scores.

For tracking to play an important role in the black-white test score gap, two facts must hold. First, blacks must differ from whites in their likelihood of assignment to the college track. To assess this possibility we investigate the determinants of track assignment. Second, track location must matter for achievement. We assess this possibility by estimating models of mathematics achievement that account for the nonrandom process of track assignment. Before these investigations we reconsider the relationship between self-reported and course-based indicators (CBIs) of track location as well as the possible role of race/ethnicity in that relationship. Throughout the analysis we also address Hispanic status and attempt to assess both the specific findings for the more recent cohort and the extent to which those findings duplicate or diverge from the previous research.

Race and Track Assignment

Little is clear about the impact of race and ethnicity on course enrollment. In a sample from Wisconsin, Robert M. Hauser, William Sewell, and Duane Alwin derived tracking indicators from coursework data but did not examine racial or ethnic differences.[5] Michael Garet and Brian Delany found mixed results when predicting students' math and science tenth-grade course enrollments in four California high schools.[6] Controlling for prior achievement, black students were more likely than whites to take general math (the lowest level), but blacks were also more likely to be found in advanced math (the highest level), with not taking math as the reference category. Black students' net probability of enrolling in general science was lower than that of whites. There were no marked differences comparing Hispanics and non-Hispanic whites in either subject. In contrast, Jeannie Oakes argued that black and Hispanic students have less access than others to high-status math and science courses such as calculus and physics.[7] However, this finding was based on gross differences in enrollment rates and did not take into account students' socioeconomic or cognitive backgrounds. It is not clear whether Oakes's finding differs from that produced by self-reported data, because the self-reports of 1980 sophomores also show disadvantages for blacks and Hispanics if socioeconomic status and previous achievement are ignored.[8] Walter Secada suggested that blacks' apparent track-assignment advantage may reflect differences in the schools attended by blacks and whites.[9] However, Gamoran and Mare took into account the racial and ethnic compositions of the schools in their sample.[10] We do so as well.

An alternative claim is that tracking works so early in the educational system that a study of high school tracking cannot assess the effect of track location on achievement or racial inequality in achievement. Clearly studies that link multiple stages of the educational system are to be encouraged. And, change in tracking regimes may make it difficult, if not impossible, to piece together findings from different studies based on different cohorts and ages. However, some of the evidence suggests that no net association exists between race and track assignment in elementary school and in middle school.[11] Thus, in this analysis we concentrate on the high school, but owing to changes in tracking we also call for continued study of different stages of the educational system, ideally with nationally representative data from a single cohort.

Tracking in U.S. High Schools

Such research will need to respond to changes in tracking while maintaining comparable measures based on past survey research. Fortunately, survey researchers have asked comparable interview questions for decades.

The survey question typically used in American studies assumes that high school tracking has a fairly simple tripartite structure, consisting of academic or college preparatory, general, and vocational programs. For example, the High School and Beyond survey asked, "Which of the following best describes your high school program?"[12] Students in response were required to indicate only one category. Although this explicit structure may have been prevalent at one time, by the 1980s it appears that most high schools did not have such clearly marked tracks.[13] The word *tracking* was generally avoided, and students tended to be divided on a subject-by-subject basis instead of for all subjects at once.[14] In a study of Boston, Chicago, New York, and Philadelphia, D. R. Moore and S. Davenport reported that

> in 1965, all four school systems had a rigid tracking process in which most students were assigned to a track that defined all of their courses. Subsequently, such formal tracks were abolished, but the reality of tracking has been preserved in many schools through a variety of mechanisms.[15]

Thus, between 1965 and 1975 both the formal labels and the programmatic assignment procedures of high school tracking apparently were discarded in many districts. Thus, by 1980, Jeannie Oakes was able to state that, out of twelve secondary schools in her national study of tracking in the United States, only four maintained the traditional form of broad program assignment.[16] The dismantling of overarching tracks continued apace in the 1990s, such that by 1991 National Center for Education Statistics survey data covering a nationally representative sample of 912 public secondary schools revealed that 85 percent of schools had neither the records nor the practices that would allow school personnel to identify students' track location.[17]

These structural changes raise ambiguity about the meaning of students' responses to the survey question. Because students are not formally divided into tracks, it is not clear what basis they use to decide which category best describes their high school programs. One possibility is that students who think they are going to college describe their program as "college preparatory," whereas those who have not thought about college call their program "general." With respect to race differences in track assignment, black students may be more likely to describe their programs as academic because, other things being equal, they are more likely to anticipate entering college. This notion is supported by previous work showing higher educational plans among blacks as compared with whites of similar achievement and family background.[18]

Structural and Social-Psychological Dimensions of Tracking

Despite the ambiguity of present-day tracking systems, one may still argue that students' reports of their track positions provide essential data. Adam

Gamoran suggested that, because students often select their courses in high schools, students' perceptions of tracking may be better predictors of achievement and attainment than school reports.[19] Tracking as measured by self-reports has been shown to exert one of the strongest and longest-lasting school-related influences on long-term educational attainment.[20] Hence, it seems unwise to dismiss self-reports as merely perceptual.

Instead, we suggest that student-reported track indicators may tap the social-psychological dimension of tracking. Writers have claimed that tracking affects achievement in part because it differentiates students in their attitudes toward school and their values toward education. Students located in high-status positions tend to accept the demands of schooling as legitimate and conform, whereas students in the lower ranks more often turn away from academic work.[21] To the extent that track effects operate by leading some students to work hard in the courses they take while leading others away from academic aspirations, self-reported data appear to be useful indicators.

At the same time, self-reports are weaker measures of the structural dimension of tracking. As a system for dividing students into organizational subunits, tracking physically separates groups of students from one another, and this structural differentiation has implications for educational outcomes. Observers report that students attending different courses are exposed to different instructional regimes, with high-track students learning more complex material at a faster pace from teachers who are more enthusiastic and who spend more time preparing.[22] Moreover, students located in different curricular programs tend to form different friendship networks, which may affect their attitudes toward schooling and their aspirations for the future.[23] Given the absence of formal labels, asking students which categories best describe their curricular programs provides an imprecise measure of such structural differentiation.

A more direct way of identifying the structural aspects of tracking is by examining the courses in which students have enrolled.[24] Typically, high schools offer courses at a variety of levels, such as honors, regular, and remedial. In some subjects, students are also differentiated by their rate of progress through curricular sequences.[25] In math, for example, those who have taken geometry may be admitted to algebra II, while those who have completed algebra I enroll in geometry, and so on. By the end of four years, students who started farther up the ladder have had the opportunity to progress farther.[26]

Students' course sequences can give rise to a variety of structural indicators. First, courses may be aggregated to describe an overall program of study.

Which students took four years of English, three years of math and science, and two years of foreign language? This might be viewed as a college preparatory program, analogous to the self-report except that it is based on students' actual positions in the school's curricular hierarchy.[27] Alternatively, because students tend to be assigned on a subject-by-subject basis, it may be more useful to examine the effects of completing a college preparatory sequence in a particular subject, on outcomes in that subject alone. A third possibility is viewing courses as completely disaggregated: Which students enrolled in honors English? Who took courses in algebra, geometry, trigonometry, and so on? How did enrollment in these specific courses affect subject-specific outcomes? Whereas the indicator of an overall program may be preferred on grounds of parsimony, the disaggregated measure may capture the curricular structure more fully. While we agree that a variety of approaches are worthy of investigation owing to the potential complexity of race and track assignment, given the existing state of knowledge as well as the different positions in the debate on tracking, study of dichotomous, summary track location is a worthwhile focus for addressing the questions posed herein. Thus, our analyses used a summary indicator of college-track location.

Still, this course-based approach contrasts with that of James E. Rosenbaum who, in comparing 1972 track reports from students and school personnel, termed the former "perceived track" and the latter "actual track."[28] Although Rosenbaum's approach may have been appropriate at the time, the absence of formal tracks in most contemporary schools means that in more recent data there would be ambiguity about school reports just as there is about student reports. Unlike school reports, course-based indicators can be held to the same standard across schools, avoiding the ambiguity caused by possible differences among schools in what it means to identify a given student's program as college preparatory.

Thus, whereas self-reports appear adequate as indicators of the social-psychological aspects of tracking, they may fail to address the structure of tracking as reflected in students' academic experiences. Course-based indicators of tracking may measure the structure more precisely and fully. Instead of viewing one measure as "true" and the other as "false," we maintain that the two are jointly determined, and thus we simultaneously assess their determination and their implications for outcomes. Consistent with this perspective, although we refer to students as either "correct" or "in error" and as "overreporting" or "underreporting" their track assignments, we do so only to ease the presentation of results. We do not claim that the CBI is correct and the self-reports are incorrect. The CBI may be a better measure of track location for some purposes, but it is not invariably correct.[29]

Table 9-1. *Cross-Tabulation of Sophomore Track Assignment Measures, 1980 and 1990 Sophomores*

	Course-based indicators, 1980 sophomores		Course-based indicators, 1990 sophomores	
Self-report	Noncollege	College	Noncollege	College
Noncollege	47.2	18.2	26.2	31.7
College	12.6	22.0	5.8	36.3

Note: Figures in the table report percentages of all cases in the sample that appear in each cell. For High School and Beyond (HS&B), N = 12,198 students; National Education Longitudinal Study (NELS), N = 7,404. HS&B analyses use the transcript sampling weights. See Calvin Jones and others, *High School and Beyond Transcript Survey 1982; Data File User's Manual* (U.S. Department of Education, National Center for Education Statistics, 1983). NELS analyses use the NELS panel sampling weights. See Steven J. Ingles and others, *National Education Longitudinal Study of 1988 Second Follow-up: Transcript Component Data File User's Manual* (U.S. Department of Education, National Center for Education Statistics, 1995).

Social-Psychological and Structural Track Location

Comparing the CBI with self-reports, table 9-1 shows that while slightly more 1980 sophomores underreported than overreported their track positions (18.2 percent to 12.6 percent), the gap between the incidence of underreporting and overreporting is far larger for the 1990 sophomores (31.7 percent versus 5.8 percent). Further, the incidence of discrepant reports is larger for the more recent cohort; whereas 30.8 percent of 1980 sophomores' self-reports did not match the structural indicator, 37.5 percent of 1990 sophomores' self-reports did not match the CBI. Further change between 1980 and 1990 is evident in that 68 percent of 1990 sophomores appear to be following a college prep program according to the CBI. In contrast, only 40.2 percent of 1980 sophomores were following a college prep program by the structural indicator.

The increase in college prep track enrollment is evident in all racial/ethnic groups studied (see table 9-2). Using the CBI as the measure of the college prep program, less than 30 percent of 1980 black sophomores were in the college prep; over 50 percent of 1990 black sophomores were college prep. About a quarter of 1980 Hispanic sophomores were college prep, whereas over 60 percent of 1990 Hispanic sophomores were. And while about 45 percent of 1980 white sophomores were college prep, over 70 percent of 1990 white sophomores were.

These increases in college prep course taking occur at the same time that the role of race in determining the relationship between the CBI and self-

Table 9-2. *Cross-Tabulation of Sophomore Track Assignment Measures,*
by Race/Ethnicity

Percent

Self-report, race or ethnicity	Course-based indicators, 1980 sophomores		Course-based indicators, 1990 sophomores	
	Noncollege	College	Noncollege	College
Blacks				
Noncollege	56.7	13.5	38.9	22.0
College	14.8	15.0	8.4	30.7
Hispanics				
Noncollege	62.7	14.1	32.7	29.1
College	12.0	11.1	7.0	31.3
Non-Hispanic whites				
Noncollege	43.4	19.5	24.2	32.9
College	12.2	24.8	5.3	37.7
Other nonwhites				
Noncollege	41.9	14.1	18.0	39.5
College	16.5	23.8	6.0	36.5

Note: Figures in the table report percentages of all cases in the sample that appear in each cell. For High School and Beyond (HS&B), N = 1,368 blacks, 1,499 Hispanics, 9,058 whites, and 273 other race/ethnicities. For National Education Longitudinal Study (NELS), N = 672 blacks, 835 Hispanics, 5,259 whites, and 638 other races and ethnicities. For other nonwhites, N = 638. HS&B analyses use the transcript sampling weights. See Calvin Jones and others, *High School and Beyond Transcript Survey 1982; Data File User's Manual* (U.S. Department of Education, National Center for Education Statistics, 1983). NELS analyses use the NELS panel sampling weights. See Steven J. Ingles and others, *National Education Longitudinal Study of 1988 Second Follow-up: Transcript Component Data File User's Manual* (U.S. Department of Education, National Center for Education Statistics, 1995).

report seems to have declined. In 1980 whites and Hispanics were both more likely to underreport than overreport their status, whereas blacks were more likely to overreport than underreport theirs. However, by 1990 these differences had dissipated; 1990 sophomores of all racial/ethnic groups were far more likely to underreport than overreport. In other words, the pattern of the social-psychological and structural track relation for 1990 sophomores appears to have changed between 1980 and 1990, leading to racial convergence in the relation between the social-psychological and structural dimensions of tracking.

However, the gross tendencies shown in table 9-2 may yet mask important differences that occur for students of similar socioeconomic and achievement levels. In table 9-3 we control for these factors as well as gender in a multino-

Table 9-3. *Multinomial Logit Model of Self-Reported and Course-Based Indicators of Track Location, 1990 Sophomores*

Independent variable	Self-reported noncollege track, course-based indicator noncollege track	Self-reported college track, course-based indicator noncollege track	Self-reported college track, course-based indicator college track
Intercept	4.927**	−0.839	−3.058**
	(0.872)	(1.372)	(0.727)
Mother's education	−0.052	−0.008	0.019
	(0.048)	(0.075)	(0.038)
Father's education	−0.068	−0.016	−0.005
	(0.050)	(0.079)	(0.041)
Father's occupation	−0.013	0.001	0.003
	(0.009)	(0.014)	(0.007)
Family income in 10,000s	−0.032	0.005	0.000
	(0.034)	(0.038)	(0.018)
Male	0.584**	0.445	−0.049
	(0.178)	(0.291)	(0.152)
Number of siblings	−0.006	−0.074	−0.134**
	(0.005)	(0.090)	(0.048)
Nonintact household	0.325*	0.057	0.188
	(0.183)	(0.309)	(0.166)
Black	−0.249	0.438	0.474*
	(0.272)	(0.432)	(0.267)
Hispanic	−0.442	0.060	0.223
	(0.280)	(0.465)	(0.265)
Other nonwhite	−0.790*	−0.205	−0.108
	(0.437)	(0.632)	(0.324)
1990 reading	−0.020	−0.012	0.016
	(0.015)	(0.025)	(0.013)
1990 mathematics	−0.069**	−0.013	0.017*
	(0.011)	(0.018)	(0.009)
1990 science	0.020	0.011	0.008
	(0.028)	(0.044)	(0.023)
1990 history	−0.021	−0.010	0.039
	(0.029)	(0.047)	(0.024)

* Coefficient discernibly different from zero ($0.05 < \alpha < 0.10$).

** Coefficient discernibly different from zero ($\alpha < .05$).

Note: Adjusted standard errors are in parentheses. Omitted category is self-reported noncollege track, course-based indicator college track. All analyses use the National Education Longitudinal Study panel sampling weights and a design effect of 6.75. See Steven J. Ingles and others, *National Education Longitudinal Study of 1988 Second Follow-up: Transcript Component Data File User's Manual* (U.S. Department of Education, National Center for Education Statistics, 1995). $N = 7,404$. Controls for missing data were included.

mial logit model for 1990 sophomores. To aid comparison with 1980 sophomores, an analogous table drawn from Lucas and Gamoran is replicated in
the appendix (see table 9A-1).[30] To highlight the contrast between underreporters and overreporters, we make all comparisons to the category of students who claim to be in a noncollege program while the course-based indicator assigns them to the college track (that is, underreporters).

The table suggests that the convergence in the structural track and social-
psychological track relation is not altered by controlling for potentially confounding factors. We observe a high degree of similarity in the relationship
between structural and social-psychological track location for all racial
groups. The only net racial difference we find is that, compared with underreporting, blacks are more likely than whites to correctly report that they are
following a college-track program. When they controlled for social class and
measured achievement, Lucas and Gamoran obtained a similar result but also
found that blacks and Hispanics were more likely than whites to overreport
than underreport their track location. For 1990 sophomores, we find no evidence of these latter racial differences in reporting.

Thus, the incidence of college prep course taking appears to have
increased from 1980 to 1990. The relationship between social-psychological
and structural track location seems to have changed, with comparatively
more students underreporting than overreporting and with racial groups con-
verging to the same pattern of relationship between the social-psychological
and structural track location. Yet, it remains to be seen whether this convergence has rendered the findings of studies of race and track assignment insen-
sitive to the measure used.

Race, Track Assignment, and Sensitivity
to the Indicator of Track Location

For tracking to be directly implicated in racial inequality in achievement,
race must matter in track assignment. We estimated two models with track
location as the dependent variable to address just this issue. In one model we
use the self-report, a social-psychological indicator of track location. In a second model we use a structural measure of track location, the CBI (see table
9-4). This analysis is similar to that conducted by Lucas and Gamoran (see
table 9A-2).

The result of our analysis of track location for 1990 sophomores is qualitatively similar to that of Lucas and Gamoran. They found that users of the
CBI and the self-report would reach different conclusions about the role of

Table 9-4. *Probit Models of Curricular Track Assignment for 1990 Sophomores: Comparison of Self-Reported and Course-Based Indicators*

	Track indicator	
Predictor	Self-report	Course-based indicator
Intercept	−3.457*	−3.871**
	(0.224)	(0.347)
Mother's education	0.007	0.030
	(0.012)	(0.019)
Father's education	0.010	0.020
	(0.013)	(0.020)
Father's occupation	0.001	0.004*
	(0.012)	(0.002)
Family income in 10,000s	0.002	−0.002
	(0.008)	(0.001)
Female	0.070	0.292*
	(0.042)	(0.065)
Number-of siblings	−0.053*	−0.016
	(0.015)	(0.023)
Nonintact household	0.183*	−0.046
	(0.066)	(0.099)
Black	0.232*	−0.059
	(0.079)	(0.116)
School mean socioeconomic status	0.022	0.022
	(0.044)	(0.068)
School percent minority	0.003*	0.003
	(0.001)	(0.002)

* Coefficient discernibly different from zero ($\alpha < 0.05$).

Note: Adjusted standard errors are in parentheses. Sample size is 12,471. All analyses use the National Education Longitudinal Study panel sampling weights and a design effect of 6.75. See Steven J. Ingles and others, *National Education Longitudinal Study of 1988 Second Follow-up: Transcript Component Data File User's Manual* (U.S. Department of Education, National Center for Education Statistics, 1995). Controls for missing data were included.

race in track assignment. Our results suggest that the conclusion of race-linked differences in assignment continues to be dependent upon the measure used.

Lucas and Gamoran showed that the self-report would lead analysts to conclude that net of social background and achievement blacks, Hispanics, and other nonwhites were more likely than whites to enter the college track. However, an analysis based on the CBI revealed no net racial difference in the likelihood of assignment to the college track for 1980 sophomores. Our analysis of 1990 sophomores replicates the earlier result.[31]

Tracking, Achievement, and Racial Inequality

We have maintained that the self-report and the course-based indicator tap two different and potentially important dimensions of tracking. The self-report captures the social-psychological aspect of tracking, while the CBI reflects the structural aspect. Although this is a defensible claim, it is possible that only one of these dimensions is important for achievement. To assess this possibility we estimated ordinary least squares regression models of achievement; we present results for 1982 and 1992 mathematics achievement.

Our dependent variable is drawn from work that uses common items across the National Education Longitudinal Study and High School and Beyond tests to place the two cohorts' test scores on the same metric.[32] Thus, our dependent variable is directly comparable across cohorts.

For the early 1980s cohort we find both the CBI and self-report to have a positive association with the test score (see table 9-5). This holds true for the 1990 cohort as well. However, while in 1980 the coefficients for the CBI and the self-report track are virtually equal, for the 1990 cohort the CBI coefficient is approximately three times larger. The coefficient for the self-report appears to have declined substantially in the period. Still, both coefficients are discernibly larger than zero for both cohorts, reinforcing the evidence that implies we may underestimate the effect of tracking if we rely exclusively on the social-psychological dimension.

The net racial gaps in achievement appear to have declined across the intervening decade. Although blacks and Hispanics lag behind whites and Asians once socioeconomic status and prior achievement are controlled, the chasm separating whites and Asians, on the one hand, and blacks and Hispanics, on the other, appears to have shrunk.

The results, suggestive though they are, do not take into account the nonrandom assignment of students to tracks. In tables 9-6 and 9-7 we present the results of endogenous switching regression models of track location and achievement, estimated for 1980 and 1990 sophomores respectively. The models we estimate are formally the same as the model Gamoran and Mare selected, a general model of track assignment and achievement.[33]

Table 9-6 contains the results for 1980 sophomores. Females and those with social background benefits are advantaged in track assignment, while Hispanics are disadvantaged in track assignment. Students at schools with more minorities and higher mean socioeconomic status are more likely to be enrolled in a college-track program. But blacks, Asians, and other nonwhites are neither advantaged nor disadvantaged in track assignment.

Table 9-5. *Ordinary Least Squares Regressions of Self-Reported and Course-Based Indicators of Track Location on Math Achievement, 1980 and 1990 Sophomores*

Independent variable	Dependent variable: math achievement	
	1982	1992
Intercept	11.468**	−0.634
	(0.835)	(0.684)
Black	−2.454**	−1.263**
	(0.267)	(0.228)
Hispanic	−2.812**	−0.764**
	(0.251)	(0.244)
Asian	2.487**	0.713**
	(1.043)	(0.362)
Other nonwhite/missing	−1.596**	−0.115
	(0.754)	(0.622)
Course-based indicator college track	2.600**	2.001**
	(0.179)	(0.174)
Self-reported college track	2.491**	0.723**
	(0.183)	(0.166)
Female	−1.263**	−1.075**
	(0.157)	(0.143)
Mother's education	0.161**	−0.030
	(0.048)	(0.040)
Father's education	0.311**	0.201**
	(0.046)	(0.042)
Father's occupation	0.010**	0.007*
	(0.005)	(0.004)
Family income in 10,000s	0.027**	0.008**
	(0.010)	(0.002)
Number of siblings	−0.014	0.032
	(0.055)	(0.051)
Nonintact household	−0.308	0.141
	(0.210)	(0.222)
1990 reading	0.113**	0.096**
	(0.012)	(0.011)
1990 mathematics	0.511**	0.795**
	(0.012)	(0.012)
R^2	0.587	0.778

* Coefficient discernibly different from zero ($0.05 < \alpha < 0.10$).
** Coefficient discernibly different from zero ($\alpha < 0.05$).
 Note: Adjusted standard errors are in parentheses. High School and Beyond analyses use transcript sampling weights. See Calvin Jones and others, *High School and Beyond Transcript Survey 1982; Data File User's Manual* (U.S. Department of Education, National Center for Education Statistics, 1983). $N = 12,198$. National Education Longitudinal Study (NELS) analyses use the NELS panel sampling weights and a design effect of 6.75. See Steven J. Ingles and others, *National Education Longitudinal Study of 1988 Second Follow-up: Transcript Component Data File User's Manual* (U.S. Department of Education, National Center for Education Statistics, 1995). $N = 12,543$. Controls for missing data were included.

Table 9-6. *Endogenous Switching Regression of Course-Based Indicator of Track Location and Math Achievement, 1980 Sophomores*

	Dependent variables		
		1982 mathematics achievement	
Independent variable	Course-based indicator	Noncollege prep	College prep
Constant	−4.411*	8.807*	7.902*
	(0.196)	(1.081)	(1.292)
Asian	0.416	2.103	3.014*
	(0.233)	(1.440)	(1.507)
Black	−0.080	−2.171*	−1.128*
	(0.069)	(0.336)	(0.418)
Female	0.245*	−0.993*	−1.373*
	(0.034)	(0.210)	(0.217)
Latino/a	−0.256*	−2.425*	−2.849*
	(0.060)	(0.309)	(0.411)
Other or missing on race	−0.232	−1.043	−1.953
	(0.176)	(0.918)	(1.252)
Nonintact household	−0.035	−0.380	−0.015
	(0.046)	(0.271)	(0.306)
Father's education	0.022*	0.352*	0.273*
	(0.010)	(0.064)	(0.060)
Mother's education	0.015	0.226*	0.120
	(0.010)	(0.068)	(0.062)
Father's occupation	0.003*	0.005	0.018*
	(0.001)	(0.006)	(0.006)
Family earnings in 10,000s	0.005*	0.036*	0.028*
	(0.002)	(0.013)	(0.013)
Number of siblings	−0.033*	−0.030	−0.018
	(0.012)	(0.072)	(0.076)
Reading test grade ten	0.015*	0.143*	0.121*
	(0.003)	(0.014)	(0.020)
Math test grade ten	0.052*	0.525*	0.634*
	(0.003)	(0.015)	(0.021)
Mean school socioeconomic status	0.148* (0.044)	—	—
Percent nonwhite in school	0.004*	—	—
	(0.001)		
Covariance with course-based indicator equation	0.000	−0.609* (0.096)	0.015 (0.077)
R^2		0.502	0.506

* Coefficient discernibly different from zero ($\alpha < 0.05$).

Note: Standard errors are in parentheses. All analyses use the High School and Beyond transcript sampling weights. See Calvin Jones and others, *High School and Beyond Transcript Survey 1982; Data File User's Manual* (U.S. Department of Education, National Center for Education Statistics, 1983). $N = 12{,}198$. Controls for missing data were included.

— = Coefficient was not estimated.

Table 9-7. *Endogenous Switching Regression of Course-Based Indicator of Track Location and Math Achievement, 1990 Sophomores*

| | | Dependent variables | |
| | | 1982 mathematics achievement | |
Independent variable	Course-based indicator	Noncollege prep	College prep
Constant	−4.555*	−0.123	0.143
	(0.266)	(1.302)	(0.985)
Asian	0.305*	1.471	0.197
	(0.141)	(0.827)	(0.445)
Black	−0.062	−1.006*	−1.069*
	(0.088)	(0.386)	(0.337)
Female	0.327*	−1.087*	−1.383*
	(0.050)	(0.270)	(0.192)
Latino/a	0.009	−0.274	−0.436
	(0.092)	(0.419)	(0.348)
Other or missing on race	−0.232	0.415	−0.653
	(0.215)	(0.872)	(1.140)
Nonintact household	−0.012	0.164	0.162
	(0.075)	(0.400)	(0.302)
Father's education	0.031*	0.228*	−0.166*
	(0.015)	(0.080)	(0.055)
Mother's education	0.013	−0.050	−0.007
	(0.015)	(0.080)	(0.052)
Father's occupation	0.003*	0.004	0.007
	(0.001)	(0.008)	(0.005)
Family earnings in 10,000s	0.002	0.004	0.009*
	(0.010)	(0.006)	(0.003)
Number of siblings	−0.017	0.072	0.016
	(0.018)	(0.092)	(0.069)
Reading test grade ten	0.015*	0.113*	0.106*
	(0.004)	(0.023)	(0.015)
Math test grade ten	0.063*	0.780*	0.821*
	(0.004)	(0.023)	(0.017)
Mean school socioeconomic status	0.074	—	—
	(0.052)		
Percent nonwhite in school	0.005*	—	—
	(0.001)		
Covariance with course-based indicator equation		−0.129	−0.168
		(0.102)	(0.115)
R^2		0.697	0.748

* Coefficient discernibly different from zero ($\alpha < 0.05$).

Note: Standard errors are in parentheses. All analyses use the National Education Longitudinal Study transcript sampling weights. See Steven J. Ingles and others, *National Education Longitudinal Study of 1988 Second Follow-up: Transcript Component Data File User's Manual* (U.S. Department of Education, National Center for Education Statistics, 1995). $N = 11,603$. Controls for missing data were included.

— = Coefficient was not estimated.

Our results for the 1980 cohort imply a track effect of 6.60 points on our cross-cohort equated test. Thus, a typical student's achievement would be about two-thirds of a standard deviation higher if assigned to the college track.

Within the noncollege and college tracks, blacks, Hispanics, and females lag behind their peers in achievement. But the black disadvantage within the college track is smaller than the black disadvantage in the noncollege track. The Hispanic and female disadvantages are larger in the college track. Still, owing to the dramatic gains associated with college-track assignment, the Hispanic disadvantage in track assignment serves to exacerbate differences between Hispanic and non-Hispanic whites. And, failure to assign more blacks to the college track also served to increase the test score gap between the groups. In short, in the 1980 cohort tracking contributed to racial/ethnic differences in achievement.

Our analysis of the more recent cohort, however, unearths some important changes that appear to have occurred in the intervening decade. A first important finding for 1990 is that, unlike the 1980 analysis, which revealed small but nonzero effects of unmeasured factors on selection into the noncollege track, we find no effects of unmeasured characteristics on track assignment. This suggests that for later cohorts selection bias is not a problem for ordinary least squares analyses of track effects that include a rich set of controls for prior conditions, when a structural indicator of track location is used.

Further, we now find that Hispanics and blacks are as likely as whites to be in the college track once other covariates are controlled. But, in contrast to 1980, in 1990 we find Asians more likely to enter the college preparatory track than whites. This change implies that race continues to be an important determinant of track location, in this case advantaging Asians in comparison to whites, blacks, and Hispanics.

Our results indicate that the track effect for 1990 sophomores was 8.03 points; that is, it appears larger than the track effect for the 1980s cohort. This translates into about eight-tenths of a standard deviation difference in mathematics achievement attributable to track assignment.

We also find that the achievement disadvantage of blacks compared with whites is virtually equal across the two tracks, unlike in 1980 when blacks in college tracks were not as disadvantaged relative to their peers as were blacks in noncollege tracks. Notably, the gap is less than half as large for both groups in 1990 than it was in 1980.

Because a large gain is associated with college prep placement, the net Asian advantage in track assessment is consequential. Clearly, it contributes

little or not at all to the black-white test score gap, but just as clearly it contributes to racial differences in measured achievement. Even after social class
and prior achievement are controlled, and even after unmeasured factors that
might affect selection are controlled, Asians are placed in college prep tracks
more than other groups. And, the premium received by college-track placement is relatively large. Thus, the net advantage in college-track placement
probabilities of Asians underlies their higher measured achievement.

Discussion

Changes in the relation between social-psychological and structural track
location, changes in the process of track assignment, and changes in the relative performance of students within the tracks have made the 1980 and 1990
stories somewhat different.

Analysis of 1980 sophomores showed that black, Hispanic, and white
tenth graders with similar coursework experiences do not always respond in
the same way to the survey question about track locations. Moreover, when
tracking is measured by a course-based indicator, and when school composition is taken into account, we found no minority advantage in track assignment, contrary to Gamoran and Mare.[34] Indeed, we found a track disadvantage for Hispanic students, as they were more likely to be assigned to the
noncollege track in 1980 than were whites after prior achievement and social
background were controlled. Even though college prep Hispanics lag further
behind their track peers than do noncollege prep Hispanics, their assignment
disadvantage exacerbated their achievement disadvantage. This occurred
because Hispanics appear to have been deprived of large gains associated with
college-track placement. Even though their gains would have been lower
than those of whites, they would have been larger than they obtained in the
noncollege track.

Gamoran and Mare's argument was directed at the issue of net inequality;
that is, inequality of results given similar initial levels of background and
achievement.[35] Taking the same questions to heart, when we analyzed the
same cohort, we found no net differences in track assignment chances for
blacks and whites and smaller black-white achievement gaps in the college
track once background factors and prior achievement are controlled. This set
of results implies that failure to place more blacks in college prep programs
may have exacerbated the achievement gap between the groups. The model
implies that, if all 1980 students had been college prep, the black-white gap
would have declined. Clearly, in models such as ours cannot predict what
would happen under massive policy change, but they can address whether

one should have confidence in the view that tracking was irrelevant to the black-white test score gap. Our results should undermine that confidence for the 1980s.

We updated our analysis by investigating a more recent cohort. We investigated the relationship between social-psychological and structural track location and the process of track assignment, and for the more recent cohort we found few differences in the reporting behaviors of blacks, whites, and Hispanics. Still, we found that one's assessment of blacks' and Hispanics' chances of being in the college track may depend on the indicator of track location used.

Blacks and Hispanics from the 1990 cohort appeared as likely to enter the college track as were comparable whites. But Asians were advantaged in the track assignment process. Further, we found gains associated with college prep track location had increased over the decade. This implies that Asians are more likely to be placed in college tracks even after several factors are controlled, and there they accrue advantages denied comparable black, white, and Hispanic students. This implies that race matters for tracking, and tracking matters for racial differences in measured achievement.

Our conclusion that race matters in both 1980 and 1990 is based on considering the complexity of race in the United States. This complexity is most important for understanding the 1990 results. Historically, analysts have focused on differences between blacks and whites. In such analyses, if the black-white difference goes to zero, researchers may conclude that race does not matter. But race is more complex in this period than simply black and white. Hence, the only way to conclude that race does not matter is to find no net differences for all groups. We found a statistically significant difference between Asians and all other groups, a difference that means that blacks, whites, and Hispanics who equal the achievement of Asians are less likely to be assigned to the college preparatory track. This is an important finding, and its implication is that race matters, even though the advantaged racial group is Asians, not whites.

Some of the changes we have documented are consistent with known changes in policy, such as the increase in graduation requirements. Increasing graduation requirements likely increased the incidence of college preparatory course taking. The nominally larger net track effect for the 1990 cohort compared with the 1980 cohort suggests, but only suggests, that little weakening in the rigor of college preparatory courses occurred in the wake of increasing graduation requirements. At the very least, whatever weakening that occurred was insufficient to keep the gains to higher placements from increasing for later cohorts relative to their older peers. And the overall implication of these results is that change, and possibly policy, is reflected in the cross-cohort comparisons.

Amidst the change, our findings also show tracking consistently plays a role in race-linked differences in achievement. By investigating additional racial groups, we were able to see the complex implications of race for tracking. Our analysis suggests that race continues to matter, but how it matters, whom it advantages, has changed. Still, what remains unaltered is the basic fact: race matters for placement, and track placement maintains or exacerbates race-linked differences in measured achievement.

Appendix 9A

Our analyses rely on data from students who were sophomores in 1980, drawing on the High School and Beyond (HS&B) base-year survey, the 1982 first follow-up, and the transcript survey.[36] Initially about thirty thousand students were included in the sample, but transcript data were gathered for a random subsample of nearly sixteen thousand cases. We use the 12,198 cases with nonmissing data for the two measures of track location and twelfth-grade mathematics achievement. Owing to the deletion of a small set of cases because they had missing data on our structural indicator, the data we use are not the same as those used by Adam Gamoran and Robert D. Mare. However, any differences in our findings are unlikely to be traced to these differences, because when we use the self-report in a similar endogenous switching regression model we replicated Gamoran and Mare's finding.

To investigate whether the key foundational findings have changed since the early 1980s, we update our analysis using National Education Longitudinal Study (NELS) data from the 1990 sophomore cohort.

Measures of Track Positions

We obtained a self-report of track location from students' sophomore-year responses to the question of which category best describes their high school programs. We collapsed the responses into two categories: college preparatory and noncollege preparatory. Our focus on the dichotomy is warranted for several reasons. First, previous work has shown that the college/noncollege distinction is much more consequential for achievement than are distinctions among the noncollege programs.[37] Second, debates about the impact of tracking on racial and ethnic inequality have centered on access to academic courses.[38] Third, evidence suggests that even though the college/noncollege dichotomy does not describe the high school curriculum and students' navigation of it, the tenth-grade curriculum is effectively summarized by the college/noncollege dichotomy.[39] Fourth, restricting our focus to the college/noncollege division permits us to replicate a key aspect of the Gamoran and Mare study.

We used course-based indicators (CBIs) of track positions, which were constructed from transcript data. The CBIs classify students' math, science, English, social studies, and foreign language courses into five categories: elite college, regular college, junior college, business/vocational, and remedial. The categorization is based on course titles and descriptions. CBIs classify some courses differently depending on when they were taken. For example, algebra I is coded regular college in grades nine and ten but lower college in grades eleven and twelve. Students' track positions in each subject in each year were then indicated by the categorization of the courses they had taken. Students who took more than one course in the same subject in a given year are scored according to the course that ended later in the year, or that took the longest time if they ended simultaneously, or according to the higher ranked course if all else was equal. We use a summary version of the CBI based on courses taken in ninth and tenth grade. The summary CBI counts students as belonging to the college preparatory track if they were enrolled in regular or elite college courses in math, English, and two of the other three subjects (science, social studies, and foreign language). Further details on the creation of the course-based indicators are provided by Samuel R. Lucas.[40]

Background and Achievement Data

For 1980 sophomores we draw background data from student questionnaires. Blacks, Hispanics, and other nonwhites are indicated by three dummy variables. Sex is coded 1 for males, 0 for females. In tables 9A-1 and 9A-2, we use a socioeconomic status (SES) scale, which is a standardized unweighted composite consisting of the nonmissing elements of mother's and father's education, father's occupation, family income, and home resources. However, in the foregoing analyses we disaggregated the components of the SES scale.

Prior achievement is assessed with tests administered in the spring of the sophomore year (1980) in math and reading. Gamoran and Mare found that controlling for all six tests available in the HS&B data set substantially reduced the impact of selection bias in the analysis of track effects.[41] However, we use only reading and mathematics in grade ten because these were the only subjects that had enough overlapping items across cohorts to allow researchers to construct a cross-cohort equated test score for these covariates.

We focus on the senior-year math test as an outcome variable when we assess the implications of tracking for achievement inequality. The math test is the most sensitive to school-related influences.[42] In addition, examining

Table 9A-1. *Multinomial Logit Model of Self-Reported and Course-Based Indicators of Track Location, 1980 Sophomores*

Independent variable	Self-reported noncollege track, course-based indicator noncollege track	Self-reported college track, course-based indicator noncollege track	Self-reported college track, course-based indicator college track
Intercept	3.408*	−0.863*	−2.432*
	(0.183)	(0.239)	(0.230)
1980 vocabulary	−0.028*	0.046*	0.073*
	(0.014)	(0.018)	(0.016)
1980 reading	−0.023	0.009	−0.004
	(0.016)	(0.020)	(0.018)
1980 math	−0.092*	−0.030*	0.028*
	(0.008)	(0.010)	(0.009)
1980 science	0.035*	0.019	0.012
	(0.016)	(0.021)	(0.019)
1980 writing	−0.050*	−0.009	0.057*
	(0.016)	(0.020)	(0.019)
1980 civics	−0.062*	0.021	0.022
	(0.024)	(0.031)	(0.028)
Socioeconomic status	−0.264*	0.286*	0.409*
	(0.058)	(0.073)	(0.065)
Black	−0.243	0.703*	0.684*
	(0.133)	(0.165)	(0.163)
Hispanic	−0.032	0.450*	0.157
	(0.123)	(0.159)	(0.161)
Other nonwhite	−0.323	0.471	0.254
	(0.255)	(0.294)	(0.278)
Male	0.302*	0.116	−0.076
	(0.081)	(0.103)	(0.092)

Source: Samuel R. Lucas and Adam Gamoran, "Race and Track Assignment: A Reconsideration with Course-Based Indicators of Track Location," paper presented at a meeting of the American Sociological Association, Cincinnati, Ohio, 1991.
* Coefficient is twice its adjusted standard error.
Note: Adjusted standard errors are in parentheses. Omitted category is self-reported noncollege track, course-based indicator college track. All analyses use the High School and Beyond transcript sampling weights. See Calvin Jones and others, *High School and Beyond Transcript Survey 1982: Data File User's Manual* (U.S. Department of Education, National Center for Education Statistics, 1983). N = 12,198. Controls for missing data on socioeconomic status, 1980 math, 1980 vocabulary, 1980 reading, 1980 science, 1980 writing, and 1980 civics were included.

Table 9A-2. *Probit Models of Curricular Track Assignment, Controlling for School Composition for 1980 Sophomores: Comparison of Self-Reported and Course-Based Indicators*

Predictor	Track indicator	
	Self-report	Course-based indicator
Intercept	−2.558*	−2.193*
	(0.159)	(0.154)
1980 vocabulary	0.042*	0.022*
	(0.007)	(0.007)
1980 reading	0.008	0.004
	(0.008)	(0.008)
1980 math	0.036*	0.053*
	(0.004)	(0.004)
1980 science	0.001	−0.009
	(0.008)	(0.008)
1980 writing	0.037*	0.041*
	(0.008)	(0.008)
1980 civics	0.035*	0.028*
	(0.012)	(0.012)
Socioeconomic status (SES)	0.234*	0.143*
	(0.031)	(0.031)
Black	0.372*	−0.029
	(0.071)	(0.071)
Hispanic	0.139*	−0.125
	(0.064)	(0.063)
Other nonwhite	0.305*	0.041
	(0.122)	(0.120)
Male	−0.107*	−0.176*
	(0.039)	(0.039)
School mean SES	0.150*	0.050
	(0.071)	(0.069)
School mean 1980 math	−0.006	−0.003
	(0.075)	(0.007)
School percent black	0.005*	0.006*
	(0.001)	(0.001)
School percent Hispanic	0.004*	0.006*
	(0.002)	(0.002)
School percent high track	0.006*	0.004*
	(0.001)	(0.001)
R^2	0.517	0.510

Source: Samuel R. Lucas and Adam Gamoran, "Race and Track Assignment: A Reconsideration with Course-Based Indicators of Track Location," paper presented at a meeting of the American Sociological Association, Cincinnati, Ohio, 1991.

* Coefficient is twice its standard error.

Note: Adjusted standard errors are in parentheses. All analyses use the High School and Beyond transcript sampling weights. See Calvin Jones and others, *High School and Beyond Transcript Survey 1982: Data File User's Manual* (U.S. Department of Education, National Center for Education Statistics, 1983). $N = 12,198$. Controls for missing data on socioeconomic status, 1980 math, 1980 vocabulary, 1980 reading, 1980 science, 1980 writing, 1980 civics, school mean 1980 math, school percent black, school percent Hispanic, and percent high track were included.

math scores allows us to compare our qualitative conclusions with those of Gamoran and Mare.[43]

School composition was indicated by aggregate measures of mean SES and principal reports of the percentage of minority students. The aggregate measures were constructed using the full base-year sample, which included a random sample of up to thirty-six sophomores in each school.

We substituted mean values when data were missing, and for each variable with missing data we created a binary variable as a control for missing data.

The data for 1990 sophomores are described in box 9A-1.

Methods

We first construct a four-category variable from the two-way cross-classification of self-reported track and CBI. We use this four-category measure as a dependent variable in multinomial logit equations to investigate the net association of race and ethnicity and jointly determined self-reported and structural measures of track position. This required us to use only cases with nonmissing data on both indicators. For HS&B, both variables had minimal missing data, but there was so much missing data in NELS that later models use the fullest set of cases possible given the dependent variable(s) under study.

To address possible race and ethnic differences in the probability of college-track assignment, and the implications of such differences for achievement, we begin by estimating probit models to address whether the substantive finding of greater black probability of college-track assignment is invariant to the measure of track location.

To investigate the effects of track placement on achievement, we use ordinary least squares to model the net association of the self-report and course-based indicators with twelfth-grade mathematics achievement. We then estimate the model of joint track location/achievement determination selected by Gamoran and Mare, except that we use the CBI as the measure of track location.[44]

Several writers have commented that standard errors generated by HS&B analyses are understated, because the clustering of students within schools in the sample means that cases within schools are not independent of one another.[45] Calvin Jones and others estimated that, in the transcript data, standard errors should be adjusted on the basis of a design effect of 3.7, and Steven J. Ingels and others calculate a design effect of 6.75 for NELS.[46] For all results we provide adjusted standard errors.

The sample size for HS&B remains stable throughout the analysis. However, owing to large amounts of missing data on the test score and the self-

Box 9A-1. Measurement of Independent Variables for 1990 Sophomores

Father's occupation. Students' responses to a seventeen-category question were recoded to the 1989 Socioeconomic Index (SEI) score of the mean of the illustrative occupations in the questionnaire using Keiko Nakao and Judith Treas's updated occupational scores for total labor force based on the 1980 census.[1] Student 1990 responses were taken unless the responses were missing, in which case the 1992 response was taken. Homemakers and military were coded as missing given that there is no SEI code for those pursuits.

Mother and father's education. Students responses to a ten-category question were recoded into the following ordered levels: 1 = less than high school graduate, 2 = high school graduate, 3 = some college only, and 4 = college degree or more.

Male. Students' self-report of sex was used.

Family income. Parents' base-year report of family income is used. Responses are coded to the midpoint of categories. The unbounded upper category is coded using the Pareto transformation for an unbounded category.

Number of siblings. Students were asked to report on the number of siblings in 1990. The codes used are 0 = none, 1 = 1 sibling, 2 = 2 siblings, 3 = 3 siblings, 4 = 4 siblings, 5 = 5 siblings, and 6 = 6 or more siblings.

Parent missing from family. Students' report of whether in 1990 or 1992 the student lived with both mother and father (0) or not (1).

Race/ethnicity. The omitted category for four dichotomous race/ethnicity indicators is white. The four variables are black, Hispanic, Asian or Pacific Islander, and other nonwhite (Native American or other) based on students' self-report.

Achievement. Four tenth-grade tests and four twelfth-grade tests are used. We use Item Response Theory—estimated number of items answered correctly in math, science, reading, and civics, history, or geography. For analyses of achievement, we use the cross-cohort equated tenth-grade reading and math tests.

Structural track location. Transcript data on students' course taking in grades nine and ten were used to classify students as noncollege (0) or college (1) track by grade ten, and their course taking in grades nine through twelve is used to classify them as noncollege (0) or college (1) track by grade twelve.

Social-psychological track location. Students' self-reports of track dichotomized as college prep (1) and noncollege prep (0).

Percent of minorities in the school. Proportion of students in the sample who are minority.

Mean SES in the school. The mean of a standardized SES scale that was produced by parents' reports of their education, occupation, and household items.

1. Keiko Nakao and Judith Treas, "Updating Occupational Prestige and Socioeconomic Status Scores: How the New Measures Measure Up," *Sociological Methodology*, vol. 24 (1994), pp. 1–72.

report, we used all cases that had nonmissing data for the dependent variables in any analysis for NELS.

Notes

We are grateful for technical assistance from Mary Rasmussen and the staff of the Social Science Computing Cooperative of the University of Wisconsin–Madison and from Carl Mason of the Demography Department of the University of California–Berkeley. We also appreciate comments on earlier drafts from Archibald Haller and Alan Kerckhoff. This paper was prepared in part at the National Center for Research on the Organization and Restructuring of Schools, Wisconsin Center for Education Research, University of Wisconsin–Madison, which is supported by a grant from the Office of Educational Research and Improvement (Grant No. OERI–R117–Q00005), and in part at the Survey Research Center of the University of California–Berkeley. Further support was provided by Samuel R. Lucas's National Science Foundation Minority Graduate Fellowship and by Adam Gamoran's National Academy of Education Spencer Fellowship. Any opinions, findings, or conclusions expressed in this paper are ours and do not necessarily reflect the views of these agencies or the U.S. Department of Education. Some portions of this paper were presented at the annual meeting of the American Sociological Association, Cincinnati, Ohio, August 1991.

1. For example, Quality Education for Minorities Project, Education That Works: An Action Plan for the Education of Minorities (Cambridge, Mass., 1990); E. Dentzer and A. Wheelock, *Locked In/Locked Out: Tracking and Placement Practices in Boston Public Schools* (Boston: Massachusetts Advocacy Center, 1990); and Jeannie Oakes, *Multiplying Inequalities: Opportunities to Learn Science and Math* (Santa Monica, Calif.: RAND, 1990).

2. K. L. Alexander, M. A. Cook, and E. L. McDill, "Curriculum Tracking and Educational Stratification," *American Sociological Review,* vol. 43 (1978), pp. 47–66; K. L. Alexander and M. A. Cook, "Curricula and Coursework: A Surprise Ending to a Familiar Story," *American Sociological Review,* vol. 47 (1982), pp. 626–40; E. James Rosenbaum, "Track Misperceptions and Frustrated College Plans: An Analysis of the Effects of Tracks and Track Perceptions in the National Longitudinal Survey," *Sociology of Education,* vol. 53 (1980), pp. 74–88; and L. Wolfle, "Postsecondary Educational Attainment among Whites and Blacks," *American Educational Research Journal,* vol. 22 (1985), pp. 501–25.

3. Adam Gamoran and Robert D. Mare, "Secondary School Tracking and Educational Inequality: Compensation, Reinforcement, or Neutrality?" *American Journal of Sociology,* vol. 94 (1989), pp. 1146–83.

4. Samuel R. Lucas and Adam Gamoran, "Race and Track Assignment: A Reconsideration with Course-Based Indicators of Track Locations," paper presented at the meeting of the American Sociological Association, Cincinnati, Ohio, 1991.

5. Robert M. Hauser, William Sewell, and Duane Alwin, "High School Effects on

Achievement," in William Sewell, Robert M. Hauser, and Featherman, eds., *Schooling and Achievement in American Society* (New York: Academic Press, 1976).

6. M. Garet and B. DeLany, "Students, Courses, and Stratification," *Sociology of Education,* vol. 61 (1988), pp. 61–77.

7. Oakes, *Multiplying Inequalities.*

8. Gamoran and Mare, "Secondary School Tracking and Educational Inequality."

9. W. Secada, "Race, Ethnicity, Social Class, Language, and Achievement in Mathematics," in D. Grouws, ed., *Handbook of Research on Mathematics Teaching and Learning* (New York: Macmillan, 1992), pp. 623–60; Garet and DeLany, "Students"; and Oakes, *Multiplying Inequalities.*

10. Gamoran and Mare, "Secondary School Tracking and Educational Inequality."

11. A. M. Pallas and others, "Ability-Group Effects: Instructional, Social, or Institutional?" *Sociology of Education,* vol. 67 (1994), pp. 27–46; and Maureen T. Hallinan, "The Organization of Students for Instruction in Middle School," *Sociology of Education,* vol. 65 (1992), pp. 114–27.

12. Jones and others, *High School and Beyond Transcript Survey 1982: Data File User's Manual* (U.S. Department of Education, National Center for Education Statistics, 1983).

13. See J. B. Conant, *The Comprehensive High School* (McGraw-Hill, 1967).

14. J. Oakes, *Keeping Track: How Schools Structure Inequality* (Yale University Press, 1985); D. R. Moore and S. Davenport, *The New Improved Sorting Machine* (Madison, Wis.: National Center on Effective Secondary Schools, 1988); and J. Oakes, A. Gamoran, and R. N. Page, "Curriculum Differentiation: Opportunities, Outcomes, and Meanings," in P. W. Jackson, ed., *Handbook of Research on Curriculum* (Washington: American Educational Research Association, 1992), pp. 570–608.

15. Moore and Davenport, *The New Improved Sorting Machine,* pp. 11–12.

16. Jeannie Oakes, *Tracking Policies and Practices: School by School Summaries, A Study of Schooling in the United States,* Technical Report Series Number 25 (University of California at Los Angeles, Graduate School of Education, 1981).

17. Nancy Carey, Elizabeth Farris, and Judi Carpenter, *Curricular Differentiation in Public High Schools: Fast Response Survey System E.D. Tabs* (Rockville, Md.: Westat, 1994).

18. Wolfle, "Postsecondary Educational Attainment among Whites and Blacks."

19. Adam Gamoran, "The Stratification of High School Learning Opportunities," *Sociology of Education,* vol. 60 (1987), pp. 135–55; and A. Powell, E. Farrar, and D. K. Cohen, *The Shopping Mall High School* (Boston: Houghton-Mifflin, 1985).

20. For a review, see Adam Gamoran and Mark Berends, "The Effects of Stratification in Secondary Schools: Synthesis of Survey and Ethnographic Research," *Review of Educational Research,* vol. 57 (1987), pp. 415–35.

21. C. Lacey, *Hightown Grammar* (Manchester, England: Manchester University Press, 1970); S. J. Ball, *Beachside Comprehensive: A Case-Study of Secondary Schooling* (Cambridge, England: Cambridge University Press, 1981); J. Abraham, "Testing

Hargreaves' and Lacey's Differentiation-Polarisation Hypothesis in a Setted Comprehensive," *British Journal of Sociology*, vol. 40 (1989), pp. 46–81; and M. Berends,
"Educational Stratification and Students' Social Bonding to School," *British Journal
of Sociology of Education*, vol. 16 (1994), pp. 327–51.

22. N. Keddie, "Classroom Knowledge," in M. F. D. Young, ed., *Knowledge and
Control* (London: Collier-Macmillan, 1971); James E. Rosenbaum, *Making Inequal-
ity* (New York: Wiley, 1976); Ball, *Beachside Comprehensive*; Merrilee K. Finley,
"Teachers and Tracking in a Comprehensive High School," *Sociology of Education*,
vol. 57 (1984), pp. 233–43; Oakes, *Keeping Track*; and Adam Gamoran and Martin
Nystrand, "Tracking, Instruction, and Achievement," paper presented at the World
Congress of Sociology, Madrid, Spain, 1990.

23. Hauser, Sewell, and Alwin, "High School Effects on Achievement."

24. Samuel R. Lucas, "Course-Based Indicators of Curricular Track Locations,"
M.S. thesis, University of Wisconsin at Madison, 1990; and Samuel Roundfield
Lucas, *Tracking Inequality: Stratification and Mobility in American High Schools* (New
York: Teachers College Press, 1999).

25. Garet and DeLany, "Students."

26. Garet and DeLany, "Students."

27. Lucas, "Course-Based Indicators of Curricular Track Locations."

28. James E. Rosenbaum, "Track Misperceptions and Frustrated College Plans:
An Analysis of the Effects of Tracks and Track Perceptions in the National Longitudinal Survey," *Sociology of Education*, vol. 53 (1980), pp. 74–88.

29. Statistical analyses of High School and Beyond data were performed using a
VAX11/780 and a MicroVAXII at the Social Science Computing Cooperative of the
University of Wisconsin at Madison and a SUN ULTRA Sparc-5 at the Survey
Research Center of the University of California at Berkeley. We used SPSSx version
3.0 for data management and cross-tabulations, LIMDEP 7.0 for the ordinary least
squares (OLS) and probit models, LIMDEP 5.1 for the multinomial logit models,
and HotzTran for the switching regressions. All analyses of National Education Longitudinal Study data were performed using a SUN ULTRA Sparc-5 at the Survey
Research Center of the University of California at Berkeley. We used SAS6.12 for
data management and cross-tabulations, LIMDEP 7.0 for the OLS, probit, and
multinomial logit models of 1990 sophomores, and HotzTran for the switching
regression models.

30. Lucas and Gamoran, "Race and Track Assignment."

31. Note that in this analysis we have disaggregated the elements of socioeconomic background. We do so because combining the factors imposes constraints that
may or may not be appropriate for a given analysis. See Claude Fischer and others,
Inequality by Design: Cracking the Bell Curve Myth (Princeton University Press, 1996).
Few of the indicators of social background are statistically significant in table 9-4.
However, when we constrain the coefficients of mother's education, father's education, father's occupation, family earnings, number of siblings, and intact-family status
to equal zero, tests show that the constrained model fits much less well than the fuller

model that estimates social background coefficients. We found this to be true for both models in table 9-4. Thus, although no single coefficient is statistically significant, the evidence suggests that social background continues to matter for track placement, regardless of whether one uses the self-report or the structural indicator of track location.

32. Mark Berends, Samuel R. Lucas, and Thomas Sullivan, "Effects of Changing Family Background Characteristics on Black-White Test Score Trends, 1972–1992," paper presented at the International Sociological Association Research Committee Number 28 Meeting, Madison, Wisconsin, August 1999.

33. We have not estimated any models that constrain the slopes to be equal across the track positions.

34. Gamoran and Mare, "Secondary School Tracking and Educational Inequality."

35. Gamoran and Mare, "Secondary School Tracking and Educational Inequality."

36. Jones and others, *High School and Beyond Transcript Survey 1982.*

37. Joel Gelb, *Beyond the Academic, Non-Academic Dichotomy: High School Curriculum Effects and Educational Attainment,* Report 273 (Johns Hopkins University, Center for Social Organization of Schools, 1979); and Gamoran, "The Stratification of High School Learning Opportunities."

38. Oakes, *Multiplying Inequalities.*

39. Garet and DeLany, "Students"; and Lucas, *Tracking Inequality.*

40. Lucas, "Course-Based Indicators of Curricular Track Locations"; and Lucas, *Tracking Inequality.*

41. Gamoran and Mare, "Secondary School Tracking and Educational Inequality."

42. V. E. Lee and A. S. Bryk, "A Multilevel Model of the Social Distribution of High School Achievement," *Sociology of Education* 62 (1989), pp. 172–92.

43. Gamoran and Mare, "Secondary School Tracking and Educational Inequality."

44. Gamoran and Mare, "Secondary School Tracking and Educational Inequality."

45. For example, A. S. Goldberger and G. G. Cain, "The Causal Analysis of Cognitive Outcomes in the Coleman, Hoffer, and Kilgore Report," *Sociology of Education,* vol. 55 (1982), pp. 103–22.

46. Jones and others, *High School and Beyond Transcript Survey 1982*; and Steven J. Ingels and others, *National Education Longitudinal Study of 1988 Second Follow-up: Transcript Component Data File User's Manual* (U.S. Department of Education, National Center for Education Statistics, 1995).

10

The Role of Federal Resources in Closing the Achievement Gap

ANN FLANAGAN AND DAVID GRISSMER

I n their landmark volume, Christopher Jencks and Meredith Phillips suggested that reducing the gap in scores between black and white students
would do more to move America toward racial equality than any other alternative.[1] They argue that eliminating the gap might eventually solve many of
the other issues that separate the races: the need for affirmative action policies
in colleges and jobs, the differences in wages, and perhaps even segregated
communities. When recommending policies that could help achieve gap
reduction, they suggest that the strongest empirical evidence exists for class-
size reductions and raising the quality of teachers by hiring those with higher
test scores as two expensive options. They also believe that programs for children before they enter kindergarten, such as prekindergarten and Head Start,
that are oriented toward teaching cognitive skills are necessary.

Jencks and Phillips emphasize the difficulty of finding politically viable
solutions. Decisive political support for programs that benefit only blacks is
unlikely, and so benefits for some whites seem necessary to build a viable
political coalition. Jencks and Phillips also were pessimistic that expanding
federal programs could play a significant role in reducing the differences in
test scores because of the distrust of federal initiatives in education.

We suggest that a federal resource role is critical to addressing the achievement gap problem and that specific programs appropriately targeted could be
effective and efficient. While significant political issues of federal involve-

ment are still present, the 2000 election and the federal surplus have probably made a broader federal role in education more likely—although still difficult. A political coalition could form to address the significant resource issues in U.S. education.

Resources and Inequality

As long as educational research was unable to provide consistent and replicable measurements on the effects of more and different uses of resources on educational outcomes, policymakers and school systems lacked perhaps the most important ingredient to improve the quality of education. Also missing were measurable educational objectives and internal incentives focused on meeting those objectives. In such an environment it is easy to understand the pessimism of the late 1980s and early 1990s about whether public education could be reformed. Effective and predictable utilization of resources that allow measurable results is a necessary condition for reforming education. But good research alone is not sufficient. It must be accompanied by internal incentives and measurable goals that motivate its use and ongoing evaluation.

Before the mid-1990s, apparent weak and inconsistent empirical evidence on the effects of resources fostered one view that public school systems could not turn additional resources into better educational outcomes.[2] Studies by Eric A. Hanushek utilized a vote-counting approach applied to published measurements. However, two re-reviews utilizing the same set of studies came to more positive conclusions. Larry V. Hedges, Richard D. Laine, and Rob Greenwald used meta-analysis that tested a specific statistical hypothesis about the distribution of previous measurements and concluded that resources showed a net positive relationship to outcomes.[3] However, wide variation in measurements still made it difficult to apply to policy. Alan B. Krueger also re-reviewed Hanushek's studies and concluded that the choice of including multiple measurements from individual studies, and the possible selectivity involved in publishing multiple measurements, was unduly influential in making the results look weak and inconsistent.[4]

Rob Greenwald, L. V. Hedges, and R. Laine utilized tighter quality criteria, but they used studies from a wider set of journals and meta-analysis to reach a conclusion that most resources showed net positive relationships with outcomes.[5] All reviews show an uncomfortably wide variance in measurement results.

Ronald F. Ferguson and Helen F. Ladd suggest that this inconsistency in previous measurements may be due to different and flawed specifications and assumptions across models.[6] David W. Grissmer and others suggest, in addi-

tion to model specification flaws, that differential bias across levels of aggrega-
tion and differential effects across types of students may partially account for
such differences.[7] In their literature review and analysis of the state National
Assessment of Educational Progress (NAEP) data, they conclude that the
weight of evidence is shifting toward a hypothesis that resources have their
largest and most efficient impact on disadvantaged and minority students.

Grissmer and others cite an emerging consistency of evidence from experimental data, explanations for previous nonexperimental analysis, and the historical pattern of score gains from 1970 to 1996. The larger gains in achievement by minority and disadvantaged white students with smaller or no gains
by advantaged white students seems difficult to explain outside of the additional resources targeted to these students or for programs that differentially
benefit these students such as pupil-teacher ratio reductions. Ronald F. Ferguson, David W. Grissmer and others, and Alan B. Krueger all suggest that
pupil-teacher ratio reductions are consistent with explaining part of the large
black score gains.[8]

The strongest evidence for effects of particular resources and possible differential effects for disadvantaged and minority students comes from experimental or quasi-experimental research on class size in Tennessee and Wisconsin.[9] Summarizing this research, David Grissmer concludes that the studies
show effects that are large and sustained into later grades for students with
small class size in K–3. The measured effects are larger for minority and disadvantaged students.[10] Hanushek details the possible flaws in the experiments that could affect these results.[11] However, empirical tests on Tennessee
data exploring the sensitivity of results to flaws in the experimental execution
have not shown sample attrition, leakage between test and control groups,
teacher assignments, and nonparticipation to significantly affect results.[12]

Perhaps as important, the Tennessee experimental research results seem to
challenge commonly used model specifications and might help explain the
inconsistency of previous nonexperimental research results. The pattern of
results suggests that inclusion of resources since school entry is important in
models and that use of previous years' test scores to control for both missing
family characteristics and earlier resources is problematic. Because these are
common flaws in specifications in previous studies, the results may help
explain the inconsistency of previous results.

If we accept the premise that money can make the most difference for disadvantaged and minority students, the next question involves the apparent
inequity in funding for advantaged and disadvantaged students. At one level,
this inequity has been repeatedly challenged within states through the
courts.[13] Starting with the constitutional challenge in California in 1971 to

the inequity across school districts in per pupil expenditures, finance reform litigation has been filed in forty-three states.[14] As of mid-2002, courts have overturned systems in nineteen states and upheld systems in twenty states, with four cases still pending.

Some states have made significant changes in the way education is financed by decreasing or eliminating reliance on the property tax to reduce inequality in per pupil expenditures. The results of such judicial intervention overturning existing financing systems seem to be increases in total state funding for education and significant narrowing of variance in spending across districts, with lower spending districts being the main beneficiaries. An analysis by William N. Evans, S. Murray, and R. Schwab also showed black and white students receiving roughly equal net spending increases due to judicial intervention.[15]

Only a few states have substantially eliminated variation in per pupil expenditures across districts, and judicial intervention seems to be required to do so. While it seems politically impossible to reduce expenditures for more advantaged students to spend more on disadvantaged students, a more achievable goal has been set out as ensuring an adequate education for all students. So courts are increasingly facing adequacy rather than equity suits.[16] Such suits will continue across the states and perhaps will be more easily won if research consistently points to larger effects of resources on disadvantaged students. However, the problem being addressed by these actions—within-state inequality in spending—is not the primary source of inequity in educational spending. Between-state inequality in spending accounts for almost two-thirds of the variance in spending while within-state inequality accounts for only one-third.[17] Equalizing spending in all states would still leave significant variation in expenditures across the nation. For instance in 1995–96, adjusting for cost-of-living differences, Mississippi spent $4,900 per pupil, while New Jersey spent $9,090 per pupil. Low-spending states are disproportionately in the Southeast, while the highest spending states are in the Northeast and the Midwest. Current federal spending narrows this gap only slightly. For instance, Mississippi in 1995–96 received approximately $590 per pupil, while New Jersey received $340 per pupil. After cost-of-living adjustments, federal spending narrows the gap by about $400 dollars a pupil, leaving a gap of $4,000 per pupil.

Setting aside the issue of the politics of more federal spending directed toward ensuring adequacy across states, the question arises as to where resources should be directed. If lower scoring students represent the most effective use of resources to increase national achievement, the question is, Where are lower scoring students located?

Exploring White and Black NAEP Scores
by Region, Locality, and State

Some of the distinct patterns present in U.S. achievement scores can be seen only by disaggregating by race, region, and locality. The racial differences are the most pronounced, and because black students are not distributed proportionately by region or locality, the aggregate region and locality scores can largely reflect the racial distributions. Significant differences also are evident by locality in the socioeconomic status (SES) of students in central cities, suburbs, and rural areas.

The problem in looking at these patterns is that the sample sizes of tests administered nationally are usually insufficient to produce robust samples at such disaggregated levels. We have combined nine national NAEP tests (main assessments) given from 1990 to 1998.[18] Table 10-1 provides the type of test and sample size for each test. These tests were given to representative national samples including public and private school students. Our analysis only includes public school students in the fourth and eighth grades. The public school sample size per test varied from around three thousand to nine thousand, with the total combined sample being approximately fifty-two thousand. The nine tests are three fourth-grade reading tests, three eighth-grade math tests, two fourth-grade math tests, and one eighth-grade reading test. The combined sample provides a composite picture of reading and math achievement at the fourth and eighth grades during the 1990s.

The NAEP main assessments are not considered basic skills tests because, in addition to multiple-choice items, they include constructed-response items requiring answers from a few sentences to a few paragraphs. NAEP data collection takes students approximately ninety minutes to complete for

Table 10-1. *Nine NAEP Main Assessments Given from 1990 to 1998*

Year	Grade	Subject	Public school sample (number)
1990	Eighth	Math	2,879
1992	Eighth	Math	6,033
1992	Fourth	Reading	5,045
1992	Fourth	Math	5,641
1994	Fourth	Reading	6,030
1996	Fourth	Math	5,215
1996	Eighth	Math	5,590
1998	Fourth	Reading	6,300
1998	Eighth	Reading	9,091

Note: NAEP = National Assessment of Educational Progress.

Table 10-2. *Black-White Gap, by Type of NAEP Test*

Type of test	Average white score	Average black score	Gap in standard deviation
Fourth-grade math	228.2	195.2	1.08
Fourth-grade reading	223.5	190.4	0.88
Eighth-grade math	276.4	238.2	1.11
Eighth-grade reading	269.4	241.6	0.86

Note: NAEP = National Assessment of Educational Progress.

a given subject. Matrix sampling of questions is used to allow testing a broad range of knowledge while limiting the time each student is tested. Bib spiraling of questions ensures that effects from the placement of questions within booklets and grouping sets of questions are minimized. Two types of exclusions from testing are allowed: Limited English Proficiency (LEP) and Individualized Education Plan/Disabled Student (IEP/DS). Approximately 1–2 percent of students nationally are excluded for LEP and about 4–6 percent for IEP/DS.

The NAEP samples are stratified to allow the reporting of scores for three mutually exclusive location types: central city, urban fringe/large town, and rural/small town. Central cities are defined as the central cities of the Standard Metropolitan Statistical Areas (SMSAs) as defined by the Office of Management and Budget (OMB). Suburban areas are densely settled places and areas within SMSAs classified as urban by OMB but outside central cities and large towns (non-SMSAs) with a population of more than twenty-five thousand. Rural areas are small towns outside SMSAs with a population of less than twenty-five thousand and all places with a population less than twenty-five hundred outside SMSAs. In our sample approximately 30 percent of K–8 students were in central cities, 50 percent in suburban areas, and 20 percent in rural areas.

Figure 10-1 shows a black-white gap of almost a full standard deviation for the composite sample. Regional and locality average scores show higher scores in the Northeast and Midwest and in suburban and rural areas. Table 10-2 shows that the black-white gap is somewhat higher for math than reading.

Summary of Locational Data

The data reveal a three-tiered pattern of achievement in the United States that can be identified by region and locality: (1) high scores in rural and suburban areas in the Northeast and Midwest; (2) average scores in rural and

Figure 10-1. *Average Scores across Nine NAEP Tests for Public School Students, by Race, Region, and Locality*

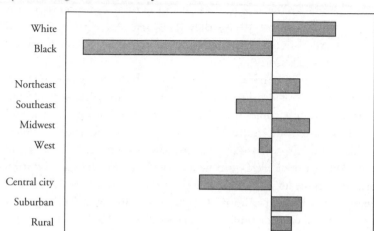

Standard deviation

Note: NAEP = National Assessment of Educational Progress. The nine tests are three fourth-grade reading tests, three eighth-grade math tests, two fourth-grade math tests, and one eighth-grade reading test.

suburban areas of the Southeast and West; and (3) low scores in central cities in all regions.

The most striking evidence comes from the Midwest and Northeast. About one-third of U.S. students live in the rural and suburban areas of the Northeast and Midwest, and these students have scores that place them near the top of international scores.[19] White students in these areas—almost 30 percent of students nationally—would likely place first in international competition.

However, central-city students in these two regions are among the lowest scoring in the nation. Black and white students in central cities in these two regions have among the lowest scores when compared with black and white students in other regions or localities. The gap between central-city and suburban scores is largest in these two regions. The states with the largest black-white score gap are Connecticut, Michigan, Minnesota, and, Wisconsin—all relatively high-spending states in the Northeast or Midwest.

The rural and suburban areas of the Southeast and West form a second tier and have average to below average scores. The third tier is central-city scores in all regions, with the lowest scores in the nation. Black students perform best in the rural and suburban areas of the Northeast, Midwest, and Southeast. Black students perform worst in the West and all central cities regardless of region. White students do best in the rural and suburban areas of the Northeast and Midwest, and they do worst in central cities in all regions and the rural Southeast. Black scores in the rural Southeast are among the highest black scores.

If we accept the premise that the lowest scoring students provide the most effective investment, the location and characteristics of the lowest scoring students in the nation become important. We use the 20th percentile and below to define low-scoring students. We find approximately equal numbers of white, black, and Hispanic students in the lowest quintile. The black and Hispanic students in the lowest quintile are highly concentrated. About 80 percent of blacks in the lowest quintile are in the Southeast or central cities in the Midwest and Northeast. About 70 percent of Hispanics in the lowest quintile are in central cities or suburbs of the Southeast and West. White students in the lowest quintile are more widely distributed. The largest groups are in the suburban areas of all regions and the rural Southeast.

The Southeast contains the largest proportion of low-scoring students— about 42 percent of low-scoring students are in the Southeast. The largest concentration of low-scoring students live in and around southern cities. One of three low-scoring students lives there. The Southeast and West together have two of three low-scoring students. The central cities of the Midwest and Northeast have only 17 percent of the nation's low-scoring students.

Examining Disaggregated Scores

The pattern that emerges when locality is disaggregated by region is shown in table 10-3. For instance, the data show that students in the suburban Northeast constitute about 11.6 percent of students nationally and have the highest score of any group—0.32 standard deviation above the national average. The rural and suburban areas of the Northeast and Midwest are grouped together at the top of the score distribution, significantly above any other group. Students in these high-scoring areas represent about one-third of students nationally (see column 3).

To get an idea of how well students in these areas perform, we made an approximate translation of their scores onto an international distribution. Eugene G. Johnson, Adriane Siegendorf, and Gary W. Phillips developed a comparison of international scores to state NAEP scores for eighth-grade math.[20] In this comparison, the average scores for the state of Iowa place it slightly below Taiwan, the highest scoring country. The average score of Iowa

Table 10-3. *Average NAEP Scores and Percent of Student Population,*
by Region and Locality

Locality	Region	Percent of total student population	Average test score (standard deviation)
Suburban	Northeast	11.6	0.32
Rural	Northeast	3.6	0.29
Suburban	Midwest	12.4	0.28
Rural	Midwest	5.4	0.26
Rural	West	3.3	0.07
Suburban	West	11.6	−0.03
Suburban	Southeast	14.8	−0.05
Rural	Southeast	7.3	−0.14
Central city	West	7.0	−0.15
Central city	Midwest	6.6	−0.22
Central city	Southeast	10.8	−0.30
Central city	Northeast	5.5	−0.46

Note: NAEP = National Assessment of Educational Progress.

students on the nine tests that are also administered across state samples (the
state NAEP tests) was 0.30 standard deviation. Thus the average scores in
rural and suburban areas of the Northeast and Midwest—about one-third of
U.S. students—would place their students near the top of international score
distributions.

Students in rural and suburban areas of the West and Southeast fall in the
middle of the distribution, while the scores of central-city students from all
regions are the lowest scores. The central-city scores in the Northeast are the
lowest, while suburban scores in the Northeast are highest. The gap between
central-city and suburban scores in the Northeast is 0.78 standard deviation—by far the largest central city-suburban gap across regions.

Table 10-4 shows the complete disaggregation by race, region, and locality. White students in rural and suburban areas of the Northeast and Midwest—the highest scoring groups—would likely rank at the top of international distributions. These students are approximately 30 percent of students
nationally. White students scoring lowest live in central cities outside the
Southeast or in the rural Southeast and West.

The average scores of white students in all areas are significantly higher
than for any black student group. However, the pattern of scores is similar in
many ways across races. The two highest scoring groups for both black and
white students live in suburban areas in the Northeast and Midwest. The
rural areas of the Northeast and Midwest are also near the top of both black

Table 10-4. *Average NAEP Scores and Percent of Student Population,*
by Race, Region, and Locality

Race	Locality	Region	Percent of total student population	Average test score (standard deviation)
White	Suburban	Northeast	9.4	0.47
White	Suburban	Midwest	11.0	0.37
White	Rural	Northeast	3.3	0.37
White	Rural	Midwest	5.1	0.31
White	Suburban	Southeast	10.1	0.23
White	Suburban	West	8.5	0.18
White	Central city	Southeast	5.1	0.17
White	Rural	West	2.9	0.16
White	Central city	West	4.6	0.15
White	Central city	Midwest	4.1	0.14
White	Central city	Northeast	2.2	0.03
White	Rural	Southeast	5.6	0.00
Black	Suburban	Northeast	1.4	−0.38
Black	Suburban	Midwest	0.8	−0.49
Black	Rural	Southeast	1.2	−0.65
Black	Rural	Northeast	0.2	−0.68
Black	Rural	Midwest	0.1	−0.71
Black	Suburban	Southeast	3.1	−0.76
Black	Central city	Southeast	3.7	−0.79
Black	Central city	Midwest	1.9	−0.79
Black	Central city	West	0.6	−0.81
Black	Central city	Northeast	2.2	−0.84
Black	Suburban	West	0.7	−0.93
Black	Rural	West	0.1	−0.99

Note: NAEP = National Assessment of Educational Progress.

and white scores. Central-city students in the Northeast of both races are
near the bottom. Western students in any locality for both black and white
students tend to rank lower, but particularly for blacks. Of all regions, black
students score lowest in the West. Rural southern scores are among the highest black scores, but the lowest white scores.

   White student scores show a different locality pattern across regions. In
the Northeast and Midwest, there are large gaps between central city and
both suburban and rural scores. In the West, scores in each locality are virtually the same, while in the Southeast, the central-city and suburban scores are
close, but both are substantially higher than white rural scores—the area of
lowest white scores.

White and Black Scores by State

Ideally, disaggregation of scores by race and locality could be done by state instead of region. Regional patterns can hide important differences across states within a region. States are the main driver of educational policy, and the pattern of black and white scores by locality within states could support a more detailed analysis including family characteristics and resources. Unfortunately the sample sizes of state NAEP scores are limited to about twenty-five hundred, and combining samples across tests is more difficult because many states either did not participate or participated in a limited number of tests.

We combined the samples of four state NAEP tests all taken by twenty-eight states. The four tests are the 1992 fourth-grade reading and math and the 1996 fourth- and eighth-grade math. Figure 10-2 shows the average black scores by state. The results show a diversity of black scores across states within regions. Some states in nearly every region are in the top, middle, and bottom of the rankings. A simple regression using an SES variable for black families by state shows a positive, but insignificant, result indicating that black family characteristics explain little of the distribution.[21] A state per pupil expenditure variable is positive, but insignificant.

The white distribution of scores across states largely follows a more familiar pattern of higher scores in the Northeast and Midwest with lower scores more often in the Southeast (see figure 10-3). Exceptions occur for Rhode Island and Texas. Simple regressions show family characteristics to be a strong predictor of the pattern of white scores, and state per pupil expenditure shows statistically significant results.

The four states with the largest black-white gap—Connecticut, Michigan, Minnesota, and Wisconsin—are among the highest spending states (see figure 10-4). In each state the white students are among the highest scoring, but the black students have average to below average scores. The smallest gaps are in Kentucky and West Virginia, where white students are among the lowest state scorers, but black students score above the average among black student groups.

The Characteristics of Students in the Lowest Quintile

While average scores across regions and localities can reveal differences for the average student, they do not take account of the variance within region and locality. Students in the lowest quintile are those 20 percent scoring lowest in the nation. The racial and ethnic distribution of the lowest quintile is

Figure 10-2. *Average Black Scores, by State, across Four State NAEP Tests,* *1992–96*

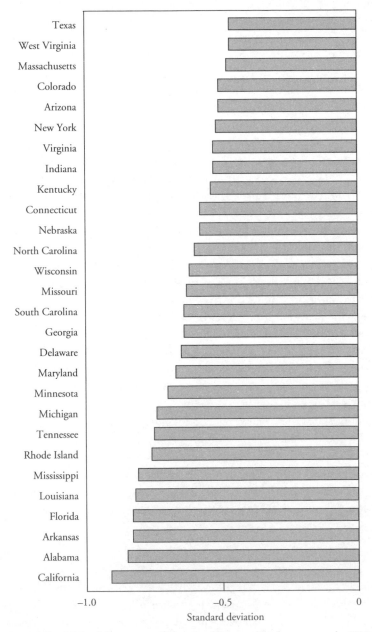

Note: NAEP = National Assessment of Educational Progress. The four tests are the 1992 fourth-grade reading and math tests and the 1996 fourth- and eighth-grade math tests.

Figure 10-3. *Average White Scores, by State, across Four State NAEP Tests, 1992–96*

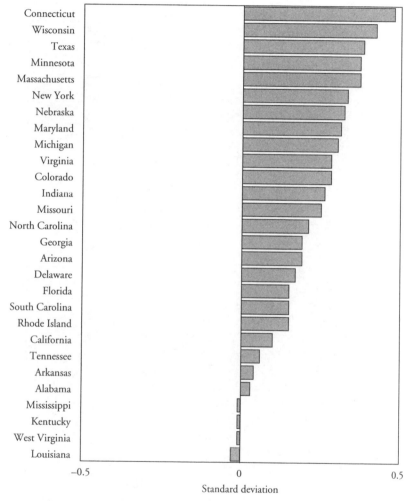

Note: NAEP = National Assessment of Educational Progress. The four tests are the 1992 fourth-grade reading and math tests and the 1996 fourth- and eighth-grade math tests.

Figure 10-4. *Average Black-White Score Gap, by State, across Four NAEP Tests, 1992–96*

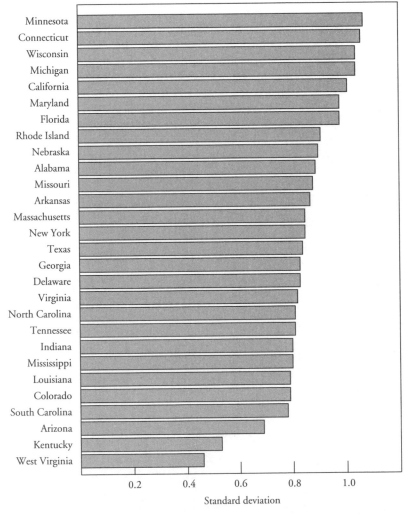

Note: NAEP = National Assessment of Educational Progress. The four tests are the 1992 fourth-grade reading and math tests and the 1996 fourth- and eighth-grade math tests.

Table 10-5. *Characteristics of Student Scoring in the Lowest Quintile on the NAEP, by Race or Ethnicity*

Race	Percent of total student population	Percent of lowest quintile population	Probability of being in the lowest quintile
White	71.9	37.6	0.11
Black	16.0	32.8	0.45
Hispanic	12.1	29.6	0.53

Note: NAEP = National Assessment of Educational Progress.

Table 10-6. *Characteristics of Students Scoring in the Lowest Quintile on the NAEP, by Region*

Region	Percent of total student population	Percent of lowest quintile population	Probability of being in the lowest quintile
Southeast	0.33	0.41	0.25
West	0.22	0.25	0.23
Midwest	0.24	0.18	0.15
Northeast	0.21	0.16	0.16

Note: NAEP = National Assessment of Educational Progress.

almost equally white, black, and Hispanic (see table 10-5). White students constitute 37.6 percent of those in the lowest quintile; black students, 32.8 percent, and Hispanics, 29.6 percent. Although only 11 percent of white students are in the lowest quintile (last column), white students constitute 71.9 percent of all students, making them the single largest group in the lowest quintile. Black and Hispanic students have much higher probabilities of being in the lowest quintile (0.45 and 0.53, respectively), but they are much smaller proportions of the national student population (16.0 and 12.1, respectively). However, these data suggest that all races might benefit from policies directed toward low-scoring students.

Table 10-6 shows similar data by region. The Southeast has the largest population of low-scoring students—41 percent of low-scoring students. The Southeast and West combined have two-thirds of low-scoring students. Table 10-7 shows the data by locality. Suburban and central-city areas have about 85 percent of low-scoring students with about equal numbers in each area. However, these aggregate statistics hide important variations by race within regions.

Low-scoring black students in central cities in the Southeast constitute 3.7 percent of the national student population and 8.5 percent of the lowest

Table 10-7. *Characteristics of Students Scoring in the Lowest Quintile on the NAEP, by Locality*

Locality	Percent of total student population	Percent of lowest quintile population	Probability of being in the lowest quintile
Suburban	50.5	42.7	0.17
Central city	29.8	42.1	0.28
Rural	19.7	15.2	0.15

Note: NAEP = National Assessment of Educational Progress.

quintile population (see table 10-8). The probability of a black student in the central cities of the Southeast being in the lowest quintile is 0.46, and 23.9 percent of all students in the lowest quintile are blacks in southern central cities—the largest single group of low-scoring students. Low-scoring black students are highly concentrated. Almost 80 percent of low-scoring black students live in the Southeast or the central cities of the Northeast and Midwest.

Hispanic low-scoring students are concentrated in four areas (see table 10-9). About 70 percent of low-scoring Hispanic students are in the suburban and central cities of the Southeast and West. Low-scoring white students are much less concentrated (see table 10-10). About 54 percent are in suburbs of the Southeast, West, or Midwest or the rural Southeast.

Table 10-11 shows the characteristics of the lowest quintile by locality and region and provides the racial percentages of the lowest quintile within each locality and region. For instance, the suburban Southeast has 14.9 percent of the total student population and 16.3 percent of the lowest quintile population. The racial and ethnic distribution of the lowest quintile students is 39.5 percent white, 43.6 percent black, and 16.9 percent Hispanic. The two largest groups of low-scoring students are in the suburban and central cities of the Southeast. Approximately one in three low-scoring students nationwide live in and around southern cities. Two out of three low-scoring students lives in the Southeast or West. Over 80 percent are in the Southeast, West, or central cities of the Northeast and Midwest.

Exploring Roles for Federal Resources

A policy agenda in K–12 education must be built on a common understanding of the strengths and weaknesses of the current system, the most important new problems and opportunities that will emerge in the next ten to fifteen years, and a recognition that the federal government should become

Table 10-8. *Characteristics of Black Students Scoring in the Lowest Quintile on the NAEP*

Race	Locality	Region	Percent of total student population	Percent of lowest quintile population	Probability of being in the lowest quintile	Distribution of lowest quintile blacks (percent)
Black	Central city	Southeast	3.7	8.5	0.46	23.9
Black	Suburban	Southeast	3.1	7.1	0.46	20.0
Black	Central city	Northeast	2.2	4.8	0.44	13.4
Black	Central city	Midwest	1.9	4.7	0.48	13.2
Black	Rural	Southeast	1.2	2.7	0.47	7.6
Black	Suburban	Northeast	1.4	2.4	0.34	6.8
Black	Suburban	West	0.7	1.7	0.53	4.8
Black	Suburban	Midwest	0.8	1.6	0.38	4.5
Black	Central city	West	0.6	1.5	0.50	4.3
Black	Rural	Northeast	0.2	0.3	0.27	0.7
Black	Rural	Midwest	0.1	0.2	0.50	0.4
Black	Rural	West	0.1	0.1	0.45	0.0

Note: NAEP = National Assessment of Educational Progress.

Table 10-9. *Characteristics of Hispanic Students Scoring in the Lowest Quintile on the NAEP*

Race	Locality	Region	Percent of total student population	Percent of lowest quintile population	Probability of being in the lowest quintile	Distribution of lowest quintile Hispanics (percent)
Hispanic	Suburban	West	2.5	5.1	0.42	21.9
Hispanic	Central city	West	1.8	4.5	0.50	19.3
Hispanic	Central city	Southeast	2.1	3.9	0.38	16.6
Hispanic	Suburban	Southeast	1.6	2.8	0.35	11.8
Hispanic	Central city	Northeast	1.0	2.1	0.40	8.9
Hispanic	Central city	Midwest	0.6	1.4	0.46	5.8
Hispanic	Rural	Southeast	0.6	1.2	0.42	5.3
Hispanic	Suburban	Midwest	0.6	0.8	0.27	3.3
Hispanic	Suburban	Northeast	0.7	0.7	0.20	2.9
Hispanic	Rural	West	0.4	0.5	0.28	2.3
Hispanic	Rural	Midwest	0.2	0.3	0.31	1.4
Hispanic	Rural	Northeast	0.1	0.1	0.23	0.5

Note: NAEP = National Assessment of Educational Progress.

Table 10-10. *Characteristics of White Students Scoring in the Lowest Quintile on the NAEP*

Race	Locality	Region	Percent of total student population	Percent of lowest quintile population	Probability of being in the lowest quintile	Distribution of lowest quintile whites (percent)
White	Suburban	Southeast	10.1	6.4	0.13	15.7
White	Suburban	West	8.5	5.8	0.14	14.1
White	Suburban	Midwest	11.0	4.9	0.09	11.9
White	Rural	Southeast	5.6	4.7	0.17	11.4
White	Central city	West	4.6	3.6	0.16	8.8
White	Suburban	Northeast	9.4	3.5	0.07	8.5
White	Central city	Southeast	5.1	3.2	0.13	7.9
White	Central city	Midwest	4.1	2.5	0.12	6.1
White	Rural	Midwest	5.1	1.9	0.08	4.7
White	Rural	West	2.9	1.8	0.12	4.4
White	Central city	Northeast	2.2	1.4	0.13	3.4
White	Rural	Northeast	3.3	1.3	0.08	3.1

Note: NAEP = National Assessment of Educational Progress.

involved only where a clear comparative advantage exists. The federal government has traditionally played a limited role in K–12 education providing only about 7 percent of expenditures. However, a strong to plausible case can be made for a comparative federal advantage in three areas.

The first area—addressing the wide inequality of educational spending across states—can be addressed only by the federal government. The second area—supporting sound research and development (R&D)—is a function typically centralized in public and private sector organizations. The federal government has a unique opportunity to strengthen the scientific research base in education. A more solid research base, in turn, could help states and districts use resources more productively. The third area where federal involvement can be efficient is in increasing the supply and quality of teachers by way of incentives.

Addressing Inequity in Spending across States

Most of the resource inequality cannot be resolved at the state level. States spending the least are southern and western states that also have a disproportionate share of the nation's minority and disadvantaged students. Only the federal government can address this issue of interstate inequality in school spending.

Table 10-11. *Characteristics of Students Scoring in the Lowest Quintile on the NAEP, by Region, Locality, and Race*

Locality	Region	Percent of total student population	Percent of lowest quintile population	Percent white in lowest quintile group	Percent black in lowest quintile group	Percent Hispanic in lowest quintile group
Suburban	Southeast	14.9	16.3	39.5	43.6	16.9
Central city	Southeast	10.9	15.7	20.8	54.4	24.9
Suburban	West	11.7	12.6	45.8	13.6	40.6
Central city	West	7.0	9.6	37.3	15.8	46.9
Rural	Southeast	7.4	8.6	54.0	31.5	14.5
Central city	Midwest	6.6	8.5	29.0	54.9	16.0
Central city	Northeast	5.4	8.3	16.9	57.7	25.4
Suburban	Midwest	12.4	7.2	67.3	22.0	10.7
Suburban	Northeast	11.6	6.6	52.8	36.7	10.4
Rural	West	3.3	2.5	72.7	5.8	21.5
Rural	Midwest	5.4	2.4	80.0	6.5	13.4
Rural	Northeast	3.6	1.6	77.3	15.9	6.7

Note: NAEP = National Assessment of Educational Progress.

Perhaps the main reason for resource shortfalls in states is their inadequate tax base. A stronger case can probably be made that the southern states lack the fiscal capacity to increase educational spending compared with what many western states could manage. California, Oregon, Utah, and Washington all have below average expenditures but may have more fiscal capacity to raise funds than many southern states.

Central cities pose a different problem than inequality between states. Addressing low suburban and rural scores in the Southeast and parts of the West may be easier than dealing with inner-city scores. Central-city resources depend heavily on the politics and judicial intervention within states. Furthermore, implementing successful interventions in inner cities may be more difficult and more expensive because of the higher cost of living and limited space.

Besides disproportionately low spending and high numbers of disadvantaged students, there are several other reasons that urban, southern, and western school districts should receive the focus of policy attention. First, students in these areas constitute a growing proportion of U.S. students, and future productivity will depend on learning how to provide better education for them. Second, recent research suggests that the achievement scores of minority and disadvantaged students respond to additional, well-targeted educational expenditures and that significant score gains could occur. Third, research also suggests that additional educational investment might be recouped through lower future social expenditures and improved economic productivity. Fourth, such policies would reduce the achievement gap between racial or ethnic and income groups—a source of continuing social and political divisions and economic costs in society. Finally, improving the United States' international standing requires lifting the scores of these students.

Addressing between-state inequality by setting an adequacy level across states near the current national average spending per pupil would require a significant expansion of federal education funding—at least $25 billion annually. The largest federal K–12 education program is Title I, an $8 billion program that directs funds to low-income school districts. This program barely begins to compensate for inequalities in spending. For instance, Title I supplies about 6 percent of educational spending in Mississippi, but less than 2 percent in many wealthier states, whereas the difference in spending in Mississippi compared with wealthy states can be over 100 percent. If additional funds were effectively spent by school districts, a significant increase in scores in the Southeast and in urban school districts could occur.

Although past evaluations of Title I have shown no compelling evidence for achievement gains, research and development provides little guidance as to how to spend the money well.[22] For instance, employing teacher aides was a common use of funds, whereas current experimental research shows compelling results favoring class-size reductions over hiring of aides. The question thus arises, Can future Title I-like programs be more effective than past ones? Any expansion of Title I programs should limit use to the strongest empirically supported interventions and have built-in experimental designs for evaluation. But significant progress appears unlikely to be made in lifting achievement nationally without significant, well-structured, well-targeted, and well-evaluated federal resources.

Federal R&D Spending on Children and Education

In most areas of national endeavor, progress is taken for granted. The basis for this progress is generally good research and development that continuously produces discoveries, innovations, and new products. The nation spends about 2–3 percent of its gross national product on R&D to fuel these results. R&D is funded through both public and private sector funding. The private sector funding in each area tends to provide a market-driven constraint that partially drives R&D spending to productive levels.

However, R&D in K–12 education and more broadly on children's issues is funded almost entirely by the federal government. Granted, this arrangement may be appropriate, because the public sector would be a prime beneficiary of discovery and innovation. State, local, and federal governments directed almost $600 billion in 1995 toward children and youth, with education being the largest component of this spending.[23] R&D that shows how to obtain better results with this spending could have significant payoff in savings for the public sector.

Furthermore, improving R&D on education and children could have other payoffs down the road. It could help avoid future expenditures on dysfunctional adult behaviors associated with poor educational outcomes. Much adult dysfunctional behavior appears rooted in developmental paths from childhood. Smoking, drinking, drug abuse, criminal behavior, depression and other mental health conditions, job performance and stability, and even factors linked to heart disease have roots in behavior and lack of educational success established while growing up. R&D that begins to understand and address these issues may decrease the substantial societal costs of these behaviors for adults. Investment in the first twenty years of life may have substantial impact on the quality of the last twenty years of life, and it easily recoups any additional investment required.

In 1995 only about 0.3 to 0.4 percent of public spending on children and education was devoted to R&D—a far smaller proportion than the average

2–3 percent spent in other areas. This R&D represented only about 5 percent of total domestic federal R&D and about 2 percent of national R&D.[24] Given that almost all R&D on children's issues is federally funded, it is problematical whether R&D seeks the most productive level. Evidence from four other domestic areas would suggest systematic underinvestment by the public sector in R&D for functions that, like K–12 education, are an almost entirely public sector responsibility: air traffic control systems, tax collection systems, postal systems, and voting systems. Each of these systems is in crisis partly because of failure of R&D to produce innovations and improved products and the slow adoption of new technology. If the public sector is inefficient in allocating R&D in areas where it bears the prime responsibility, perhaps progress in education and improving outcomes for children have not surprisingly been slow and uncertain.

Past research in education has been notable for its inconsistency and inability to provide compelling results. Under such circumstances, low funding might have been appropriate. Evidence has emerged that future R&D on education and children could be more scientifically productive.[25] Two central concepts underlie these assertions.

First, a restructuring of educational research around the model used in health research would improve its scientific quality. Health research—widely hailed for advancing knowledge and producing new discoveries, innovations, and technology—is undergirded by solid basic and applied research based on the use of clinical trials and of major ongoing longitudinal studies tracking health behavior and status focusing on virtually every health problem.

Health research also has an institutional infrastructure based on teaching hospitals, schools of public health, and academic research centers that closely link research to training, practice, and public education. Another component of this infrastructure is extensive cross-training among disciplines and between researchers and practitioners. All of this is aided by a central federal funding agency—the National Institutes of Health (NIH)—guided by scientific peer review and able to set priorities and achieve more efficient investment in infrastructure.

By contrast, research on children, besides their physical health, often lacks a vibrant basic research component, has almost no scientifically structured clinical trials, has relatively few major longitudinal surveys, and has no equivalents of teaching hospitals or schools of public health that combine research with practice. The R&D community is fragmented across disciplines and federal departments that invest in infrastructure, making investment inefficient. Research centers tend to be university-based and far removed from schools or communities where children's learning and development occurs. Research on children can strengthen its scientific basis by moving toward the health model.

Second, new opportunities for breakthroughs in understanding children's cognitive development are emerging in current brain research. This work promises to illuminate the basic processes underlying cognitive, emotional, and physical development in children. Just as physics and chemistry needed understanding of atomic and nuclei structure and electron movement in solids to spawn revolutions in R&D and technology, and medicine and biology needed access to cells and genes to move forward, research on children needs a basic understanding of the organ that centrally governs all development in children—the brain. Each of these past revolutions occurred with advances in instrumentation that allowed deeper or more precise penetration into matter; that is, particle accelerators, electron microscopes, lasers, and radio telescopes.

The new brain instrumentation promises to provide the same penetration allowing increasingly precise knowledge of the links between brain processes and behavior. This knowledge will ultimately spawn a revolution in understanding and the related capacity to address developmental problems in children.

A strong scientific infrastructure must emerge that links this basic brain research to more applied areas of cognitive, emotional, physical, and social development and to training and practice. It takes at least ten years to substantially restructure areas of research. Such restructuring has occurred in the area of health in the 1960s and 1970s, in computer science when it emerged from the field of electrical engineering in the same period, and in engineering in the last fifteen years. Federal funding was instrumental in nurturing and building these new fields through support for research, funding for new undergraduate and graduate programs, and writing of new textbooks and curriculums.

The federal government needs to develop a longer term strategy for accomplishing this restructuring to shape and guide research on K–12 education and children. Some in Congress have recommended doubling budgets for NIH and the National Science Foundation over five years, which would increase R&D spending alone by more than $20 billion. However, only a small portion of this—about $1 billion—would naturally flow to children's R&D. A small boost in the portion of scheduled federal R&D increase toward children's research could double R&D spending on children—currently at around $3 billion. Such increases should occur gradually and only with a plan that ensures better research productivity.

Improving Teacher Quality

Perhaps the most important emerging issue in education amenable to federal involvement is the potential shortage of certified and qualified K–12 teachers in the next ten years. The demand for new teachers is expected to increase because a disproportionately large number of teachers are nearing retirement, increasing demand from smaller class size, rising enrollments, and rising teacher attrition levels due partly to a highly competitive labor market.[26] Expanding the supply of new teachers to meet rising demand may be difficult given the highly competitive labor market for new college graduates and noncompetitive wages for teachers. Shortages may be particularly severe for science and math teachers, as the gap between wages inside and outside teaching is very large.

Shortages of certified teachers are usually addressed through increasing teacher salaries at the school district level or hiring uncertified teachers or both. Unfortunately, teacher salaries are raised by increasing salaries for all teachers—an inefficient and expensive process as salaries for beginning teachers are most closely linked to decisions by college students to teach. Because teacher salary and benefits consume over 50 percent of educational expenditures, rising salaries for all teachers could consume a considerable portion of the growth in education expenditures over the next decade, leaving little for implementing more effective reform initiatives.

When teacher shortages occur, they fall disproportionately on inner-city schools and lower paying school districts, predominately in the Southeast. These areas not only will need to hire more teachers to meet their rising demand, but they also will need to replace many current teachers who will take jobs that open up in higher paying districts. Inner-city teachers will take suburban jobs, and interstate competition may drive teachers north. Thus, southern and urban school districts will be hardest hit—exactly those districts that constitute the major problem areas for U.S. education.

The federal government can efficiently increase teacher supply and raise the quality of incoming teachers through several programs aimed at beginning and younger teachers. These include college loan forgiveness programs, undergraduate scholarships, and a graduate level GI Bill–type program. These kinds of programs have been used to increase the quality of officer and enlisted personnel in the armed forces. A contributory GI Bill would allow the federal government to provide matching funds that could be used for pursuit of advanced degrees after a specified number of years of teaching. This program would appeal mainly to college graduates who have plans for graduate school but are uncertain of career choice or lack funds. Such candidates are likely to be of higher quality on average than typical college students choosing teaching.

Such programs can also be more heavily targeted toward types of teachers in short supply (math and science, inner city) or teachers with superior grades or credentials (a math degree instead of an education degree), thereby increasing even more the quality of incoming teachers. All of these programs essentially provide the equivalent of more front-end compensation for younger teachers that does not get built into the entire salary scale, thus making them efficient. These programs could ease the need for across-the-board salary increases and leave more discretionary funds at the state and local level for effective initiatives—especially in urban and southern schools. The long-term cost of such programs that would on average provide the equivalent of a 10 percent salary increase for younger teachers would be around $2 billion to $3 billion annually.

Notes

This research was supported by grants from the Secondary Analysis Program, National Assessment of Educational Progress; the Office of Program Evaluation and Services, U.S. Department of Education; and the Center for Educational Excellence and Diversity, a research center funded by the Office of Educational Research and Improvement, U.S. Department of Education.

1. Christopher Jencks and Meredith Phillips, eds., *The Black-White Test Score Gap* (Brookings, 1998).

2. Eric A. Hanushek, "The Impact of Differential Expenditures on School Performance," *Educational Researcher,* vol. 18, no. 4 (1989), pp. 45–51; Eric A. Hanushek, *Making Schools Work: Improving Performance and Controlling Costs* (Brookings, 1994); and Eric A. Hanushek, "Outcomes, Costs, and Incentives in Schools," in Eric A. Hanushek and Dale Jorgenson, eds., *Improving America's Schools: The Role of Incentives* (Washington: National Academy Press, 1996), pp. 29–52.

3. Larry V. Hedges, Richard D. Laine, and Rob Greenwald, "Does Monday Matter? Meta-Analysis of Studies of the Effects of Differential School Inputs on Student Outcomes," *Educational Researcher,* vol. 23, no. 3 (1994), pp. 5–14.

4. A. B. Krueger, "An Economist View of Class Size Reductions," mimeo, Princeton University, 2000; and chapter 2 in this volume, Alan B. Krueger and Diane M. Whitmore, "Would Smaller Classes Help Close the Black-White Achievement Gap?"

5. Rob Greenwald, L. V. Hedges, and R. Laine, "The Effect of School Resources on Student Achievement," *Review of Educational Research,* vol. 66, no. 3 (Fall 1996), pp. 361–96

6. Ronald F. Ferguson and Helen F. Ladd, "How and Why Money Matters: An Analysis of Alabama Schools," in Helen F. Ladd, ed., *Holding Schools Accountable* (Brookings, 1996), pp. 265–98.

7. David W. Grissmer and others, *Improving Student Achievement: What Do State NAEP Scores Tell Us* (Santa Monica, Calif.: RAND, 2000).

8. Ronald F. Ferguson, "Can Schools Narrow the Black-White Score Gap?" in Christopher Jencks and Meredith Phillips, eds., *The Black-White Test Score Gap* (Brookings, 1998), pp. 318–74; David Grissmer and others, "Why Did the Black-White Score Gap Narrow in the 1970s and 1980s?" in Christopher Jencks and Meredith Phillips, eds., *The Black-White Test Score Gap* (Brookings, 1998), pp. 182–226; and A. B. Krueger, "Experimental Estimates of Education Production Functions," *Quarterly Journal of Economics,* vol. 114 (1999), pp. 497–532.

9. Jeremy Finn and C. Achilles, "Tennessee's Class Size Study: Findings, Implications, and Misconceptions," *Educational Evaluation and Policy Analysis,* vol. 20, no. 2 (Summer 1999), pp. 97–109; Krueger, "Experimental Estimates of Education Production Functions"; Alex Molnar and others, "Estimated Achievement and Teacher Time Allocation Effects from a Quasi-Experimental Class Size Reduction in Wisconsin," *Educational Evaluation and Policy Analysis,* vol. 20, no. 2 (Summer 1999), pp. 165–77; and Barbara Nye, Larry V. Hedges, and Spyros Konstantopoulos, "The Long Term Effects of Small Classes: A Five-Year Follow-up of the Tennessee Class Size Experiment," *Educational Evaluation and Policy Analysis,* vol. 20, no. 2 (Summer 1999), pp. 127–42.

10. David Grissmer, "Effects of Class Size: Assessing the Evidence, Its Policy Implications and Future Research Agenda," *Educational Evaluation and Policy Analysis,* vol. 20, no. 2 (Summer 1999), pp. 231–48.

11. Eric Hanushek, "Assessing the Empirical Evidence on Class Size Reductions from Tennessee and Non-Experimental Research," *Educational Evaluation and Policy Analysis,* vol. 20, no. 2 (Summer 1999), pp. 143–63.

12. Krueger, "Experimental Estimates of Education Production Functions"; Nye, Hedges, and Konstantopoulos, "The Long Term Effects of Small Classes"; and Barbara Nye, Larry V. Hedges, and Spyros Konstantopoulos, "The Effects of Small Class Size on Academic Achievement: The Results of the Tennessee Class Size Experiment," University of Chicago, Department of Education, 1999.

13. Helen Ladd, Rosemary Chalk, and Janet Hansen, eds., *Equity and Adequacy in Education Finance* (Washington: National Academy Press, National Research Council, 1999).

14. William N. Evans, Sheila Murray, and Robert Schwab, "Schoolhouses, Courthouses, and Statehouses after Serrano," *Journal of Policy Analysis and Management,* vol. 16 (January 1997), pp. 10–31; and William N. Evans, S. Murray, and R. Schwab, "The Impact of Court-Mandated School Finance Reform," in Helen Ladd, Rosemary Chalk, and Janet Hansen, eds., *Equity and Adequacy in Education Finance* (Washington: National Academy Press, National Research Council, 1999), pp. 72–98.

15. Evans, Murray, and Schwab, "The Impact of Court-Mandated School Finance Reform."

16. Helen F. Ladd and Janet S. Hansen, *Making Money Matter: Financing America's Schools* (Washington: National Academy Press, 1999).

17. Evans, Murray, and Schwab, "The Impact of Court-Mandated School Finance Reform."

18. I. V. S. Mullis and others, *NAEP 1992 Mathematics Report Card for the Nation and the States: Data from the National and Trial State Assessments* (U.S. Department of Education, National Center for Education Statistics, 1993); J. R. Campbell and others, *NAEP 1994 Reading Report Card for the Nation and the States: Findings from the National Assessment of Educational Progress and Trial State Assessments* (U.S. Department of Education, National Center for Education Statistics, 1996); C. M. Reese and others, *NAEP 1996 Mathematics Report Card for the Nation and the States* (U.S. Department of Education, National Center for Education Statistics, 1997); and Patricia L. Donahue and others, *NAEP 1998 Reading Report Card for the Nation,* NCES 199–459 (U.S. Department of Education, National Center for Education Statistics, 1999).

19. Eugene G. Johnson, Adriane Siegendorf, and Gary W. Phillips, *Linking the National Assessment of Educational Progress (NAEP) and the Third International Math and Science Study (TIMSS): Eighth-Grade Results* (U.S. Department of Education, Office of Educational Research and Improvement, May 1998).

20. Johnson, Siegendorf, and Phillips, *Linking the NAEP and the TIMSS.*

21. We used a socioeconomic status variable constructed from 1990 census characteristics for black families by state weighted by coefficients from equations derived from the National Education Longitudinal Study. The variable includes parental education, family income, family size, average age of mother at child's birth, and single parent. A more detailed description is provided in Grissmer and others, *Improving Student Achievement.*

22. Michael J. Puma and others, *Prospects: Final Report on Student Outcomes* (Cambridge, Mass.: ABT Associates, 1997).

23. Office of Science and Technology Policy, *Investing in Our Future: A National Research Initiative for America's Children for the 21st Century* (The White House, April 1997).

24. Office of Science and Technology Policy, *Investing in Our Future.*

25. David W. Grissmer and Ann Flanagan, "Moving Educational Research toward Scientific Consensus," in David W. Grissmer and Michael Ross, eds., *Analytic Issues in the Assessment of Student Achievement,* NCES 2000–050 (U.S. Department of Education, National Center for Educational Statistics, 2000).

26. William J. Hussar, *Predicting the Need for Newly Hired Teachers in the United States to 2008–09,* NCES 1999-026 (U.S. Department of Education, National Center for Education Statistics, 1999).

Contributors

JOHN CHUBB
Edison Schools

A. GARY DWORKIN
University of Houston

KAREN EHRLE
University of Wisconsin–Milwaukee

ANN E. FLANAGAN
RAND

ADAM GAMORAN
University of Wisconsin–Madison

DAVID GRISSMER
RAND

ANKE HALBACH
University of Wisconsin–Milwaukee

ANTWANETTE N. HILL
University of Houston

WILLIAM G. HOWELL
University of Wisconsin–Madison

DAVID KLEIN
California State University–
Northridge

ALAN B. KRUEGER
Princeton University

JON LORENCE
University of Houston

TOM LOVELESS
Brookings Institution

SAMUEL R. LUCAS
University of California–Berkeley

NANCY MADDEN
Success for All Foundation

ALEX MOLNAR
Arizona State University

PAUL E. PETERSON
Harvard University

ROBERT E. SLAVIN
Johns Hopkins University

PHIL SMITH
University of Wisconsin–Milwaukee

ABIGAIL THERNSTROM
Manhattan Institute

STEPHAN THERNSTROM
Harvard University

LAURENCE A. TOENJES
University of Houston

DIANE M. WHITMORE
University of California–Berkeley

JOHN ZAHORIK
University of Wisconsin–Milwaukee

Index

Accountability systems, 109–30; compared to voucher programs, 55; debate over, 109. *See also* Texas accountability system

Achievement Council (Los Angeles), 166–67

Achilles, Charles M., 18, 21, 24

ACT. *See* American College Test

African American students: comparison with Latinos in voucher programs, 59–66; KIPP Academy (NYC), 139–45; math achievement and tracking, 182–87; SAGE outcomes, 91–108; Success for All outcomes, 77, 79–88; TAAS scores, 112–17; track assignment, 177–89; underachievement, 131, 138, 148; voucher outcomes, 36–37, 53–55, 66–67, 76; vouchers vs. class-size reduction, 36–37, 54. *See also* Black-white achievement gap

Alabama: Success for All program, 79

Alwin, Duane, 172

American College Test (ACT): accountability system effect on scores, 123; class size effect on scores, 3, 27–33

Anekwe, Juliet, 161

Arizona: Success for All, 79

Arkansas: Success for All, 79

Armor, David J., 136

Asian American students: Hobart Elementary School, 139–45; home culture and academic achievement, 145–49; TAAS scores, 113–15; and tracking, 8, 182–87

Baltimore: Success for All, 77, 79, 81

Bennett-Kew Elementary School (Los Angeles), 7, 158–61; bilingual students, 160; composition of student body, 158; math program, 159–61; placement of entering students, 160; teacher selection, 160–61

Beyond the Classroom (Steinberg), 145

Bilingual programs: adaptation of Success for All program, 83; administra-